The Freudian Left

The Freudian Left

Wilhelm Reich
Geza Roheim
Herbert Marcuse

PAUL ROBINSON

Cornell University Press
Ithaca and London

First published, Cornell Paperbacks, 1990 by Cornell University Press.

International Standard Book Number 0-8014-9716-7
Library of Congress Catalog Card Number 89-28749
Printed in the United States of America

Library of Congress Cataloging in Publication Data
Robinson, Paul A., 1940–
    The Freudian left : Wilhelm Reich, Geza Roheim, Herbert Marcuse /
Paul A. Robinson.
        p. cm.
    Reprint. Originally published : New York : Harper & Row, 1969.
    Includes bibliographical references.
    ISBN 0-8014-9716-7 (alk. paper)
    1. Psychoanalysis—History.   2. Reich, Wilhelm, 1897–1957.
3. Róheim, Géza, 1891–1953.   4. Marcuse, Herbert, 1898–1979.
I. Title.
BF173.R552   1990
150.19′52′0922—dc20   89-28749

♾ The paper used in this publication meets the minimum requirements
of the American National Standard for Permanence of Paper for Printed
Library Materials Z39.48–1984.

CONTENTS

———◆———

ACKNOWLEDGMENTS

———— ◆ ————

The author wishes to make acknowledgment to the following firms for allowing the use of copyrighted material in this book:

George Allen & Unwin Ltd., for permission to quote from *Australian Totemism* by Geza Roheim.

Basic Books, Inc., for permission to quote from *The Life and Work of Sigmund Freud*, Volume III, by Ernest Jones, and from *Psychoanalytic Pioneers*, edited by Franz Alexander, Samuel Eisenstein, and Martin Grotjahn.

Beacon Press, for permission to quote from *Eros and Civilization* and *One-Dimensional Man* by Herbert Marcuse, and to cite passages, in my own translation, from *Kultur und Gesellschaft* (© 1965 by Suhrkamp Verlag), which appear in a different translation in *Negations* (© 1968 by Beacon Press).

Daedalus, journal of the American Academy of Arts and Sciences, for permission to quote from "Remarks on a Redefinition of Culture" by Herbert Marcuse.

Farrar, Straus & Giroux, Inc., for permission to quote from *The Function of the Orgasm, Character-Analysis, The Sexual Revolution, Listen, Little Man!* and *The Murder of Christ* by Wilhelm Reich, and from *Reich Speaks of Freud*, edited by Mary Higgins and Chester M. Raphael.

Sigmund Freud Copyrights Ltd., the Institute of Psycho-Analysis, and the Hogarth Press Ltd., for permission to quote from *The Standard Edition of the Complete Psychological Works of Sigmund Freud.*

The Hogarth Press Ltd., for permission to quote from *The Riddle of the Sphinx* by Geza Roheim.

Humanities Press, Inc., for permission to quote from *Reason and Revolution* by Herbert Marcuse.

International Universities Press, Inc., for permission to quote from *The Eternal Ones of the Dream* and *Psychoanalysis and Anthropology* by Geza Roheim.

Alfred A. Knopf, Inc., for permission to quote from *Moses and Monotheism* by Sigmund Freud.

Liveright Publishing Corporation, for permission to quote from *Group Psychology and the Analysis of the Ego* by Sigmund Freud.

Thomas Nelson & Sons, for permission to quote from *Psychoanalysis: Evolution and Development* by Clara Thompson.

W. W. Norton & Company, Inc., for permission to quote from *New Introductory Lectures* by Sigmund Freud.

Random House, Inc., for permission to quote from *Love's Body* by Norman O. Brown.

The Wilhelm Reich Infant Trust Fund for permission to quote from *The Mass Psychology of Fascism* and *Cosmic Superimposition* by Wilhelm Reich, and from *The Psycho-Analytic Reader,* edited by Robert Fliess.

Routledge & Kegan Paul Ltd., for permission to quote from *Animism, Magic, and the Divine King* by Geza Roheim, from *Reason and Revolution, Eros and Civilization,* and *One-*

Dimensional Man by Herbert Marcuse, and from *Life Against Death* by Norman O. Brown.

Wesleyan University Press, for permission to quote from *Life Against Death* by Norman O. Brown.

PREFACE TO THE 1990
PAPERBACK EDITION

———————◆———————

A quarter century has passed since I got the idea for this book, and I can't read it today without an almost Proustian sense of time past. It conjures up forgotten people, places, and passions. Much of this, I would have to admit, is garden-variety nostalgia, of the sort that any author approaching fifty might feel about a book written in his twenties. But in one respect, at least, my sentiments can perhaps lay claim to broader interest. I have in mind the very different attitude I now hold toward the tradition of thought the book examines, the tradition of Freudian radicalism. When I wrote the book, I found it remarkably easy to identify with my three protagonists. Although not uncritical of their views and eager to locate them correctly in the history of ideas, I readily confessed to sharing "many of their prejudices and convictions" (p. 4). I certainly couldn't make that confession today. In a word, I've grown more conservative, and the enthusiasms, both Freudian and radical, of Reich, Roheim, and Marcuse no longer hold the charm for me they once did.

Doubtless it is uninteresting to learn that yet another intellectual has moved to the right with age. From William Wordsworth to Norman Podhoretz the pattern has become one of the great biographical clichés of the modern world. In this instance, however, the story is more than personal: over the past two decades the whole world has grown more conservative, and the tradition of Freudian radicalism has fallen into neglect alongside virtually the entire leftist enterprise. Reich and Roheim are now largely ignored, while Marcuse (who died in 1979) is actively reviled. Moreover, the tradition has had, as far as I am aware, no significant heirs. For all practical purposes, it has passed irredeemably into history.

What accounts for the collapse of its fortunes? I suggest that important intellectual and political developments during the past two decades have effectively undermined the conceptual pillars on which the tradition rested. We can take the measure of those developments by briefly contemplating three questions: What has happened to radicalism? What has happened to sex? And what has happened to Freud?

Political radicalism was a central assumption of the Freudian Left, particularly of Reich and Marcuse. It entailed, first of all, a profound alienation from the established culture, the conviction that its institutions and practices were fundamentally hostile to human fulfillment. It also entailed a commitment to the revolutionary transformation of those institutions and practices. Even Roheim, the most conservative of the three, considered himself very much a critical intellectual, and his writings seethe with hatred for the existing order.

As we all know, political radicalism has been set thoroughly on the defensive by the Reagan Revolution and its European counterparts. The intellectual fallout, moreover, has been enormous. Most immediately in this regard one thinks of the many former leftists who have become neo-conservatives. At the same time, those figures who have remained true to their radical origins, such as Noam Chomsky, now seem hopelessly isolated, as if locked in a time-warp. Above all, the rightward displacement of the entire ideological spectrum has resulted in a virtual redefinition of political discourse, so that what in the 1960's counted for a centrist is now a leftist, and a traditional conservative like George Bush can pose plausibly as a moderate. In such a political universe, genuine radicalism of the sort presumed by Reich and Marcuse has become marginalized. Indeed, it has been all but obliterated.

What has happened to Marxism is merely a local variation on this theme. Marx was of course essential to the Freudian Left. In particular, the effort to work out an intellectual synthesis of Marx and Freud was among the defining preoccupations of the tradition. But the past two decades have seen Marxism fall from grace. The historian Tony Judt, for example, has written that we are "at the tail end of the history of Marxism as a living idea" (*Marxism and the French Left* [Oxford, 1986], p. 18). For one thing, the advancing sclerosis and the recent outright collapse of Communist regimes in Eastern Europe have contributed to the discrediting of Marxism as an intellectual tradition. The equation is of course unfair, since Western Marxists—not least of all Reich and Marcuse—have always expressed their firm for distaste for Soviet-style Communism. But the distinction between theoretical Marxists on the one hand and practicing Communists on the other no longer enjoys the authority it once did. Perhaps more important, the central intellectual movements of the past two decades, notably structuralism and post-structuralism, have effectively bypassed the familiar per-spectives of Marxism. The "linguistic turn" in intellectual affairs, with its abstract, hermetic, and (I would argue) deeply apolitical style, has rendered Marx old-fashioned. To the extent that he still attracts adherents, they are for the most part academic sociologists and historians, who continue to find class analysis a useful intellectual tool (and even they feel themselves an embattled minority). As a broad-gauged critique of the human condition—and it was precisely in this sense that Marxism interested Reich and Marcuse—it has lost its grip on the Western imagina-tion.

The representatives of the Freudian Left distinguished themselves from other radicals, and from Marxists in par-ticular, by their critique of the sexual repressiveness of modern civilization. They excoriated the established order as much for its erotic as for its social and economic defi-ciencies, and they anticipated (albeit Roheim rather less emphatically than Reich and Marcuse) a more libidinal organization of human society in the future. Their radical-ism, in short, was sexual as well as political. Accordingly, their collective reputation has suffered as sex itself has fallen on hard times.

Speaking somewhat more precisely, we can identify two developments on the sexual front that have blunted the erotic enthusiasms urged by the Freudian Left. In the first instance, the sexual revolution has been domesticated by its very success. Marcuse himself identified this ten-dency when, in *One-Dimensional Man* (1964), he devel-oped the concept of "repressive desublimation," which for him denoted the manner in which sexual expression had been co-opted by capitalism. In effect, sexual indulgence, including many forms of erotic behavior traditionally proscribed, has proved to be entirely compatible with political quietism. Sex has been put to work in the market economy, and in the process it has lost much of its ideological bite.

More recently sex has fallen victim to the fears inspired by the AIDS epidemic and to the new asceticism championed by such figures as Allan Bloom, William Bennett, and Roger Scruton. It is now entirely respectable—indeed, for homosexuals it is nothing more radical than a commitment to survival—to endorse the virtues of monogamy and to regret the sexual extravagances of the 1960's and 1970's. Had he lived, Marcuse might well have welcomed the revolutionary promise of these developments, since he considered sex most dangerous when it was most repressed. But a simpler reading of the situation forces us to concede that under the current sexual freeze all talk of a more libidinal culture, such as Reich and Marcuse envisioned (and such as Roheim claimed to have found among his beloved Australian aborigines), seems at best quaint, at worst vaguely unhealthy.

And what of Freud? By definition, Freud lies at the intellectual heart of the project whose history this book seeks to trace. By and large, the Freud Reich, Roheim, and Marcuse admired was the speculative cultural critic and metapsychologist, the author of *Totem and Taboo* and *Civilization and Its Discontents*. Moreover, when properly understood—or, in the case of Reich, when loyal to his deepest convictions—Freud was, in their view, a profoundly oppositional figure, a thinker who had identified the erotic depredations of modern life and whose intellectual system contained the seeds of a cultural criticism no less exigent than Marx's.

Freud has suffered a complex fate over the past two decades, and the history of his reputation in the 1970's and 1980's has tended to undermine the radical version of his thought advanced by Reich, Roheim, and Marcuse. The first signs of trouble came from the feminists. Betty Friedan and then, more systematically, Kate Millett and Germaine Greer charged that, far from being a figure of the left, Freud was an architect of the patriarchal reaction. In particular, they took him to task for his unreconstructed views on female psychology and sexuality. To be sure, some feminist intellectuals, notably Juliet Mitchell, Nancy Chodorow, and Jane Gallop, continue to claim him for their cause. But for the most part feminists have cast him as one of the enemy.

Moreover, to the extent that Freud has remained a vital intellectual presence, he has done so less as a cultural critic or metapsychologist than as a hermeneutician. Freud the interpreter—whether of dreams, of parapraxes, or, more generally, of language—has proved highly sympathetic to certain literary critics, especially as seen through the philosophical prism of Lacan and Derrida. In terms of the Freudian corpus, the case histories have displaced the cultural writings as the center of attention, and while this has encouraged a decidedly abandoned style of exegesis, a kind of hermeneutic riot, today's literary Freudianism is at best politically neutral. It is certainly a far cry from the revolutionary doctrine conjured up by Reich, Roheim, and Marcuse.

Freud himself has come under sharp attack in recent years, leading to a widespread sense that his reputation is now at risk. Frank Sulloway and Jeffrey Masson have raised doubts about his intellectual development in the 1890's, especially about his theoretical debt to Wilhelm Fliess and his abandonment of the seduction theory. The philosopher of science Adolf Grünbaum has returned attention to the vexed issue of his methodological soundness, suggesting that many of his ideas lack sufficient empirical grounding. In general, these criticisms seem to be unrelated, or at best very indirectly related, to the cultural and metapsychological themes so important to the adepts of Freudian radicalism. Nonetheless, the destabilization of Freud's reputation has served to undermine the easy authority that he enjoyed in their writings. Put another way, Freudian radicalism flourished when Freud was in the ascendant, and to the extent that his stature has slipped, it too has been diminished.

Freud has not been without his defenders. The most prominent among them is Peter Gay, whose recent biography bears the significant subtitle, *A Life for Our Time*. But Gay's portrait offers small comfort to the beleaguered Freudian Left. The "timely" figure who emerges from his pages is an eminently stoic bourgeois, a man altogether suited to our Thermidorian sensibilities. In effect, Gay returns us to the Freud of Philip Rieff's *The Mind of the Moralist* (1959), which locates him within the great tradition of conservative moral philosophers. At the center of this interpretation stands the disabused realist who, as he himself eloquently expressed it, aimed at "transforming . . . hysterical misery into common unhappiness." His Freud is light years removed from the crypto-revolutionary imagined by Reich, Roheim, and Marcuse.

My own view of Freud is now closer to Rieff's than to

Marcuse's. Under these circumstances the reader might legitimately wonder how I wish to recommend the present book. As a historian, I have no difficulty answering that question. While the Freudian Left may have fallen into neglect, perhaps even into disrepute, it nonetheless constituted a significant development within psychoanalytic opinion during the middle years of the century and thus remains a deserving subject of historical interest. Moreover I am willing to go beyond this purely academic recommendation to suggest that these thinkers have a continuing moral claim on our attention, and perhaps even our respect. Although their hopes for a more libidinal culture now seem utterly utopian and their version of Freud no longer persuades, the social and psychological reality they set out to criticize is, I would argue, as bad as it ever was. Precisely because we live in an age of regnant conservatism, their unrelenting hostility to that reality comes as a bracing antidote. At the very least, it may keep us from adding our voices to the triumphant counterrevolution, both sexual and political. This is a modest enough achievement, and hardly what Reich, Roheim, and Marcuse intended. But it is perhaps the best we can hope for in these dispiriting times.

PAUL ROBINSON

Stanford University
January 1990

PREFACE

IN THIS book I have examined a particular tradition in the history of psychoanalysis, which I call the radical or left-wing tradition. The book seeks to define this school of interpretation through an analysis of its three most important representatives: Wilhelm Reich, Geza Roheim, and Herbert Marcuse. In effect, the study consists of three intellectual biographies, in which I follow the development of the radical tradition in psychoanalysis from the 1920's to the 1960's. The story begins in Central Europe (in Germany, Austria, and Hungary), but shifts to America with the emigration of my three protagonists in the 1930's. I have divided my efforts between an analysis of each thinker's development into a Freudian radical and a comparative examination of their respective brands of radicalism. At the same time I have sought to relate the evolution of the radical tradition to the history of the psychoanalytic movement as a whole, and to the general course of European and American social thought in the nineteenth and twentieth centuries.

I am anxious to thank a number of friends for the help they have given me in completing this book. My primary indebtedness is to David Hunt, with whom I have carried on a dialogue, sometimes Freudian, always radical, since we first came to Harvard as graduate students in 1963; he is my best psychoanalytic critic, and each chapter of this book has profited from his conscientious scrutiny. I also wish to thank Professor H. Stuart Hughes of Harvard, who supervised an earlier version of this study, giving generously of his time and enthusiasm. The manuscript was read very thoroughly by Ann Shorter, and I'm grateful to her for eliminating many ambiguities and infelicities of expression. Chapters or parts of chapters were also read by Scott Massey, William Beik, Edward Shorter, Christopher Lydon, and by various members of my family, including my brother and sister-in-law, James and Joan Robinson, my mother, Mrs. Beryl Robinson Gore, and my aunt Mrs. Margery Robertson. To them also, thanks.

Finally, I wish to acknowledge a pair of debts which date from the very earliest and the very latest stages of the book's evolution. The first is to Albert LaValley, who gave me my first copy of Herbert Marcuse's *Eros and Civilization* nearly a decade ago, and whose personal and intellectual style has been perhaps the most important influence in the development of my own thinking. The second is to Herbert Marcuse himself, who graciously consented to read the chapter of the book which treats his work. In the midst of very trying times in the summer of 1968, with the American Legion and reactionary congressmen harassing him, and while literally hiding out following a threat on his life, Professor Marcuse somehow managed to find time to read my account of his earlier, more purely intellectual skirmishes. It was not only an act of kindness on his part, it was also a testimony to his goodwill and remarkable personal composure.

Stanford University
February, 1969

INTRODUCTION: FREUDIAN RADICALISM

WE ARE just beginning to see Freud in perspective. His great discoveries were made over half a century ago, and they no longer represent the immediate data of our own culture. In effect, Freud now appears in our intellectual history as a figure whose achievement must be subjected to the kind of historical analysis and evaluation which we afford Marxism or Hegelianism.

Unfortunately, the effort to understand Freud historically has been complicated by the divided character of the man and his work. There has been no single great debate over psychoanalysis, but rather a number of lesser controversies about particular tensions in Freud's intellectual makeup. There is, first, the question of whether psychoanalysis should be considered a scientific psychology or an imaginative metaphysics. We have on the one hand Freud the clinician, heir to the scientific tradition of experiment and observation, preoccupied with discrete therapeutic problems; and on the other hand

Freud the speculative philospher who dabbled in anthropology and political theory and set out to diagnose the universal neurosis of mankind. There is also the question of whether psychoanalysis was the final product of nineteenth-century positivism, or an early manifestation of the revolt against positivism with which our century began. Here one contrasts Freud the product of the Helmholtz school of physiology, infatuated throughout his life with mechanical and electrical metaphors, always insisting that psychology would one day be a branch of physics or chemistry, attacking religion as if the nineteenth century had never happened, with the Freud who in the 1890's made the revolutionary discovery that men fall ill because of memories, the man who read Dostoevski with enthusiasm and wrote about Leonardo with sympathy and insight, who characterized himself as a conquistador rather than a scientist, and who, at the end of his life, identified his own intellectual venture with the religious mission of Moses. Finally, there is the issue of rationalism versus instinctualism—Freud the loyal son of the Enlightenment, struggling to uphold the values of reason and humanity and to defend the embattled ego against the assaults of instinct and conscience, versus Freud the doctor and sometime apologist of the passions, who portrayed man as licentious and murderous, the victim of unconscious impulses, truly himself only in his most childish and irrational moments.

These tensions are all very real, and historians of Freudianism have acted legitimately in attempting to resolve them. However, there is, I think, a larger dichotomy under which the others might be subsumed. It is the question of Freud's ideological location along the spectrum from conservatism to radicalism. The question can be formulated in both political and sexual terms. Did Freud's theoretical achievement imply a revolutionary or a reactionary attitude toward the human situation? Was Freud truly the apologist of sexual and political repression, drawing a picture of inevitable unhappiness, unfreedom, and aggression, or did his new science contain within it the promise of gratification, liberty, and peace? Put another way, was psychoanalysis basically critical or conformist? By and large, I think, the verdict, both on Freud himself and on the science he created, has been on the conservative side. Freud has most frequently been identified, along with Weber, Durkheim, Pareto, and even Spengler, as one of the great antiutopians of the early twentieth century, the man who dealt the final blow to the revolutionary aspirations of Marxism. Yet there remains the haunting suspicion that Freud was up to something mischievous, that psychoanalysis, despite its overt historical pessimism, refuses to adapt itself peaceably to the established political and sexual order. Certainly many European and American conservatives have found Freud most unsettling—indeed, no less dangerous than Marx himself.

This study is devoted to a group of European intellectuals who explored the radical potential of psychoanalytic theory. They were unwilling to accept the majority sentiment that Freud's great enterprise implied instinctual renunciation and political reaction. Instead, they found in Freud's work the rudiments of a radical political and sexual philosophy, which served to undermine the established culture. The result of their collective endeavors was to offer a corrective to the prevailing interpretation of

Freud as conservative. In the writings of Wilhelm Reich, Geza Roheim, and Herbert Marcuse, Freud emerges as the architect of a more erotic and more humane organization of man's communal life. He appears as heir to the critical impulse in European social thought, a prophet in the tradition of Karl Marx.

I have chosen to study Reich, Roheim, and Marcuse as the foremost representatives of the radical tradition in psychoanalysis. Several years ago I came to the conclusion that by understanding how certain intellectuals managed to view psychoanalysis as a revolutionary or critical doctrine, I might better be able to come to terms with Freud himself. In other words, it was my feeling that one could most successfully get at the radical component in Freud's own intellectual constitution via the circuitous route of his left-wing disciples. Thus I harbor no illusions concerning the bias of the interpretations I have chosen to analyze. On the contrary, I find such interpretations useful precisely because of their one-sidedness: they pose the issue in clearly focused terms, offering the intellectual historian a vantage point from which to view the master himself.

I feel I owe the reader a more precise characterization of the radicalism I detect in Reich, Roheim, and Marcuse. I have assigned the concept several different meanings in the course of this study. The common denominator linking all three thinkers, and the primary criterion I have used in selecting my protagonists, is sexual radicalism. Reich, Roheim, and Marcuse are all convinced of the unparalleled significance of sex, both in individual psychology and in the evolution of civilization. In this they do not, I suppose, differ markedly from Freud himself.

What makes them sexual radicals is their unqualified enthusiasm for sex, their belief that sexual pleasure is the ultimate measure of human happiness, and their pronounced hostility to the sexual repressiveness of modern civilization. I have frequently been asked why my study omitted a man like Erich Fromm, who has made a considerable reputation as a psychoanalytic radical. The answer is quite simple: while Fromm undoubtedly stands to the left of Freud politically, he is a rabid sexual conservative, denying both the importance attributed to sexuality by Freud himself and the value assigned to it by Reich, Roheim, and Marcuse.

The second connotation of Freudian radicalism is political. Reich, Roheim, and Marcuse share the conviction that politics and sexuality are intimately connected with one another. Their radicalism consists of regarding sexual repression as one of the principal mechanisms of political domination. I have also used radicalism in the more familiar sense of advocating political, social, or economic revolution. However, I have not been able to insist on this criterion, since only Reich and Marcuse can be characterized as political revolutionaries in the traditional sense. Roheim's critical attitude toward politics never resulted in a commitment to political activism; in this respect he was much like Freud. Moreover, Roheim did not share Reich's or Marcuse's Marxian sympathies, and he did not follow them in attempting to work out a synthesis of Marx and Freud—an enterprise which I have also taken as a characteristic, if not mandatory, feature of Freudian radicalism.

The third sense in which I have used the concept radicalism is somewhat less precise. It might be called stylistic radicalism. What I have in mind is a propensity for extreme statement, for pursuing a line of argument in a relentless, some would say inflexible, fashion. Reich, Roheim, and Marcuse all exhibit a categorical quality of mind. Reich fixed upon a single idea, the orgasm, and elevated it to a universal exegetical principle. Roheim was a ruthless leveler, subjecting all cultural artifacts to the most uncompromising sort of psychoanalytic reductionism. And Marcuse has enthusiastically committed himself to the most extreme, and apparently outlandish, psychoanalytic concepts, at once embracing Freud's death instinct and rising to a lofty vision of universal erotic gratification. All three thinkers are eminently injudicious; they harbor only contempt for the pluralistic tolerance of the liberal imagination.

Although I have treated these three thinkers as exemplars of a certain tradition in psychoanalysis, I have also respected their individuality. That is, while attempting to place their ideas in the evolving tradition of Freudian radicalism, I have also been preoccupied with the logic of their individual intellectual development. I suggested a moment ago that these intellectuals could be used as steppingstones to Freud. But they are also interesting theorists in their own right, and I have tried to do justice to the cohesiveness of their thought. This concern has frequently led me far afield from psychoanalysis—into the history of anthropology, political theory, and philosophy. In effect, I have found it important to place Reich, Roheim, and Marcuse within the larger context of European intellectual history in the modern period.

Finally, let me indicate that I have made no pretense to neutrality in this essay. I consider the Weberian ideal of a *wertfreien* science misguided and, in the final analysis, illusory. In general I think it advisable for the intellectual historian to approach his subject with sympathy, although without forfeiting his critical perspective. Moreover, I should confess that it has been easy for me to deal generously with Reich, Roheim, and Marcuse, since I share many of their prejudices and convictions. I do not intend to argue whether any one of them is a thinker of the first rank, but I admire them all. Most important, I am persuaded that they offer a legitimate and important corrective to the prevailing understanding of Freud. I cannot be convinced that Freud was anything less than a revolutionary, the man who rendered for the twentieth century services comparable to those Marx rendered for the nineteenth.

WILHELM REICH

———————————◆————————————

WILHELM REICH is a difficult intellectual, and I should admit right at the start that my attitude toward Reich is ambivalent. I am impressed by his frequent incisiveness, his obvious theoretical boldness, and his humane generosity. But I do not want to identify myself with his alarming intellectual simplicity. In short, I appreciate Reich's radicalism, but I am bothered by his insensitivity to the complexity of things. I have attempted to cope with this ambivalence by reading Reich with all the sympathy I could muster. At every point I have tried to distinguish what is valuable, or at least interesting, in his work from what is merely perverse.

Reich's thought was clearly of a piece, despite the efforts of orthodox psychoanalysts to draw a line (around 1934) between the good Reich and the bad. I do not wish to argue that Reich never changed his mind. In fact, he possessed one of the most volatile imaginations of the twentieth century. It is precisely the development of Reich's thinking that I have emphasized in this chapter. Little or nothing has been written on his work from the particular perspective of the intellectual historian. The one genuinely sophisticated treatment of his thought to have appeared in recent years, a long chapter in Philip Rieff's *The Triumph of the Therapeutic*, offers a number of interesting historical insights, but in general Rieff's approach is analytical rather than chronological. My tack has been just the opposite. Without ignoring the important continuities underlying the successive phases of Reich's career, I have tried to be scrupulous in distinguishing the ideas and rhetoric of one phase from those of another. Moreover, wherever possible I have related Reich's theoretical development to his practical activities, as well as to the general evolution of psychoanalysis and the broader intellectual currents of the time.

My point of reference in this chapter, as in the entire study, is classical Freudian psychoanalysis. I have chosen to examine Reich as a particularly arresting example of the kind of social theory and philosophical vision that evolved out of Freud. It is important to point this out, since the true Reichian is convinced that Reich's greatest contributions lay not in the field of psychology or even sociology, but in biophysics and astronomy. From my perspective, however, Reich is of interest principally as the social philosopher who, perhaps more consistently than anyone else, worked out the critical and revolutionary implications of psychoanalytic theory.

I

Wilhelm Reich belonged to the second generation of Freud's psychoanalytic critics. It was a generation that fell between that of the earliest deviants (Jung, Adler, and Stekel) and the later generation of revisionists and ego-psychologists who began their work in the 1930's (Fromm, Horney, Sullivan, Anna Freud, Ernst Kris, Heinz Hartmann, and Erik Erikson). Besides Reich, the two principal representatives of this middle generation were Sandor Ferenczi and Otto Rank. It was not birth dates which united Reich, Ferenczi, and Rank: Reich himself was born in 1897, Rank in 1884, and Ferenczi in 1873. But all three men made their most significant contributions to psychoanalysis at approximately the same time, in the 1920's, and all three experienced an almost simultaneous falling out with Freud in the early 1930's. Most important, the three shared a similar concern during the period of their greatest impact on psychoanalysis, namely the problem of technique. Clara Thompson has characterized the postwar era as "a period of growing pessimism about the therapeutic effectiveness of psychoanalysis."[1] Rank, Ferenczi, and Reich addressed themselves precisely to this crisis in therapy. Each ultimately abandoned Freud's "talking cure" in favor of a more active, more dramatic, and, it was hoped, more effective therapeutic method. And in each case the break with

[1] Clara Thompson, *Psychoanalysis: Evolution and Development* (New York, 1950), p. 172.

classical Freudian therapy was followed inevitably by a deviation from the master's general psychological conceptions and *Weltanschauung*.

Reich became a member of the Vienna Psychoanalytic Society in 1920, while still a medical student at the University of Vienna.[2] It was rather unusual for so young a man to be accepted among the elders of the psychoanalytic movement, but it should be borne in mind that Reich, like most Europeans of his generation, was old beyond his years. The experience of the war, in which he had fought from 1915 to 1918, was already behind him. Before the war were the happier years spent on his father's large farm in the German-Ukrainian part of the Austrian Empire. As an adolescent he took part in the yearly agricultural routine, and in his spare time he maintained plant and insect collections, as well as his own breeding laboratory.[3] Indeed, the most striking feature of Reich's childhood was its bucolic setting. Perhaps this closeness to nature explains his later antipathy to "mechanistic" industrial civilization, as well as the prominent role which the eighteenth-century rhetoric of "naturalism" assumed in his social criticism.

Once accepted within the psychoanalytic movement, Reich lost little time establishing himself as an expert on technique. In 1922 he helped found the Vienna Seminar for Psychoanalytic Therapy, which he led from 1924 to 1930. The "technical seminar" was a branch of the Vienna Psychoanalytic Society devoted to the improvement of

[2] Reich, *The Function of the Orgasm* (New York, 1961), pp. 27–29.
[3] "Biographical Note," in *Wilhelm Reich: Selected Writings* (New York, 1961), pp. 3–4.

therapeutic technique "through systematic case studies."[4]
The members of the seminar worked exclusively with case
histories which had successfully resisted traditional analysis.[5] As head of this seminar Reich established his reputation as a brilliant therapist, and out of his experiences in
the seminar he developed the basic components of his
own psychological system: the theory of the orgasm, the
theory of character, and the technique of character
analysis.

Although Reich's career was regularly punctuated with
earth-shaking discoveries, the greatest discovery of all
was undoubtedly the function of the orgasm. The orgasm
was his *idée fixe*. It stood at the heart of his theory of man
and society, and it ultimately became the rubric under
which he interpreted the entire cosmos. The simplicity
and consistency of this vision are at once magnificent and
appalling.

Reich became aware of the importance of sexual life
even before he officially affiliated himself with the psychoanalytic movement:

> An entry in my diary, of March 1, 1919, runs: "Perhaps
> my own morality objects to it. However, from my own
> experience, and from observation of myself and others, I
> have become convinced that sexuality is the center around
> which revolves the whole of social life as well as the
> inner life of the individual."[6]

[4] *The Function of the Orgasm*, p. 40.
[5] Walter Briehl, "Wilhelm Reich," in *Psychoanalytic Pioneers*,
Franz Alexander, Samuel Eisenstein, Martin Grotjahn, eds. (New
York, 1966), p. 431.
[6] *The Function of the Orgasm*, p. 4. Reprinted by permission of
Farrar, Straus & Giroux, Inc.

Eight years elapsed between this original insight and the first systematic presentation of the orgasm theory in *Die Funktion des Orgasmus.*[7] Like Freud, Reich developed his basic ideas in an effort to explain the etiology of the neuroses. All neuroses, he contended, were accompanied by a disturbance of genitality. Freud had stated earlier that no neurosis arose without sexual conflict, but he had meant "sexual" in the widest possible sense. For "sexual" Reich now substituted "genital," thus undermining that broadening of our erotic sensibilities which had been one of Freud's hardest-won accomplishments. To be sure, Reich never denied that there were nongenital manifestations of sexuality, but beside the monumental importance of the genital act they paled into insignificance.[8]

As Reich was well aware, his genital theory of the

[7] *The Function of the Orgasm* (1942) is *not* a translation of *Die Funktion des Orgasmus* (1927). Much of the material from the 1927 monograph was included in the later work, but they are, for all practical purposes, two separate books. This bibliographical anomaly is perhaps the most obvious example of the sorry editorial state in which Reich's writings find themselves. By twentieth-century standards Reich was remarkably prolific. An official list of his publications, compiled by the Orgone Institute Press, notes twenty-six books and almost a hundred articles ("Appendix 3," in *Selected Writings*). Most of Reich's more popular books went through several editions and translations during his lifetime, and at every turn he took it upon himself to bring his ideas up to date—without, unfortunately, always bothering to inform the reader. It is not unusual, for example, to come upon a reference to the Nazi-Soviet pact in a work supposedly written in 1935. Clearly what is needed is a critical edition of Reich's works, but I'm afraid nothing of the sort is in the offing.

[8] Reich, *Die Funktion des Orgasmus* (Leipzig, Vienna, Zurich, 1927), pp. 7, 13–14; *The Function of the Orgasm*, p. 87.

neuroses had been anticipated by Freud himself. In the 1890's Freud had distinguished, according to their origin, two major categories of neuroses: the psychoneuroses and the actual neuroses. The psychoneurotic suffered from memories; the origins of his illness lay in the repressed longings and traumas of a distant childhood. In the case of the actual neuroses ("actual" in the French or German sense of "present-day"), the victim fell ill from a *contemporary* disturbance of genitality, such as excessive masturbation or asceticism.[9] Having made the distinction, Freud went on to devote his career to a study of the psychoneuroses; his later psychological conceptions and, most clearly, his therapeutic technique were geared to the historical (as opposed to contemporary) concept of neurotic disorders. The actual neuroses were simply forgotten.

Reich now proposed to reverse Freud's procedure. He would revive the concept of the actual neuroses and make it the centerpiece of his systematic pathology.[10] A good deal was at stake in this shift of emphasis, more even than the difference between a historical and a contemporary conception of mental illness, important though that may be. The most significant implication, I would suggest, was that it involved opting for a quantitative rather than a qualitative notion of psychic functioning. Freud had explained the dynamics of the actual neuroses in terms of what he later called the "economic" perspective on mental life, that is, in terms of the metaphor of psychic energy.

[9] Cf. Sigmund Freud, "Sexuality in the Aetiology of the Neuroses," in *The Standard Edition of the Complete Psychological Works of Sigmund Freud*, James Strachey, ed. (London, 1953–1966), III.
[10] *Die Funktion des Orgasmus*, pp. 9–10.

The actual-neurotic symptom was "nourished" by undischarged libido. The extent to which Freud intended this metapsychological formula to be taken seriously is still a much-debated issue. We simply cannot say for certain how strongly he was committed to the nineteenth-century positivist vision of a scientific psychology, which would ultimately deal in measurable and manageable quantities, as in hydraulics or electricity. However, if our assessment in Freud's case has to be hedged with ambiguity, we need not be so diffident where Reich is concerned. He reveled in precisely those aspects of Freud's scientism that most later commentators found slightly embarrassing, particularly the vocabulary of "blocks," "cathexes," and "displacements." He invented the term "sex-economy," with its suggestion of a synthesis of Freud and Marx (but in fact more like an amalgam of Freud and Adam Smith), to designate the science of biopsychic energy.[11] One could characterize the entire course of Reich's intellectual development as an elaboration of Freud's concept of libido, in the process of which the original "metaphor" hardened into that very concrete stuff, Cosmic Orgone Energy.

I have oversimplified Reich's theory for purposes of contrasting it with Freud's. His basic contention was indeed that neurotics fall ill because of a disturbance of genitality, or, more precisely, because of their inability to achieve a satisfactory orgasm. But he did not completely abandon Freud's concern for the psychological (or historical) origins of the neuroses. The Oedipal situation, in particular, continued to provide the fantasy material, the "content," of the neuroses.[12] Reich adopted a Marxian

11 *The Function of the Orgasm*, p. xvii.
12 *Die Funktion des Orgasmus*, p. 79.

vocabulary to illuminate this process: dammed-up sexual energy was the basis of symptom formation, but the neuroses also had a "psychic superstructure."[13] Reich was hard put to explain how the disturbance of genitality came about in the first place, and on one occasion he actually admitted that at the beginning of all neurotic development stood a psychic conflict.[14] The point to emphasize, however, is that he was concerned almost exclusively with the economic analysis of the neuroses. In the end it was the orgasm, the release of sexual energy, which made the difference between sickness and health.

Not surprisingly, Reich was frequently required to defend his theory against the objection that many neurotics had "a completely healthy sex life."[15] And he was, I think, equal to the task. On closer inspection the orgasm theory turns out to be much subtler than was at first apparent. Reich coined the phrase "orgastic potency" to designate with greater precision the phenomenon he had in mind. Not every sexual contact resulting in climax measured up to his criteria for a true orgasm. Orgasm had to be heterosexual, without irrelevant fantasies, and of an appropriate duration. Above all, a true orgasm had to result in the complete release of dammed-up libido. In other words, orgastic potency was *defined* in economic terms; it was "the capacity for complete discharge of all dammed-up sexual excitation through involuntary pleasurable contractions of the body."[16]

In the light of this definition, Reich's contention that

13 *The Function of the Orgasm*, p. 68.
14 *Die Funktion des Orgasmus*, p. 198.
15 *The Function of the Orgasm*, p. 75.
16 *Ibid.*, p. 79; *Die Funktion des Orgasmus*, pp. 18–28.

"not a single neurotic individual possesses orgastic potency"[17] becomes at once more plausible and more elusive. Who was to say whether the sexual habits of a particular individual fulfilled the economic criteria of orgastic potency? Reich was not about to have his theory refuted by eager empiricists. Of course he did offer certain minimal empirical measurements of orgastic potency, but he also left himself plenty of territory to haggle over.

I would like to make three final observations about the orgasm theory. First, one should note the radical difference between the Reichian and the traditional Christian notions of the function of sexual pleasure. In the popular mind (which in this matter, at least, has remained remarkably loyal to Christian orthodoxy), the orgasm is the sugar coating with which the Creator (or Nature) has disguised the bitter pill of reproduction. True, it may be our highest pleasure, but basically we can get along without it. It is vital only to the survival of the race. For Reich, on the contrary, the orgasm was no longer an experience on the periphery of biological or psychic life. It was instead the central regulating mechanism of the closed energy system called man. Failing the proper sexual release, man would surely fall ill, either in body or in mind, because undischarged libido would be channeled into the formation of psychic or physical symptoms.

Second, if the orgasm was the central outlet for the bodily economy, it followed quite naturally that uninhibited genitality was the goal of therapy. Reich embraced this conclusion enthusiastically, although he was

---

[17] *The Function of the Orgasm,* p. 79.

reluctant to announce it openly in the early years of the technical seminar.[18] By 1927, however, when *Die Funktion des Orgasmus* was published, he felt enough confidence in his theory to state without qualification that the object of psychoanalytic therapy was "the establishment of orgastic potency."[19]

Finally, I would like to come to Reich's defense in his preoccupation with the "mechanistic" metaphor of psychic energy. I mentioned a moment ago that many commentators have found Freud's libido theory a rather unattractive manifestation of his residual positivism. Historically speaking, the theory undoubtedly had nineteenth-century roots. However, I think that in dismissing this conception as dated we fail to do justice to its critical implications. The materialistic concept of psychic energy opposed itself to any spiritualization of sexuality. It seems to me no accident that those schools of psychoanalysis which have abandoned or radically attenuated the libido theory (neo-Freudianism and, increasingly, ego-psychology) have also been most prone to shortchanging sexuality. Reich's orgasm theory, on the contrary, preserved and accentuated the critical impetus of Freud's "mechanistic" conception.

II

Die Funktion des Orgasmus was dedicated to Freud, but it was given a rather tepid reception by the old

[18] *Ibid.*, p. 98.
[19] *Die Funktion des Orgasmus*, p. 193.

man.[20] It seems certain that Reich would never have established a major reputation on the basis of the orgasm theory alone. The very enthusiasm with which he accepted and elaborated Freud's hypothesis of a libidinal economy tended to isolate him from the principal concerns of his generation of psychoanalysts. Quite the opposite, however, was the case with his theory of character. In this instance his work was very much in the mainstream of psychoanalytic thought during the 1920's and 1930's. In fact, Reich must be counted among the pioneers of Freudian ego-psychology, which (along with its heretical deviation, neo-Freudian revisionism) has dominated the psychoanalytic movement down to the present day. Yet even here, as we shall see, Reich was curiously out of step, for his concept of character, worked out between 1926 and 1934, was designed expressly as a companion piece to the theory of the orgasm.

Reich arrived at his idea of character by way of the clinical problem of resistances. He noted that quite often it was not a particular piece of conscious or unconscious trickery that interfered with analytic progress, but rather the patient's general personal "style," his "character structure." For example, instead of resisting the therapeutic process by raising putative intellectual objections to psychoanalysis (the classic example of resistance), a patient might achieve the same ends by reacting to the analyst with exaggerated politeness. Reich would call this politeness a "character resistance";[21] it served the same function as the more easily recognized resistance of classical

---

[20] *The Function of the Orgasm*, pp. 140–41.
[21] Reich, "On Character Analysis" (1928), in *The Psycho-Analytic Reader*, Robert Fliess, ed. (London, 1950), p. 108.

analysis, i.e., diverting the analyst from the investigation of dangerous unconscious material, but it had the distinct advantage of being "built into" the patient's general mode of behavior.

Through a slight, but significant, shift of emphasis, Reich came to treat the character resistance itself as the central manifestation of the patient's illness. The phrase "character resistance" gave way almost imperceptibly to "character neurosis." This definition of neurosis in terms of character was one of the more interesting of Reich's ideas, and it signaled an important historical change in the concept of mental illness. With Reich the analyst's attention was diverted from the easily identifiable neurotic symptom which had concerned Freud in the 1890's (a paralysis, a tick, an irrational or compulsive ritual) to the malfunctioning of the personality as a whole. From Reich's point of view, a symptom in the classical sense was only the manifestation of a general psychic disorder, "a concentrate of the neurotic character,"[22] and it was not necessarily present in all neuroses. Whereas the symptom corresponded to a definite experience or specific wish in the patient's past, the character neurosis was the product of his entire history.[23]

[22] *Ibid.*

[23] *Ibid.*, p. 111. This conception of neurosis may lack the sharp outlines of the original Freudian theory, but it is clearly more in keeping both with the contemporary lay use of the word "neurotic," and with our intellectual prejudice against any overly precise or mechanistic explanation of how the personality functions. Curiously, the term "neurosis," used to describe a clinical syndrome, seems to be going out of fashion altogether, perhaps because the suggestion of a foreign body within the fabric of an otherwise healthy personality still clings to it. Instead one now speaks of

Reich's theory of character was one manifestation of the general revival of ego-psychology during the 1920's. Freud's great discovery, of course, was the unconscious, and it was therefore not at all surprising that the earliest efforts of the psychoanalytic movement were devoted to an exploration of this uncharted dimension of the personality. With the publication of *The Ego and the Id* (1923), however, Freud shifted the focus of attention back to the traditional psychological problem of the conscious self, the ego.[24] To be sure, this ego was still conceived as evolving out of the darker, unconscious dimensions of the mind, and it led a most precarious existence between the demonic sensuality of the id and the militant prudery of the superego. But if Freud's ego lacked the moral fiber and sheer energy with which the neo-Freudians were to endow it, or even the autonomy which the ego-psychologists have granted it, it was nevertheless portrayed with considerable compassion and admiration. In general Freud's attitude seemed to be that the ego's lot was not a happy one and that it deserved all our sympathy and consideration.

Reich's theory of character was in reality a theory of the ego. Technically, I suppose, this statement is incorrect, since the concept of character was used by Reich (as by psychoanalysts in general) to designate a type of behavior rather than a structural component of the per-

---

"character disorders," and Reich's concept of character neurosis clearly marked an important milestone in this shift in perspective.
[24] "Ego" and "conscious" are, of course, not absolutely identical, since important ego functions are unconscious. Cf. *The Ego and the Id, The Standard Edition* . . ., Vol. XIX.

sonality.[25] Still, what was at stake here was essentially the pre-Freudian, conscious self. The striking feature of Reich's treatment of character, the feature isolating him from all his contemporaries, was the uncompromising hostility with which he regarded this dimension of the personality. Where he had originally spoken of "character neurosis" or "neurotic character," he soon slipped into the habit of treating character *tout court* as a disease.[26] Character was a kind of "armoring," a rigid outer shell which protected the individual from the hard knocks of reality, but at the same time limited his ability to experience life, both within and without him, in its full intensity.[27] Reich's most famous work, *Character-Analysis*, in which he brought together in book form the articles he had written on the subject between 1928 and 1933, was in effect a prolonged and quite often ill-tempered assault on the ego.[28]

[25] Reich, "The Genital Character and the Neurotic Character" (1929), in *The Psycho-Analytic Reader*, p. 125. Character is defined here as "the typical mode of reaction of the ego towards the id and the outer world." Perhaps character might best be thought of as the "style" of the ego.

[26] Reich, *Character-Analysis* (3rd ed.; New York, 1963), p. 145.

[27] Reich, "On Character Analysis," p. 111; "Psychic Contact and Vegetative Current" (1935), in *Character-Analysis*, p. 342.

[28] I have somewhat oversimplified Reich's position in order to emphasize what I feel is the implicit logic of his characterology. The notion that character is itself a disease is suggested in statements such as "Character is primarily and essentially a narcissistic protection mechanism" ("Genital and Neurotic Character," p. 125), and "The character consists in a *chronic* alteration of the ego which one might describe as a rigidity" (*Character-Analysis*, p. 145). By way of contrast, I should note that Reich frequently attempted to distinguish between good and bad character struc-

The contrast between Reich's hostility toward the ego and Freud's compassion for it exactly reflected the difference in their respective attitudes toward the instincts. Freud tended to regard the unconscious animal depths in man with distrust. He portrayed the id as "a cauldron full of seething excitations,"[29] and the unconscious as peopled with hideous specters and murderous desires. Reich did not deny the existence of this unconscious, in all its ugliness, but it remained for him the distortion of a more basic reality which was essentially healthy.[30] His confidence in the instincts was practically unlimited. He ultimately came to think of the human personality in terms of a three-tiered model. At the deepest level were man's "*natural* sociality and sexuality, *spontaneous* enjoyment of work, [and] *capacity for love*." When these wholesome instincts were repressed, as in our sex-negating culture, a second layer arose, "the Freudian 'unconscious,' in which sadism, greediness, lasciviousness, envy, [and] perversions of all kinds" held sway. This layer was in turn

---

tures, between what he called the "genital" and the "neurotic" character. But when examined closely this distinction proves to be illusory. The good character, the genital character, turns out to be a kind of anticharacter. It represents an ego-style which is utterly transparent to the desires of the id. Put another way, the genital character seems to me not so much a meaningful structural type as an aggregate of all conceivable virtues, libidinal and otherwise. Cf. "Genital and Neurotic Character," pp. 136–37.

[29] Freud, *New Introductory Lectures, The Standard Edition* . . ., Vol. XXII, p. 73.

[30] *The Function of the Orgasm*, p. 148: "Beneath [the] neurotic mechanisms, behind all [the] dangerous, grotesque, irrational phantasies and impulses, I found a bit of simple, matter-of-fact, decent nature."

covered over and kept in check by the characterological superstructure, "the artificial mask of self-control, of compulsive, insincere politeness and of artificial sociality."[31] Character, then, had a kind of functional justification; it represented a necessary stopgap in the face of the perversion of instinct which repression had already brought about. But in the final analysis, character was itself a disease, all the more pernicious because it was not recognized as such. Thus Reich took as his special mission the denunciation of the ego and all its works. The unconscious could take care of itself; its hideousness was apparent even to the naked eye. Much less obvious, however, was the fundamentally sick nature of the ego's response to the perverse Freudian unconscious, that is, the ego's character structure.

Behind Reich's analysis of character lay the familiar economic conception of psychic life which we have found to be the leitmotiv of his orgasm theory. Character was in fact the economic antithesis of the orgasm. It developed, quite literally, at the expense of the orgasm; it "consumed" the psychic energy not discharged in sexual intercourse.[32] Therefore the establishment of orgastic potency, which was the goal of therapy, involved the dissolution of character and the liberation of psychic energy from its characterological prison.[33] It was to this end that Reich developed his famous technique of character analysis. He invariably professed that character-analytic therapy was only a prologue to the traditional

---

[31] *Ibid.*, p. 204.
[32] "Genital and Neurotic Character," p. 128.
[33] *Character-Analysis*, p. 127.

exploration of the unconscious by means of free associations.[34] But Reich rarely got past the preliminaries. A careful reading of *Character-Analysis,* or any of the clinical writings, reveals that the detection and dissolution of character resistances absorbed his entire therapeutic energies.

The first objective of Reichian analysis was to discover the precise nature of the patient's characterological armor. It was in the art of detection that Reich demonstrated his genuine technical virtuosity. He drew attention to a new realm of evidence, previously either unnoticed or dismissed as meaningless, which, to the alert observer, revealed clues to the patient's true character. Freud had made a similar breakthrough when he discovered meaning in such overlooked aspects of behavior as dreams, slips, and jokes. Reich now supplemented Freud's evidence with a new set of data: "the patient's manner of speech, the way in which he looks at the analyst and greets him, the way he lies on the couch, the inflection of his voice, the measure of his conventional politeness."[35] These, along with many other mannerisms and postural attitudes, were the raw material with which the analyst worked. It was no longer so important to notice *what* the patient said as *how* he said it; the form rather than the content of his revelations was decisive. In fact, the patient need not say anything at all; he revealed himself even in his bodily motions and facial expressions. Where traditional analysis had emphasized intellectual or, more precisely, verbal exchange (the "talking cure"),

[34] "On Character Analysis," p. 122.
[35] *Ibid.*, p. 112.

Reich conceived of both patient and doctor as actors in the flesh.

It would be an understatement to say that Reichian therapy lacked the decorum and austerity of classical Freudian analysis. Reich's style was unabashedly melodramatic. His basic tactic was to isolate a particular character trait and confront the patient with it repeatedly, even threatening to terminate the analysis if this procedure was objected to. Ultimately the patient was forced to experience his mannerism "like a distressing compulsive symptom."[36] The result of this heightened awareness was the dissolution of the character trait, and with it the release of imprisoned libido.

In some respects this procedure was in keeping with the original Freudian formula. In traditional analysis the bringing to consciousness of a repressed infantile memory relieved the patient of his neurotic symptom. With Reich, too, consciousness, now of one's present character structure rather than of past traumas, was the key to mental health. But this healing consciousness could be achieved only through a vigorous policy of intervention on the part of the analyst and a ruthless exploitation of the emotional tie between patient and doctor (the transference).[37] It was this emphasis on the active role of the therapist and the affective reaction of the patient that separated Reich from Freud and united him with Ferenczi and Rank. Reich warned that this aggressive procedure was not without its dangers; in every case, "character analysis gives rise to violent emotional outbursts."[38] Reich would

[36] *Ibid.*, p. 116.
[37] *Character-Analysis*, pp. 126–28.
[38] "On Character Analysis," p. 122.

frequently provoke such reactions with the most outlandish behavior, and it was not unusual for an analytic session to culminate in a gross physical attack on the doctor. The ultimate goal of therapy, however, was love. In every instance, successful treatment meant loosening the patient's character armor and heightening his capacity for genital pleasure.

III

The theory of character and the technique of character analysis established Reich in the vanguard of the psychoanalytic movement during the late 1920's. In the meantime, however, his relations with the elders of the movement had deteriorated seriously. Within the psychoanalytic establishment, Paul Federn, Ernest Jones, and Otto Fenichel were among the earliest of Reich's detractors, and according to his own account it was their constant "digging" which ultimately succeeded in turning Freud against him.[39]

Reich's relationship with Freud seems to have followed the classic pattern of infatuation and disillusionment so characteristic of psychoanalytic friendships. Freud is said to have thought very highly of Reich as a young man, enough so to have included him within the inner circle of friends who met once a month in Freud's home.[40] For

[39] Reich, Reich Speaks of Freud, Mary Higgins and Chester M. Raphael, eds. (New York, 1967), pp. 8, 10, 101–2, 105, 153, 195, 213.
[40] Ernest Jones, The Life and Work of Sigmund Freud, Vol. III (New York, 1957), p. 191; Reich, The Function of the Orgasm, p. 165; Reich Speaks of Freud, pp. 41–42.

Reich's part, it is evident from scattered remarks throughout his writings that the acquaintance with Freud was the great event in his life.[41] On the basis of these facts one can legitimately assume that the friendship between the two men took on at least some of the characteristics of a father-son relationship. This hypothesis is supported by two circumstances: first, the age difference between the two men (forty-one years), and secondly, the fact that Reich's father had died in 1914, when Reich was only seventeen years old.[42] If I am correct here, then Reich's break with Freud was as much a personal as an intellectual necessity. This interpretation also helps explain the ambivalent nature of the break, at least on Reich's side. We love our fathers even though we slay them; in fact we seek their approbation for our murderous act. Thus Reich always maintained that it was Freud who had rejected him, not vice versa, and he even argued that underneath it all Freud actually approved of his heresy.[43]

Reich, it must be noted, was fully aware of the psychological dimension of his difficulties with Freud. He readily confessed his "father fixation," and he recognized his personal need "to make a clean break."[44] But he also insisted that the break was a personal necessity for Freud as well. Reich argued that several psychological factors had prevented Freud from accepting the equation of genital satisfaction and psychic health. He pointed first of all to Freud's residual Judaism, with its sexual rigidity and

[41] See, *The Function of the Orgasm*, pp. 17–18.
[42] "Biographical Note," in *Selected Writings*, p. 4.
[43] *The Function of the Orgasm*, pp. 105, 187, 197; *Character-Analysis*, p. xviii.
[44] *Reich Speaks of Freud*, p. 213; cf. also p. xiii.

historic commitment to monogamy. He also suggested that Freud was the victim of an unhappy marriage—that he was "very much dissatisfied genitally"—and thus unconsciously frightened by the orgasm theory.[45] Above all else, Reich attributed Freud's disenchantment to the burdens of success. After years of obscurity and struggle, Freud had lived to witness the general recognition of psychoanalysis in the 1920's. According to Reich, he was now too old and too weary to risk alienating his public (and his conservative disciples within the psychoanalytic movement) by espousing Reich's sexual radicalism. He thus tolerated the emasculation of the libido theory at the hands of pupils whom he secretly despised. In the end, Reich argued, it was this "seductive admiration" which kept Freud from pursuing his great discovery to its logical conclusion.[46]

I find Reich's analysis of Freud at least plausible, if exaggerated. Undoubtedly Reich's theoretical commitment to complete sexual fulfillment was a source of anxiety to the aging Freud, and to other members of the psychoanalytic elite as well. Moreover, the difficulty was compounded by Reich's private behavior in sexual matters. Reich later admitted to having affairs with his patients: "It happened once or twice that I fell in love with a patient. Then I was frank about it. I stopped the treatment and I let the thing cool off. Then we decided either yes or no to go to bed."[47] His first wife, Annie Pink, was a former patient, and in 1932, when the conflict with Freud was coming to a head, Reich divorced Annie and

[45] Ibid., pp. 20, 33–34, 129–30.
[46] Ibid., p. 35; cf. also pp. 21–25, 34–36, 59, 62, 66–67.
[47] Ibid., p. 103.

took up residence with another woman, Elsa Lindenberg. Reich himself later emphasized the importance of these private sexual circumstances in isolating him from Freud and the other psychoanalytic leaders.[48]

Reich's defection from the ranks of the orthodox was not a sudden development. Nor was it the result of a single theoretical disagreement. There had been a number of vaguely unpleasant confrontations with Freud as early as 1926, situations in which Freud either expressed strong reservations about the orgasm theory or criticized Reich's therapeutic methods.[49] However, it was Freud's hypothesis of a death instinct and his theory of the inexorable dialectic of civilization and repression that occasioned the final falling out.

Reich considered *Civilization and Its Discontents* an unmitigated disaster. Ironically, he also held himself indirectly responsible for the book's appearance.[50] On the

[48] *Ibid.*, pp. 102–3, 105–7, 112.
[49] *The Function of the Orgasm*, pp. 140–43.
[50] Here is his own account, from *The Function of the Orgasm* (pp. 165–68): "On December 12, 1929, I gave my talk on the *prophylaxis of the neuroses*, in Freud's inner circle. These monthly sessions at Freud's home were open only to the officers of the psychoanalytic society and a few guests. Everybody knew that the discussions at these meetings were of far-reaching importance. . . . In the course of these evenings at Freud's home, devoted to a discussion of the prophylaxis of the neuroses and the problem of culture, Freud for the first time clearly stated those views which in 1931 [*sic*] were published in 'Das Unbehagen in der Kultur' and which were often strictly contradictory to his views as expressed in 'Die Zukunft einer Illusion.' . . . Only a very few know that Freud's 'Unbehagen in der Kultur' originated from these discussions on culture, which took place in order to refute my maturing work and the 'danger' which was supposed to arise from it. The book

surface of things, one might have expected Reich to show considerable admiration for Freud's ideas about civilization and repression. After all, the argument of *Civilization and Its Discontents* was based quite explicitly on the hydraulic theory of psychic energy: the energy which made civilization possible was "subtracted from" direct erotic experience.[51] A few passages in Reich's early writings seemed to reflect an acceptance of this argument.[52] But by 1930, when the first version of *The Sexual Revolution* was published,[53] he unquestionably counted himself among the opponents of Freud's cultural philosophy.

Reich's critique of *Civilization and Its Discontents* was not particularly forceful. He claimed to have discovered an internal contradiction in Freud's argument:

> Two facts are at variance: On the one hand, the child has to suppress its instincts in order to become capable of cultural adjustment. On the other hand, it acquires, in this very process, a neurosis which in turn makes it in-

contains sentences which Freud used in our discussion to oppose my views."
[51] Freud, *Civilization and Its Discontents, The Standard Edition* . . ., Vol. XXI. See, in particular, pp. 103–4.
[52] *Die Funktion des Orgasmus*, p. 162; "Genital and Neurotic Character," p. 129.
[53] *The Sexual Revolution* is an editor's nightmare. The book which circulates under that title in a Noonday Press paperback edition (New York, 1962) is a translation and revision (1944) of *Die Sexualität im Kulturkampf*, which was first published in 1936. The latter, in turn, is really two books in one: the first half is an "enlarged" (p. xxxi) version of *Geschlechtsreife, Enthaltsamkeit, Ehemoral,* published originally in 1930; part two is entitled "The Struggle for the 'New Life' in the Soviet Union," and it seems to have been written in 1935.

capable of cultural development and adjustment and in the end makes it antisocial.[54]

This was of course not a contradiction at all; it was in fact the very dilemma Freud set out to expound. The contradiction, or better, the paradox existed not in Freud's mind, but in the objective process of civilization. Reich scored a more stylish point when he accused Freud of generalizing incorrectly from the repressiveness of Western civilization to a universal equation of culture and repression.[55] Here he was able to join in the general chorus of cultural relativists who criticized Freud's work, sometimes quite unfairly, for its insensitivity to non-European (or even non-Victorian) societies. Reich fully concurred in Freud's estimation of the repressive character of Western culture, but he maintained, as we shall see, that this was to be explained by the economic, social, and political peculiarities of Western history. Culture as such was not incompatible with sexuality. Indeed, the theme of the "unity of culture and nature" recurs throughout Reich's writings.[56] Sexual satisfaction, far from undermining creativity, was its foremost prerequisite. "The few bad poems which occasionally are created during abstinence are of no great interest."[57] However, Reich did not neglect the economic perspective in his defense of culture; he kept his libidinal budget balanced by arguing that cultural activities were

[54] Reich, *The Sexual Revolution* (New York, 1962), p. 12. Reprinted by permission of Farrar, Straus & Giroux, Inc.
[55] *Ibid.*, p. 10.
[56] *Ibid.*, p. 269; *The Function of the Orgasm*, p. xx.
[57] Reich, *The Sexual Revolution*, p. 66; cf. also *The Mass Psychology of Fascism* (New York, 1946), p. 252.

financed by sublimating not genital, but pregenital, libido.[58]

The same motives which led Reich to take issue with Freud's pessimistic cultural philosophy forced him to reject the death instinct as well. The hypothesis of a death instinct was Freud's way of expressing a characteristic modern uncertainty about human nature. In the course of the last hundred and fifty years, the notion of an innocent natural man corrupted by a perverse social order has given way to a deep sense of ambiguity about our instinctual makeup. It is commonplace to remark that the twentieth century is in this respect closer to the Middle Ages than to the Enlightenment. Freud's death instinct appears to be our modern equivalent of the doctrine of original sin. Reich, however, was more thoroughly entrenched in the Enlightenment tradition than Freud, and it was only in some of his final utterances that he transcended this eighteenth-century inheritance. At the time of the clash over the death instinct, he was unable to appreciate Freud's sense of the complexity of the human situation.

Of course, to have had reservations about the death instinct was nothing unusual, even within orthodox circles. Few seemed to take to the notion with any enthusiasm. It was not until the 1950's, and the writings of Herbert Marcuse and Norman O. Brown, that Freud's idea was examined with real seriousness. In *Die Funktion des Orgasmus* Reich still went along with Freud on the matter of innate aggression, although even here he argued that repressed libido could "augument" the destructive

[58] *Die Funktion des Orgasmus,* p. 188; "Neurotic and Genital Character," pp. 139–40.

impulses.[59] It was inevitable, however, that sooner or
later he would be forced to reject Freud's hypothesis
altogether. There was no place within his instinctual
monism for doubts about the basic goodness of human
nature.

The explicit refutation of the death instinct came in an
article entitled "The Masochistic Character," which Reich
published in the *Internationale Zeitschrift für Psychoanalyse* in 1932 and subsequently incorporated into
Character-Analysis. His point was a simple one, despite
the apparent sophistication of the argument: masochism
was a derivative rather than a primary psychic phenomenon. Anyone familiar with Reich's general style of
thought, particularly his infatuation with Freud's economic metaphor, could easily have anticipated the form
his argument would take. Destructiveness, like everything
else undesirable, was in reality a manifestation of repressed libido: "It is the inhibition of sexuality . . .
which makes aggression a power beyond mastery, because
inhibited sexual energy turns into destructive energy."[60]

I have, up to this point, treated Reich's clash with
Freud over the death instinct and the relation of culture
to repression as the result of the very different intellectual
and psychological predilections of the two men. This is,
however, only part of the story. Crucial practical matters
were at stake as well. If the argument of *Civilization and
Its Discontents* was correct, then any commitment to
sexual liberation necessarily involved a readiness to ac-

[59] Pp. 94–97, 153, 168–69, 196. Reich even suggested that the
First World War was caused by the unsatisfactory sex lives of the
Kaiser and the German aristocracy (p. 169).

[60] *Character-Analysis*, p. 290.

cept its radical cultural consequences: the end of art, industry, and ultimately even communal life itself. Reich was in fact convinced that Freud's pernicious cultural philosophy had been designed expressly to undermine his practical activities in the cause of sexual reform. Freud had placed his scientific authority "at the disposal of a conservative ideology";[61] he had supervised the "development of psychoanalysis into an *anti*sexual theory."[62]

If Freud's cultural philosophy undermined Reich's activities as a sexual reformer, the hypothesis of a death instinct was yet more tendentious. It made even a commitment to radical *social* and *political* criticism impossible, or at least pointless.[63] The death instinct implied that human suffering was inevitable, under socialism as well as capitalism. Thus Reich, like Adler before him, was forced to separate himself from psychoanalysis as much for political as for intellectual reasons. Freud, too, was fully aware of the ideological nature of his disagreement with Reich. He claimed, most unfairly, that Reich's article on masochism "culminated in the nonsensical statement that what we have called the death instinct is a product of the capitalistic system."[64] Freud even went so far as to state that "The Masochistic Character" had been written "in the service" of the Communist party.[65]

[61] *The Function of the Orgasm*, p. 195.
[62] *The Sexual Revolution*, p. 247.
[63] *Character-Analysis*, p. 214.
[64] Jones, *Sigmund Freud*, III, 166.
[65] Cf. "Translator's Note" to "The Masochistic Character," *Character-Analysis*, p. 209. The manner in which Freud overreacted to Reich's article on masochism lends weight to Reich's own psychological analysis of Freud, as I recounted it a few pages back. "The

Reich's membership in the International Psychoanalytic Association was officially terminated at the Lucerne Congress in 1934. Ernest Jones reported incorrectly (and with a certain amount of bad faith, I suspect) that Reich "resigned" from the Association at Lucerne.[66] In fact, Reich had already been secretly expelled from the German Psychoanalytic Society (and thus from the International Association) a year earlier. He learned shortly before the Lucerne Congress that his name would not appear on the calendar listing the members of the Association. Appar-

---

Masochistic Character" was a perfectly legitimate piece of psychoanalytic theorizing, without political obiter dicta. Yet it so annoyed Freud that for a while he insisted that it could not appear in the *Internationale Zeitschrift* without the following editorial comment:

> Special circumstances have caused the publisher to direct the reader's attention to a point that is usually taken for granted. Within the framework of psychoanalysis this journal gives every author who submits a paper for publication full freedom of opinion, and in turn does not assume any responsibility for these opinions. In the case of Dr. Reich, however, the reader should be informed that the author is a member of the Bolshevist party. Now it is known that Bolshevism sets similar limits to scientific research as does a church organization. Party obedience demands that everything contradicting the premises of its own dogma be rejected. It is up to the reader of this article to clear the author of such suspicions; the publisher would have made the same comment if he had been presented with a work of a member of the S.J. (*Reich Speaks of Freud*, p. 155. Reprinted by permission of Farrar, Straus, & Giroux.)

Freud continued his harassment the following year, when, in his capacity as editorial director of the International Psychoanalytic Publishers, he was party to the decision to cancel publication of Reich's *Character-Analysis*. (*Reich Speaks of Freud*, pp. 159–61.)

[66] Jones, *Sigmund Freud*, III, 191.

ently he was told that the publication of *The Mass Psychology of Fascism* (1933) had made him a liability to the psychoanalytic movement.[67] Thus Reich's break with psychoanalysis was inextricably bound up with his role as political activist and social philosopher. We must now retrace our steps in order to follow the evolution of Reich's political ideas and involvements in the late 1920's and early 1930's. This was in many respects the most interesting phase of his career: the period of his attempted synthesis of Marx and Freud, as well as the earliest anti-Fascist polemics. It was also a surprisingly brief phase, since by the mid-thirties Reich had already turned his attention to more pressing problems in the realm of biology.

IV

In the preface to the first edition of *Character-Analysis*, Reich asked how it was possible to justify writing a book on individual analytic technique when "in a city like Berlin there are millions of people who are neurotically ruined in their psychic structure."[68] The real task, he admitted, was not therapy but prophylaxis. However, under the existing regime of social, political, and particularly sexual repression, Reich felt that prevention was impossible. Thus he concluded his apology by arguing that until the preconditions for prevention had been cre-

[67] *The Function of the Orgasm*, p. 265; *Reich Speaks of Freud*, pp. 189, 255–61.
[68] *Character-Analysis*, p. xx.

ated by "a basic revolution in social institutions and ideologies," one's efforts were best devoted to a thorough study of the causes and cures of individual psychic disturbance.[69] Then, at least, it would be possible to introduce the proper prophylactic measures after the revolution.

In practice Reich was able to maintain no such neat distinction between the individual psychology of the present and the mass psychology of the future. Almost from the beginning of his professional career, he attempted to find some institutional synthesis of his political and psychological commitments. As a member of the Austrian Communist Party, he hit upon the idea of establishing socialist sex-hygiene clinics, which would make psychoanalytic advice available to the masses and at the same time arouse in them an awareness of the sexual reforms that must accompany the revolution. Between 1928 and 1930, six such clinics were established in the Vienna area.[70] Reich invested a good deal of his own money in these institutions, and he claimed later that thousands of men and women had crowded in to hear his lectures and receive advice on sexual matters.[71] Apparently the clinics were popular enough to cause the party fathers to fear a sapping of energy from the political and economic struggle. As a result, they were closed down in

[69] Ibid., pp. xx–xxi.
[70] "Biographical Note," Selected Writings, p. 5; The Function of the Orgasm, p. 169; Reich Speaks of Freud, pp. 32–33, 48–50, 78–82.
[71] Reich, Listen, Little Man! (1948) (New York, 1965), p. 102; The Function of the Orgasm, p. 165.

1930. Reich then moved to Berlin, where he joined the German Communist Party and once again set up his clinics.[72]

Paralleling Reich's practical efforts to fuse socialist politics and psychoanalytic therapy were his attempts to work out an intellectual reconciliation between Marx and Freud. From 1929 to 1935, in no less than six different books,[73] he struggled with this monumental task of synthesis. What resulted was not a coherent or finished body of social theory, for Reich lacked the patience, the discipline, and, it must be admitted, the raw intelligence of a truly great social theorist. His synthesis often amounted to little more than a crude hyphenation of Communism and psychoanalysis, quite literally a "Freudo-Marxism."[74] There were many loose ends, insufficiently digested arguments, and even outright contradictions. Yet when all these concessions have been made, there remains, I think, much that is incisive in Reich's effort to bridge the gap between the two dominant intellectual traditions of the nineteenth and twentieth centuries.

[72] Mildred E. Brady, "The Strange Case of Wilhelm Reich," *New Republic*, May 26, 1947, p. 21. In the Berlin KPD Reich was a member of the same cell as Arthur Koestler. Cf. Koestler in *The God That Failed*, Richard Crossman, ed. (New York, 1963), p. 43.

[73] *Dialektischer Materialismus und Psychoanalyse*, 1929; *Geschlechtsreife, Enthaltsamkeit, Ehemoral*, 1930; *Der Sexuelle Kampf der Jugend*, 1932; *Der Einbruch der Sexualmoral*, 1932; *Massenpsychologie des Faschismus*, 1933; *Die Sexualität im Kulturkampf*, 1936.

[74] Philip Rieff claims that Reich explicitly called himself a "Freudo-Marxist." He may have used the phrase occasionally (I can recall only a single instance—in the preface to the second edition of *The Sexual Revolution*), but he certainly never employed it with any consistency. Cf. Rieff, *The Triumph of the Therapeutic* (New York, 1966), p. 143.

The first difficulty Reich faced was persuading his fellow Marxists that psychoanalysis was not an "idealistic" diversionary maneuver of the decaying bourgeoisie, the spiritual counterpart, so to speak, of imperialism. He addressed himself to this task in a short work entitled *Dialektischer Materialismus und Psychoanalyse* (1929), perhaps the most tightly argued piece he ever wrote.

Reich contended, in this tract, that psychoanalysis shared several important presuppositions with Marxism. In the first place, psychoanalysis was basically a materialist science, although not in the mechanistic sense which equated "material" with "measurable" or "touchable." Like Marx, Freud focused on real human needs and experiences. He began with the concrete material facts of love and hunger, and he followed the tragic fate of these instincts as they came up against the equally concrete hostility of nature and society.[75] Furthermore, Reich argued, psychoanalysis was a dialectical science. As evidence for this contention, he marshaled a whole series of psychoanalytic concepts and arguments.[76] The underlying dialectical theme in all of Freud's work was the notion of psychic conflict. As Marxism was a conflict sociology, so

[75] Reich, *Dialektischer Materialismus und Psychoanalyse* (Copenhagen, 1934), pp. 9–10, 12–17.

[76] For example, Reich argued that Freud had shown how the libidinal development of the child followed, in dialectical manner, from the conflict between instinct and external reality. The child progressed from one stage of libidinal fixation to another, not because of any "innate principle of development" (which would have been both metaphysical and undialectical), but as a result of the repeated clashes between instinct and society, desire and frustration, which forced instinct to seek ever new outlets. *Dialektischer Materialismus*, pp. 30–31.

Freudianism was a conflict psychology. Rather than stress the harmonious functioning of the components within the whole, whether the self or society, both Marx and Freud chose to underline the antagonisms which threatened the whole with dissolution.[77]

Reich's demonstration that psychoanalysis and Marxism were at one in their materialist metaphysic and dialectical methodology was uncharacteristically academic. Much more to the point was his assertion that psychoanalysis was at bottom a revolutionary science. Here his argument was quite ingenious. He suggested that just as Marxism represented a critique of bourgeois economics brought forth by the contradictions within capitalism itself, psychoanalysis was a critique of bourgeois morality which, in dialectical fashion, arose out of the contradictions inherent in sexual repression. The very repressiveness of bourgeois sexual mores brought about an intensification of neurotic disorders, and this situation in turn called forth its antithesis: the great scientist who diagnosed the source of modern nervousness and pointed an accusing finger at our "civilized" sexual morality.[78] Bourgeois society, of course, had done everything in its power either to destroy psychoanalysis or to neutralize its critical impact. And to a certain extent it had been successful in this effort. Reich admitted sadly that psychoanalysis seemed to be losing its sense of mission. Analysis had become "good business," and discussing one's complexes had developed into a stylish cocktail-party pastime. Worst of all, psychoanalysis had retreated theoretically. *The Ego and the Id*

[77] *Ibid.*, pp. 25 ff.
[78] *Ibid.*, pp. 40–42, 46.

(1923) had ushered in an era in which it was no longer popular to talk about libido. Psychoanalysts, like the most unregenerate reactionaries, warned that sex wasn't everything.[79] Reich deeply deplored this whole course of development, much as Lenin deplored the accommodations which Marxism itself had made with bourgeois society. But none of these feeble compromises with the existing order could erase the fundamentally revolutionary message of Freud's new science.

With this apology for psychoanalysis, Reich apparently hoped to prepare the way for his reinterpretation of classical Marxian social theory. It was his fundamental contention that the existence of an unjust social order could not be accounted for, as the vulgar Marxist would have it, simply in terms of the economic and political power of the ruling class. Similarly, one could not explain the failure of revolution solely as the result of the relative economic weakness of the oppressed classes. Marx, of course, had recognized the existence of a gap between economic substructure and ideological superstructure, politics included. For one thing, economic groups sometimes failed to act in accordance with their real interests (the role of the French peasantry in the revolutions of 1789 and 1848 was a case in point). Furthermore, the entire political and ideological structure of a society could lag far behind economic realities. Marx's explanation, often only implicit, for such discrepancies was "false consciousness." But this notion fitted rather badly with his categorical pronouncements (in *The German Ideology*) about the dependence of consciousness on real economic condi-

[79] *Ibid.*, pp. 43–45.

tions. It was to this dilemma that Reich addressed himself in his political writings. How could one explain the apparently autonomous force of ideology?

Reich's answer was that ideology became internalized, or "anchored," in the character structure of the individual.[80] It was this psychological fact that classical Marxian analysis had neglected. To be sure, ideas, moral imperatives, and religious tenets reflected economic and technological developments, but these were not simply matters to which the members of society gave intellectual assent. They actually became embedded in personality structure; as a result of the impact of ideology, men not only thought differently, they *were* different.[81]

The notion that ideology became anchored psychologically made it possible to understand how politics might fail to reflect economic realities, particularly in a society undergoing rapid change. Ideology was internalized in character structure, but since character structure was formed in childhood, it embodied the ideological forms of an earlier era. This was the meaning of "the force of tradition."[82] It was precisely because tradition was built into men's personalities that it was capable of maintaining a social order completely at odds with the logic of economic development and the reality of human needs.

Reich was not satisfied merely with the bald assertion that ideology was anchored in personality structure. He also explained where and how the process took place. The

[80] *Mass Psychology of Fascism*, p. 13.
[81] *The Sexual Revolution*, pp. xxv–xxvii; *Character-Analysis*, pp. xxii–xxiii; *Mass Psychology of Fascism*, p. 67.
[82] *The Function of the Orgasm*, p. 161; *Mass Psychology of Fascism*, pp. 14, 16.

vehicle for this all-important development was the family. Freud had shown that we become what we are, for better or for worse, as a result of the conflicts and crises of family life. The peculiarities of the child's relationship with his father and mother determined the larger contours of his adult experience. For Reich the domestic drama was of even greater significance. The fate not merely of the individual but of entire nations and races was decided within the confines of this narrow stage. The family, which was itself the historical product of definite economic constellations, created, through the process of child rearing, the type of character structure which supported the political and economic order of the society as a whole.[83]

Stated thus in its most general form, Reich's social theory offers an imaginative conceptual tool for sociological and historical research. It suggests that one must look at the family structure and child-rearing practices of a culture or historical epoch to understand how economic realities are translated into politics, ethics, and religion, indeed even to understand how the economic order itself is maintained. The theory suggests further that one could analyze the major social forces *within* a given society in terms of typical family situation and character structure. Reich, however, disappoints us here. The crude, undisciplined character of his mind did not lend itself to a patient empirical elaboration of his basic insight. In this respect, as in so many others, he fell short of the greatest social theorists, who never considered scholarly historical research beneath their dignity. The examples of Marx's

[83] *The Sexual Revolution*, pp. 71–79.

studies of the French revolution of 1848, Weber's analysis of the Reformation, and Durkheim's monograph on suicide come to mind immediately.

Reich's lone attempt to apply the fruits of his theoretical ruminations to a concrete social problem was his analysis of Fascism, and the results were not altogether satisfying. A decade before Erich Fromm, and two decades before Theodor Adorno (*et al.*), Reich asserted that the triumph of Nazism in Germany could not be understood simply in terms of Hitler's charisma or the machinations of German capitalists. Reich was the mass-society theorist par excellence. Absolutely nothing could be explained in terms of individuals or elites.[84] Nazism, like any political movement, was grounded in the psychological structure of the German masses.[85]

One comes away from reading Reich's *Mass Psychology of Fascism* (1933) with the unavoidable impression that this book must have significantly influenced Erich Fromm's *Escape from Freedom* (1942). The parallels are simply too striking to be fortuitous. Like Fromm, Reich described the psychological foundations of Nazism as an ambiguous relationship to authority characteristic of the German lower middle classes. The petty bourgeois at once craved authority and rebelled against it. He therefore submitted to the absolute dictatorship of the rebellious

[84] Reich, *Mass Psychology of Fascism*, pp. 29, 278; *Murder of Christ* (1953) (New York, 1966), p. 142.

[85] Ironically, Reich's mass-psychological analysis of the German problem bore a striking resemblance to the apologies of such German conservatives as Friedrich Meinecke and Gerhard Ritter, who, in their anxiety to excuse the German elite (whether cultural, political, or military), were quick to put the blame on the hoi polloi.

corporal, and at the same time assumed an authoritarian attitude similar to the Führer's toward those below him.[86] For Fromm, this authoritarian syndrome was a product of the typical economic anxieties of lower-middle-class life, in particular the feeling of being caught between the wealthy capitalists on the one hand and the increasingly class-conscious proletariat on the other. He argued that the economic crises of the Weimar Republic brought these fears to a head, although their origin lay as far back as the first stirrings of German capitalism during the Reformation.[87]

Reich was unable to match Fromm's historical scholarship, but he was in every respect the more conscientious Freudian of the two. He maintained that one could not explain character structure without examining the family, and particularly the manner in which the family handled infantile and adolescent sexuality. The distinguishing feature of lower-middle-class life was the correspondence of familial and economic structures; the small farm or small business was worked by members of the family. Therefore, the father's familial authority was reinforced by his economic authority. He could much more effectively insist upon sexual abstinence than could, say, the proletarian father, whose children might escape into the relative anonymity of the factory, and who himself was separated from the family by the nature of his employment. Reich argued it was precisely the ruthless sexual repression to which the lower-middle-class child was exposed that cre-

[86] *Mass Psychology of Fascism,* pp. xi, 4, 30–31, 34, 39.
[87] Erich Fromm, *Fear of Freedom* (London, 1960), particularly Chapters Three and Six. I have used an English paperback edition of the book originally published as *Escape from Freedom* (1942).

ated the authoritarian fixation upon which Nazism fed.[88]

This very interesting analysis of the sociological and sexual roots of Nazism occupied only a small fraction of Reich's attention in *The Mass Psychology of Fascism*. Needless to say, he made no attempt to test the argument empirically. Moreover, it becomes apparent as one reads through the book that Reich was not particularly interested in charting the vicissitudes of German history. His was a loftier calling: to diagnose the ills of humanity as a whole. All the categories of his analysis of Nazism collapse as the book progresses. Nazism, it turns out, was not an exclusive or even typical lower-middle-class phenomenon, but rather one supported by the character structure of all Germans. In fact, it was not even an explicitly German development, since Fascism was, after all, international. Nor was it limited to the twentieth century: Hitlerism was only the most highly developed form of a malady which had plagued mankind for centuries, namely mysticism.[89] In the end Fascism simply revealed in undisguised form the disease from which we all suffer, and have suffered for a long time. " 'Fascism' is only the politically organized expression of the average human character structure, a character structure which has nothing to do with this or that race, nation or party but which is general and international."[90] Thus did Reich flee from the particular to the universal, the one realm of discourse in which he felt completely at home.

Instead of pursuing a careful historical analysis of

[88] *Mass Psychology of Fascism*, pp. 40–45, 162–63; *The Function of the Orgasm*, pp. 213–14.

[89] *Mass Psychology of Fascism*, pp. 97–98, 300.

[90] *Ibid.*, p. ix.

different family structures and child-rearing practices, Reich simply reduced all history to two basic family types: permissive matriarchy and authoritarian patriarchy. There was only one important watershed in human history, that separating the age of matriarchy from the age of patriarchy (circa 4000 B.C.). In comparison with this great event, the transition from feudalism to capitalism faded into insignificance. Likewise, there were only two character structures of historical importance: the genital character of matriarchal society, capable of genuine self-determination, and the neurotic character of patriarchal society, whose basic political posture was submissiveness.[91]

The bulk of Reich's political writings was devoted to an analysis (and denunciation) of the patriarchal family. The patriarchal family, supported by the institution of monogamous marriage, served as "a *factory for authoritarian ideologies* and conservative [character] structures."[92] To Reich it was inconceivable that the exploitative economic order and authoritarian political regime of our culture could have maintained themselves without this institution. In fact, the patriarchal family had emerged precisely in order to shore up the system of exploitation and domination.[93] It fulfilled its purpose by performing a single function: that of suppressing all manifestations of genital sexuality in children and adolescents. The family might serve other ends as well, but its raison d'être was sexual repression.

[91] *Ibid.,* p. xxiii; *The Sexual Revolution,* pp. xxvii–xxviii.
[92] *The Sexual Revolution,* p. 72.
[93] *Mass Psychology of Fascism,* p. 88.

The connection between sexual repression and the authoritarian social order was simple and direct: the child who experienced the suppression of his natural sexuality was permanently maimed in his character development; he inevitably became submissive, apprehensive of all authority, and completely incapable of rebellion.[94] In other words, he developed exactly that character structure which would support a regime of injustice and exploitation. The first act of suppression prepared the way for every subsequent tyranny. Here at last was the answer to the riddle of sexual repression. Reich concluded that repression existed not for the sake of moral edification (as traditional religion would have it), nor for the sake of culture (as Freud had claimed), but simply in order to create the character structure necessary for the preservation of an authoritarian social regime.

In an effort to highlight the repressive function of the patriarchal family, Reich, like Freud before him, indulged in an anthropological fantasy. But unlike Freud, who had constructed his myth of human origins on the basis of Sir James Frazer's study of totemism, Reich began with the analysis of matriarchy in the writings of Johan Bachofen, Lewis Morgan, Friedrich Engels, and Bronislaw Malinowski. Their investigations had established as "a historically proven fact" that matriarchy was the familial organization of "natural society."[95] In political terms matriarchy was characterized by the absence of any system of domination. Economically, it corresponded to Marx's era of primitive communism. It was, in effect, a

<hr />

[94] *Ibid.*, pp. 23–26; *The Sexual Revolution*, p. 79; *The Function of the Orgasm*, p. 198.

[95] *Mass Psychology of Fascism*, p. 73.

society without state and without class, held together only by the loose clan comprising all the blood relatives of a common mother. Most important, matriarchal society was completely permissive with regard to infantile and adolescent sexuality.[96] Sexual repression was, of course, unnecessary in such a society. There was neither economic exploitation nor political domination, and therefore no need to create the submissive character structure which would support these institutions. The child was even spared the confused longings and brutal punishments of the Oedipal crisis, since the rigidly defined triad (father-mother-child) of the nuclear family had not yet come into being.[97]

In Reich's mind the tragedy of human history was that this idyllic maternal order had, in the end, succumbed to the tyrannical dictatorship of the father. I'm afraid, however, that Reich's effort to recount the series of events which led to this catastrophe was not very successful. His

[96] *Ibid.*, pp. 203–4; *The Sexual Revolution*, pp. 161–62, 236.

[97] It should be noted that Reich felt that the theory of primal matriarchy ruled out a priori Freud's account of the origins of civilization in *Totem and Taboo*. Freud had assumed that the Oedipus complex was the prime mover in this development: the brothers desire their mother, kill their father to obtain access to her, and then, out of a profound sense of guilt, create the first piece of social legislation, the incest taboo. The trouble with this theory, according to Reich, was that it ignored the cultural relativity of the Oedipus complex. Here Malinowski, in particular, was called upon to bear witness. In the original matriarchal society the Oedipus complex simply didn't exist. Thus, far from being the prime mover in the dialectics of civilization, the Oedipus complex turned out to be itself a result of the authoritarian patriarchal order. *Mass Psychology of Fascism*, pp. 47–48; *Dialektischer Materialismus*, pp. 38–39.

argument was fuzzy and inconclusive, and it in no way measured up to the standards set by Freud in *Totem and Taboo*. In fact, it was only in the last years of his life, more than two decades after he had first committed the theory of primal matriarchy to print, that he finally came to grips with the origins of repression. In the meantime, the real purpose of Reich's anthropological detour was not so much to explain how matriarchy gave way to patriarchy, as simply to contrast the evils of the present order with the delights of a long-forgotten past.

V

Reich was at heart a policy maker rather than a social theorist. The analysis of ideology, the theory of primal matriarchy, and the dissection of Fascism were all meant to serve a single purpose: that of lending scientific authority to his call for a sexual revolution. These theoretical studies were important nevertheless, since they demonstrated, in Reich's mind, the crucial interdependence of social and sexual liberation. The sexual revolution was not merely desirable "in addition to" the political and economic revolution. On the contrary, the political revolution itself was doomed to failure unless accompanied by the abolition of repressive morality. "To define freedom is the same as to define sexual health."[98]

Reich felt that the disastrous outcome of the Russian Revolution substantiated this contention. To be sure, the Soviet Union had taken important steps in the direction of

[98] *Mass Psychology of Fascism*, p. 297.

sexual reform. In particular Reich admired the socialist collectives, which, to a limited extent, had undermined the authority of the patriarchal family.[99] But the reforms had been much too tentative. Most important, the education of children in the Soviet Union had remained "sex-negative." Thus the degeneration of Lenin's social democracy into the dictatorship of Stalin was a foregone conclusion. The submissive character structure of the Russian masses had remained unchanged.[100]

All of Reich's work as psychologist, social theorist, and political commentator pointed inevitably to a single conclusion: the need for a revolution which would secure once and for all the sexual rights of children and adolescents. Of course, Reich did not neglect the inequities of adult sexual life. In particular he was an ardent defender of the sexual rights of women. His feminism was as pronounced as Freud's misogyny. He was likewise a severe critic of the traditional ideal of marital fidelity. The compulsive marriage of existing society was to be eradicated, since every individual had the right to seek a new partner whenever his sexual happiness so demanded.[101]

However, Reich was at his most impassioned when portraying the sexual miseries of the young. The child was "godlike" in his natural sensuality and innate sociability. Only through the brutal repression of his natural impulses was he transformed into a neurotic, self-abasing adult. The sexual revolution, therefore, involved providing the child with legal protection against the sexual tyranny of

[99] *The Sexual Revolution*, pp. 162–63; 232–33.
[100] *Ibid.*, p. 238; *Mass Psychology of Fascism*, p. 213.
[101] *The Sexual Revolution*, pp. 123–25, 142–43.

disregards & overshadow the problem of guilt

& drive theory

his parents. In particular, he was to be guaranteed the right to masturbate and to play sexually with children of his own age.[102]

The dilemma of adolescence moved Reich even more deeply than that of childhood, reflecting a subtle shift in his psychological perspective away from the almost exclusive emphasis on early childhood in classical Freudian thought.[103] The sexual abstinence demanded of adolescents in repressive society led to juvenile delinquency, to neuroses, to perversions, and, of course, to political apathy.[104] Thus, above all else, the sexual revolution involved not merely permitting but actually encouraging adolescent sexual intercourse. Reich pursued this radical conclusion even into its most mundane administrative details. He devoted numerous pages to the problem of providing adolescents with the private quarters and contraceptive devices necessary for the fulfillment of their sexual needs.[105] One is easily amused that Reich apparently considered himself both the Marx and the Lenin of the sexual revolution, at once grand theoretician and bureaucratic strategist. But his compassion for the very real miseries of adolescence testified to his humane and

[102] *Ibid.*, pp. 75, 258–59; *Murder of Christ*, pp. 18–19.
[103] Even the distinction between childhood and adolescence tended to disappear in Reich's psychology. The latency period of Freud's developmental schema turned out to be a product of our repressive civilization. Just as the end of repression would undermine the Oedipus complex, it would also eliminate the supposedly "natural" period of sexual abstinence between early childhood and adolescence. *The Function of the Orgasm*, p. 212; *The Sexual Revolution*, p. 75.
[104] *The Sexual Revolution*, pp. 80, 102–6, 257.
[105] *Ibid.*, 111–15, 191, 263.

generous sensibilities. Even his inappropriately concrete preoccupation with administrative detail—his disregard for the niceties of academic discourse and its concern with maintaining the proper level of abstraction—has a refreshing quality about it.

Reich's sexual revolution was not without its disturbing corollaries. Although no advocate of polymorphous perversity, Reich's attitude toward sexual deviance was at least passably progressive. Homosexuality, which, like all our problems, resulted from the suppression of heterosexual impulses during childhood and adolescence, would disappear in the wake of the revolution. In the meantime, Reich urged an attitude of toleration.[106] But authoritarian tendencies revealed themselves in his characterization of the nonrepressive society of the future. For example, there was to be a considerable amount of sexual management. All large institutions would contain "sexologically well-trained functionaries" who would supervise activities "in conjunction with a central sexological agency."[107] An even less attractive feature of Reich's utopia was its unexpectedly puritanical character. The sexual revolution marked the end of pornography and foul language. This was, of course, perfectly logical. One of the ironies of a nonrepressive society is that it eliminates that need for sexual escape which forms the basis of our erotic subculture. In short, the end of repression would mean no more dirty jokes, a conclusion

[106] *Ibid.*, p. 211. Reich also proposed to counteract the development of homosexuality with what might be termed "co-militarism": "the inclusion of female youth in the life of the army and the navy." *The Sexual Revolution*, p. 264.

[107] *The Sexual Revolution*, p. 262.

already implicit in Freud's analysis of humor and repression in *Jokes and Their Relation to the Unconscious*.[108]

Reich was completely unsuccessful in his efforts to persuade the European left to incorporate the sexual revolution into its political platform. The hygiene clinics which he established in Berlin, like those in Vienna, were a failure.[109] Reich was expelled from the Communist Party, just as he had earlier found it necessary to abandon the Social Democratic Party. In 1932, according to his own account, both the socialists and the communists in Germany prohibited the distribution of works published by the Verlag für Sexualpolitik, the private press he had established in Berlin. The communists denounced *The Mass Psychology of Fascism* in particular as "counterrevolutionary."[110] Thus Reich suffered a falling out with the Marxists even before the termination of his official relationship with psychoanalysis. By the end of 1933, when he left Germany for Scandinavia, he had been rejected by both camps.

Nineteen thirty-four marked an important turning point in Reich's career. In the summer of that year, he accepted an invitation to teach character analysis at the University of Oslo. The appointment gave him access to a laboratory and the opportunity to undertake his first biophysical experiments.[111] Reich thereupon retired from the politi-

---

[108] *Ibid.* "Somebody once said that among his numerous acquaintances there was only one he had never heard tell a dirty joke; I was the one." *Listen, Little Man!*, p. 65.

[109] *Listen, Little Man!*, pp. 61–62.

[110] Brady, "The Strange Case of Wilhelm Reich," p. 21; Reich, *Mass Psychology of Fascism*, pp. xiii–xvi.

[111] *The Function of the Orgasm*, p. 326.

cal scene to devote the rest of his life, first in Norway and later in America, to the elaboration of the most remarkable biological myth.

However, there is considerable evidence that things might have turned out quite differently. Reich could well have gone the way of the small-time political revivalist, becoming the perennial presidential candidate of some "socialist sex-reform" party. His writings are filled with oblique references to his political ambitions.[112] And for a moment Reich actually succumbed to the temptation of politics. After fleeing from Germany and before receiving the call to Oslo, he spent several months in Denmark; during his stay there he persuaded one of his followers to run for the Danish Riksdag on a sex-political platform. For a while it looked as though a new political movement might be launched. But such was not to be. Reich's Danish visa was not renewed, and he was forced to leave the country.[113]

As Reich grew older he became more and more intolerant of the entire political process. The politician, he wrote, was "a cancer on the body social."[114] To be "unpolitical" now became the supreme virtue, whereas earlier Reich had regarded it as a sure sign of psychic rigidity. The only hope for mankind was to put an end to all politics and get about the practical tasks of life.[115] Reich did not seem to be bothered by the fact that this latterday attack on the politicians was incompatible with his

[112] *Mass Psychology of Fascism*, pp. 280, 326.
[113] "The Strange Case of Wilhelm Reich," p. 21.
[114] *Mass Psychology of Fascism*, p. 181.
[115] *Ibid.*, pp. 172–73, 182, 310–11.

earlier (and more trenchant) analysis of the mass-psychological character of all political behavior.

Reich's rejection of politics brought with it the inevitable alienation from his political mentor, Karl Marx. He never explicitly admitted the break, but it was evident in all his later writings. He dismissed class analysis as fundamentally wrongheaded. In particular, he asserted that no meaningful correlations existed between class situation and character structure.[116] This critique of Marx had been implicit in his earlier reduction of history to a matriarchal and a patriarchal age. In fact, only the analysis of Fascism had remained completely within a Marxian frame of reference. But now Reich openly admitted the uselessness of differentiating between "proletarian" and "capitalist," to say nothing of finer economic distinctions.

Behind Reich's rejection of Marx lay the same basic motives that led to his break with Freud. An observation which Reich himself made, and which I have already noted, suggests this comparison. In *Dialektischer Materialismus und Psychoanalyse* he had argued that both Freud and Marx interpreted reality in terms of conflict, be it the struggle between classes or that between instincts. Reich had pointed to this parallel with apparent approval at the time, but his own predilections, both psychological and sociological, lay in an entirely different direction. I have already argued that his break with Freud resulted from his unwillingness to accept the pessimistic implications of Freud's dualistic theory of the instincts. He refused to believe that man could be divided against himself, any more than culture could be at odds with nature.

[116] *Ibid.*, pp. 330–31; *The Sexual Revolution*, pp. xvii–xviii.

In similar fashion, Reich ultimately found Marx's doctrine
of class struggle incompatible with his own inclination to
view social life as at bottom conflict-free. Antagonisms
within society had no basis in reality; they were the
artificial creation of political ideologies, Marxism itself
being among the worst offenders in this respect. Underneath the apparent conflicts was a basic community of
interest which united all productive individuals.[117] In
the end Reich obviously preferred Bentham to Marx. His
utopian bias led him to discount the stresses and strains of
communal life, as he had those of psychic life. Freud and
Marx may indeed have been fellow revolutionaries, as
Reich had argued in 1929, but they were also realists.
Reich, on the other hand, was a romantic, as much in his
politics as in his psychology.

VI

The last two decades of Wilhelm Reich's career are in
every respect the most difficult to deal with. If Reich's
political ideas were utopian, his biological and cosmological speculations can only be called insane. Yet a strange
logic underlies even his most extreme formulations, and
the student who has immersed himself in Reich's early
work will find the science of Orgonomy curiously familiar.
In this brief consideration of his final biological writings, I
want to stress those strands of continuity which link
Reich's early psychological and sociological theories to his
ultimate philosophical vision. The details of the science of

[117] *Mass Psychology of Fascism*, p. 265.

Orgonomy hold little interest for the intellectual historian, but the larger contours of Reich's mythology are
certainly important for our understanding of his intellectual development.

Since the 1930's it has become standard practice to
distinguish between two major traditions within psychoanalysis: "biologically-oriented" orthodox Freudianism on
the one hand, and "culturally-oriented" neo-Freudian revisionism on the other, with the ego-psychologists strad-
dling the fence between them. Crudely stated, the issue
between these two schools has been the relative importance of cultural as opposed to instinctual factors in
psychic development. The neo-Freudians have accused
the orthodox of ignoring the social and economic influences on personality formation, while the orthodox have
denounced the revisionists for soft-pedaling the unpleasant facts of sexuality and aggression. One of the many
anomalies of Reich's thought is that it defies classification
in terms of this well-established dichotomy. As a result,
Reich has remained a complete enigma to both camps.
The neo-Freudians wanted very much to claim him as one
of their own.[118] After all, Reich was among the first to
recognize the importance of social factors in psychic development. He broke with Freud's narrow "biological"
emphasis and directed attention to "the whole personality," including its cultural environment. And yet it was
Reich who pushed psychoanalysis to the utmost biological
extreme, reducing all of psychic life to a manifestation of
bodily streamings and spasms. From the beginning he had

[118] Cf., for example, Thompson, *Psychoanalysis: Evolution and
Development*, pp. 189–91.

been fascinated by Freud's penchant for explaining psychic phenomena in terms of energy concepts derived from the natural sciences. In the final phase of his career, Reich simply pursued Freud's hypothesis of sexual energy to its logical "scientific" conclusion: to the horror of Freudians and neo-Freudians alike, he discovered the physical reality of libido.

The line separating the psychic from the somatic had never been sharply drawn in Reich's thought. Even in *Die Funktion des Orgasmus* he had argued that libido stasis could lead to physical as well as mental disease. Furthermore, a physical disease which developed in this fashion was not the product of some mysterious psychic phantom. Reich wanted no part of Georg Groddeck's psychosomatic theories.[119] If the dualism of mind and body was to be resolved at all, it would be resolved in favor of the body. Sexual energy was the very concrete product of "inner secretory processes."[120] Thus the physical disease brought about by the damming up of libido had just as "real" a cause as that resulting from infection or mechanical failure.

Although the orgasm theory of the mid-1920's already contained the seeds of Reich's later biological preoccupations, it was only during the 1930's that he turned his full attention to the physiological foundations of psychic life. The first indication of this shift in perspective was a revised theory of the neuroses and a corresponding transformation of his therapeutic technique. By 1935 "muscular armoring" had replaced "character armoring" as the principal manifestation of psychic disease. Reich now

[119] *The Function of the Orgasm*, pp. 44–45.
[120] *Die Funktion des Orgasmus*, p. 150; cf. also pp. 68–72.

argued that sexual energy was imprisoned not so much in the patient's psychic defense mechanisms, in personality traits and mannerisms, as in his muscular rigidity.[121] The neurotic was a person with a stiff body. Therefore, character-analytic therapy was abandoned in favor of what Reich called "vegetotherapy," a curious amalgam of yoga and chiropractics. Muscular rigidity was relieved through deep-breathing exercises and massages.[122] The talking cure was given up altogether, since words, Reich contended, only got in the way of therapy. The body alone spoke truth. Similarly, in vegetotherapy one was no longer concerned with memories, with dreams, or with associations.[123] Instead, Reich confined his entire therapeutic attention to an attack on the body. Successful psychotherapy involved relaxing taut muscular structures, beginning with the forehead and progressing downward toward the pelvis. With the elimination of the final muscular blocks, the patient would break down in involuntary convulsions, which Reich termed the "orgasm reflex."[124] In short, the therapeutic process culminated in a physical acting out of sexual intercourse in the doctor's office. And with the orgasm reflex came a revolution in the patient's

[121] "Psychic Contact and Vegetative Current," pp. 341–54; *The Function of the Orgasm*, pp. 240–41, 266–68.
[122] Reich, "The Schizophrenic Split" (1948), in *Character-Analysis*, pp. 411, 418; "The Expressive Language of the Living in Orgone Therapy" (1948?), in *Character-Analysis*, pp. 377–80; *The Function of the Orgasm*, p. 274.
[123] "The Expressive Language . . . ," pp. 361–62, 379; "The Schizophrenic Split," p. 448; *The Function of the Orgasm*, p. 267.
[124] *The Function of the Orgasm*, p. 311; "The Expressive Language . . . ," pp. 370–72.

entire psychic makeup. To change a man's body was in effect to change his *Weltanschauung*.[125]

Paralleling this biological revolution in therapy were Reich's first efforts to uncover the physiological reality of libido. He began his quest for the essence of sexuality in the realm of electricity. From 1934 to 1937 he conducted a series of bizarre experiments, designed to measure "whether the sexual organs, in a state of excitation, . . . show an increase in their bio-electric charge."[126] The results, as with all of Reich's experiments, were most gratifying. Sexual excitation was found to be identical with an increase of electrical charge on the surface of the organism, particularly in the genitals, while anxiety and other unpleasurable emotions corresponded to a withdrawal of electrical energy into the center of the body. Freud's concept of libido as a measure of psychic energy was "no longer a mere simile."[127] Libido was electricity, and the orgasm a spectacular electrical storm. Reich nicely summed up the results of his experiments when he wrote, "We are all simply a complicated electric machine."[128]

Reich did not long rest content with his electrical theory of sexuality, although he never repudiated it explicitly. The theory simply contained too many inconsistencies. For one thing, "bio-electric" energy violated almost all known laws of electrical behavior. Even more

[125] See the "Case History" in *The Function of the Orgasm*, pp. 276–92; Reich, *Ether, God and Devil* (Rangeley, Maine, 1949), pp. 45–52.
[126] *The Function of the Orgasm*, p. 327.
[127] *Ibid.*, p. 335.
[128] *Ibid.*, p. 24.

important, it seemed inappropriate that sexuality should be merely a variant of electricity. In the meantime, Reich's research into microscopic plant and animal life had revealed that not merely sexuality, but life itself functioned according to the orgastic pattern of tension and discharge, expansion and contraction.[129] From this insight to the hypothesis of a special kind of energy unique to life and to sexuality was but a short leap. In 1939 Reich discovered just such a life force. He christened it Orgone energy, and he devoted the rest of his career to investigating its characteristics and harnessing its immense therapeutic powers.

Orgone energy was Reich's *élan vital*. In fact, Reich explicitly claimed Bergson as an intellectual forebear, along with Giordano Bruno and Johannes Kepler.[130] But unlike Bergson's *élan vital*, Kepler's *vis animalis*, or any other metaphorical evocation of the forces of life, Orgone energy was "visible, measurable and applicable."[131] Orgone energy was indeed embarrassingly concrete. It was blue in color and could be observed in such natural phenomena as the bluish glimmer of "red" blood corpuscles or the blue coloration of sexually excited frogs. It could be measured with an Orgone Energy Field Meter, as well as with an electroscope and a Geiger counter. It could be collected in the Orgone Energy Accumulator. And, perhaps most important of all, Orgone energy could

---

[129] *Ibid.*, pp. xxi, 255, 257.
[130] *Ibid.*, p. 6; *Ether, God and Devil*, pp. 17, 71, 75, 79; *Murder of Christ*, p. 104.
[131] "Psychic Contact and Vegetative Current," p. 304 n.

be used to cure any number of psychic and physical ills, from hysteria to cancer.[132]

Besides marking the discovery of the Orgone, 1939 was also the year in which Reich came to America. His emigration was quite unlike that of many other Central European intellectuals who made the trip across the Atlantic during the 1930's and 1940's. He was not driven out of Europe by the Nazis, although he undoubtedly would have been eventually. His biophysical research came under fire first from scientists and then from the liberal press in Norway. The newspaper compaign resulted in a royal decree stipulating that all psychoanalysts were to be licensed by the government, and with the pressure on, Reich accepted an invitation from a representative of the American psychosomatic medicine movement, Theodore P. Wolfe. In May of 1939 he moved his entire Orgone Energy Laboratory to Forest Hills, New York.[133]

Reich adjusted quickly and easily to his new life in America. In this respect also, I suspect, his experience was

[132] *The Function of the Orgasm*, pp. 341–42; *Ether, God and Devil*, pp. 123–24.

[133] Brady, "The Strange Case of Wilhelm Reich," pp. 21–22; Briehl, "Wilhelm Reich," p. 436; "Biographical Note," in *Selected Writings*, p. 5. The anthropologist Bronislaw Malinowski, who was both a friend and an admirer of Reich's, helped arrange his emigration to America. At the time of Reich's difficulties with the Norwegian government, Malinowski wrote a public letter on his behalf which contained the following appreciation: "Both through his published work and in personal contacts [Dr. Wilhelm Reich] has impressed me as an original and sound thinker, a genuine personality, and a man of open character and courageous views." *Reich Speaks of Freud*, p. 19. Cf. also pp. 219–26.

unlike that of the typical European emigrant. From 1939 to 1941 he held the post of Associate Professor of Medical Psychology at the New School for Social Research in New York City, and he soon established a lucrative private practice in Forest Hills. By 1942 he had accumulated enough money to purchase over two hundred acres near Rangeley, Maine, where he set up a private research institute called "Orgonon."[134] There in the Maine woods, aided by a dozen co-workers, he carried on his strange experiments, held "Orgonomic Conventions," and fired off angry messages to Congress demanding legislation for the protection of the sexual rights of children and adolescents.[135]

It should come as little surprise to find that Reich liked America very much. His reaction to this country was, in fact, just the opposite of that of many other European exiles of psychoanalytic persuasion, such as Erich Fromm, Theodor Adorno, and Herbert Marcuse, who were disturbed by the authoritarianism which lurked beneath America's democratic façade. To Reich, however, America was the only country in the world where one could "stand up for the pursuit of happiness and the rights of the living."[136] Not even the McCarthy experience dimmed his enthusiasm. In fact, he seems to have joined wholeheartedly in the anticommunist debauch of the early 1950's. He fretted over the spineless liberals, who

[134] "The Strange Case of Wilhelm Reich," p. 20; "Biographical Note," p. 5.
[135] Reich, *Murder of Christ*, pp. 163–64; *Cosmic Superimposition* (Rangeley, Maine, 1951), p. 9.
[136] Reich, "Preface" to the 4th edition of *The Sexual Revolution*, p. xv.

would deliver America "to the habitual spies of the reactionary Russian empire," and he denounced our supposed allies (particularly the British) for "doing business with the red dictators."[137] The thought of returning to Europe after the Allied victory seems never to have entered his mind. And although the last years of his life were anything but serene, it is undeniable that Reich felt much more at home in America than he ever had in Europe.

Reich's basic biological discoveries were made before he set foot on American soil. His intellectual activities in the new world consisted principally in a fantastic elaboration of the cosmological and, ultimately, religious implications of the discovery of the Orgone. He published book after book in which ever more extravagant claims were made for his new science. He respected none of the traditional academic boundaries. In fact, he disregarded even the restrictions of his own definitions. Orgone energy had been defined originally as the form of energy unique to life, but in 1951 Reich announced that it was the primordial stuff out of which all reality evolved.[138] Matter itself was created through the sexual embrace or "superimposition" of two Orgone energy streams. The galactic systems, the aurora borealis, hurricanes, and gravity were likewise various manifestations of Orgone energy.[139] In brief, Reich propounded a unified-field theory more ambitious than even the most undisciplined physicist could have imagined. Every aspect of reality from schizophrenia to the Milky Way was encompassed within his system.

[137] Reich, *Murder of Christ*, p. 217; *The Oranur Experiment* (1951), in *Selected Writings*, p. 357.
[138] *Cosmic Superimposition*, p. 12.
[139] *Ibid.*, pp. 15, 22–23, 53, 65, 87.

Only nuclear energy retained its autonomy. In fact, Reich came to conceive of the history of the cosmos as a titanic struggle between Orgone energy and atomic energy. Remarkable as it seems, the inveterate monist had arrived at a dualistic cosmology not unlike Manichaeanism. The eternal antagonism between Eros and Thanatos, of which Freud spoke so movingly in the final pages of *Civilization and Its Discontents*, now received its scientific confirmation. The struggle of love against hate was only the psychological manifestation of a more basic cosmic antipathy.[140]

Like Hegel, Reich considered his science the culmination of Western intellectual history. He argued that Western man's sense of reality had been fractured into two antagonistic intellectual traditions. Natural science had interpreted the universe according to rigid mechanical laws, and thus drained the cosmos of vitality. As a result, all consciousness of the living, surging forces in the universe had been relegated to religion, which, unfortunately, interpreted these energies in a distorted, "mystified" form.[141] Orgonomy, however, transcended the dichotomy of science and religion, in that it represented a scientific (i.e., concrete, tangible, and measurable) comprehension of the forces which religion grasped only obscurely and impressionistically.[142]

The most remarkable feature of this meta-intellectual

[140] *The Oranur Experiment, passim,* especially p. 355.

[141] *Ether, God and Devil,* pp. 33–34, 92; *Cosmic Superimposition,* p. 10; *The Function of the Orgasm,* pp. 6–7; *Mass Psychology of Fascism,* p. 295.

[142] *Cosmic Superimposition,* pp. 5–6; *Murder of Christ,* p. 200; *The Oranur Experiment,* pp. 422–23.

history of Western civilization was Reich's new-found sympathy for religion. He had begun his career as a Voltairian anticlerical. Yet in the end he concluded that religion, reactionary though it might be, was the legitimate precursor of his own science. He even undertook to reinterpret the principal Christian doctrines in terms of their "Orgonotic" meanings. "God" represented an anthropomorphic projection of man's awareness of the Cosmic Orgone Ocean.[143] The Kingdom of Heaven was the "vibrating of living Life in Christ as in all men on earth," and Christ himself was the archetypal genital character, in direct communication with the cosmic Orgone forces.[144] Reich was even prepared to admit that the relentlessly antisexual gospel of St. Paul was historically justified, given "the pornographic, filthy, sick mind of man in sexual matters."[145]

Much as did Weber in *The Protestant Ethic*, Durkheim in *The Elementary Forms of the Religious Life,* and Malinowski in *Magic, Science and Religion,* Reich abandoned his Enlightenment prejudices in favor of an interpretation of religion as psychologically and sociologically "functional." Religion was not simply an opiate, a piece of trickery with which the rich prevented the poor from claiming their just share of the wealth of the earth. On the contrary, religion represented a positive good, since it alone had preserved man's awareness of the forces of life. It is of course somewhat misleading (although not altogether so) to compare Reich's writings on religion with those of the

[143] *Listen, Little Man!,* p. 25; *The Function of the Orgasm,* p. 319; *Ether, God and Devil, passim.*
[144] *Murder of Christ,* pp. 31, 33.
[145] *Ibid.,* p. 193.

great social scientists of the first quarter of the century. Weber, Durkheim, and Malinowski had written about religion as outsiders, although sympathetic outsiders, to be sure. It is more than questionable whether the same can be said of Reich. Historians are often much too glib in characterizing secular philosophies and political ideologies as, at bottom, religious faiths, and in general I feel this is an analogy to be avoided. But the evidence in Reich's case is overwhelming. The science of Orgonomy was as fantastic and elaborate as any theological system, and its content was identical with that of the great religions of salvation: it promised both a total interpretation of reality and a total therapy for man's individual and social ills.

As with all religious thinkers, Reich's most persistent intellectual difficulty was the problem of evil. He had already wrestled with the matter in his anthropological writings, where he attempted to explain how primal matriarchy gave way to repressive patriarchy. But, as I suggested earlier, the solution which he had worked out in the early 1930's was quite unsatisfactory. His cosmological speculations concerning the eternal antagonism of Orgone energy and atomic energy might have suggested a way out of the dilemma, but Reich never pursued that alternative.

The problem of evil was in effect the problem of human sickness: why was it that, of all living creatures, man alone had managed to fall ill? By the late 1940's Reich was no longer able to believe that man's muscular and psychic armoring could be explained in terms of repressive social and economic influences. The malignant socioeconomic regime was itself a manifestation of some more basic disorder.[146] Taking his theme from the Tree of Knowledge myth in Genesis, Reich concluded ultimately that self-consciousness was at the root of human malaise. "In thinking about his own being and functioning, man turned involuntarily against himself."[147] Reich stood Descartes and Hegel on their respective heads. Man was indeed a thinking animal, and human history was the process through which "the cosmic orgone energy [read "the Spirit"] becomes aware of itself."[148] But rationality and self-consciousness had at the same time robbed man of his emotional and biological spontaneity. Terrified by "the deep experience of the Self,"[149] man had armed himself against the biological forces within him by erecting the psychological barrier of character structure and the sociological barrier of repressive patriarchy. Almost in spite of himself, Reich, like Freud, concluded that the source of human unhappiness lay within man himself. At the same time the anti-intellectual bias implicit in all of his thought finally achieved explicit formulation: man knew too much for his own good.

Despite the relative peace and undeniable prosperity of his life in America, Reich grew increasingly misanthropic and embattled in his final years. As his self-esteem exceeded all limits of sanity, not to speak of modesty, he developed a sense of persecution which was nothing short of paranoic. He identified with every great martyr from Socrates to Marx, and with none so intimately as Jesus

[146] *Cosmic Superimposition*, p. 112.
[147] *Ibid.*, pp. 116–17.
[148] *Ibid.*, p. 104.
[149] *Ibid.*, p. 119.

Christ.[150] He hypostatized all critics of his theories as "the Emotional Plague,"[151] proving himself more than Freud's equal in the art of *ad hominem* argument. Reich seemed to fear his would-be admirers even more than his critics. He was haunted by the thought that men with dirty minds would misuse his authority to unleash "a free-for-all fucking epidemic."[152] Once again he revamped his terminology, in the hope of heading off the pornographic exploitation of his discoveries. The word "sex," "abused and smutted into a horrible nightmare, into a rubbing of cold penises within stale vaginas," was abandoned altogether, and for "sexual intercourse" he substituted "the genital embrace."[153]

Reich's elaborate rituals of avoidance strike us as a little comic, and his fears of persecution as exaggerated to the point of madness. But in a sense he was justified on both counts. In so far as his work elicited any response at all, it was from very questionable quarters: among the poets and novelists of the Beat Generation, in particular William Burroughs and Allen Ginsberg, who fused Reichian rhetoric with a most un-Reichian apology for homosexuality and hallucinatory drugs.[154] And surely the unhappy conclusion of Reich's career lent a certain credibility to his sense of persecution. In 1954 the Federal Food and

[150] *Murder of Christ*, pp. 76, 87.
[151] Reich, "The Emotional Plague" (1945), in *Character-Analysis*, pp. 277–78; *Listen, Little Man!* p. 9.
[152] *Murder of Christ*, p. 94.
[153] *Ibid.*, p. 102.
[154] See, in particular, William Burroughs, *Nova Express* (New York, 1964), and William Burroughs and Allen Ginsberg, *The Yage Letters* (San Francisco, 1963).

Drug Administration initiated a complaint against him for renting a fraudulent therapeutic device, the Orgone Energy Accumulator, across state lines. The Accumulator was a six-sided box, the size of a telephone booth, made of metal on the inside and wood on the outside. It was Reich's ultimate therapeutic recourse, employed when both character analysis and vegetotherapy had failed: the patient simply sat in the box and absorbed concentrated Orgone radiation.[155] When Reich refused to appear in court on what he considered a matter of scientific research, an injunction was issued against the device. Finally, in 1956, he was brought to trial for disregarding the court order. On November 3, 1957, Reich died of a heart attack in the federal penitentiary at Lewisburg, Pennsylvania, having served eight months of his two-year sentence.[156] Such was the sad but (one can't help feeling) appropriate end to a career so utterly serious and hopelessly grandiose that it faded imperceptibly into farce.

[155] Brady, "The Strange Case of Wilhelm Reich," p. 22; Reich, "The Schizophrenic Split," pp. 463–64.

[156] *The New York Times,* November 5, 1957, 31:4; "Biographical Note," pp. 5–6. Cf. Appendix I to *Selected Writings,* where the decree of injunction and Reich's protestations are reprinted.

GEZA ROHEIM

GEZA ROHEIM's radicalism was less obvious than that of Wilhelm Reich. Roheim was apolitical, as was Freud himself, and he never projected his cultural criticism in the form of a sexual utopia, as did Reich. Nevertheless, he definitely belongs in any study of the "Freudian Left." In the most general sense, Roheim was a revolutionary by virtue of the single-mindedness with which he applied psychoanalytic categories to the study of culture. Indeed, professional anthropologists frequently deplored the inflexibility of his interpretations. From the perspective of this study, however, it is precisely the relentlessness with which Roheim pursued the psychoanalytic interpretation of culture, even to its absurd conclusions, which qualifies him as a Freudian radical. Moreover, above and beyond this stylistic radicalism, the explicit content of Roheim's thought was essentially critical. At every opportunity he took it upon himself to denounce the repressiveness of modern civilization. He was sublimely contemptuous of

75

all ideologies and intellectual traditions which in any fashion served to justify the established cultural order. Thus, although Roheim's hostility to culture was not without a characteristic Freudian ambivalence, it was nonetheless much more explicit, much less hedged, than Freud's own. One might say that his work represented a halfway house between the tortured acquiescence of Freud and the unqualified opposition of Herbert Marcuse.

Roheim was a very consistent thinker. Once he had accepted psychoanalysis, he remained staunchly orthodox. To a great extent, therefore, his intellectual development simply paralleled the vicissitudes of Freud's career. Still, his thought did undergo a considerable evolution, and, as in the case of Reich, I have examined both the important watersheds and the underlying continuities in his development as a social theorist. Appropriately reflecting Roheim's intellectual stability was the relative uneventfulness of his life. He was, in a word, an academic. The political involvements of Reich's odyssey would have been utterly incongruous in the context of his very predictable professional career. There was in effect only one event in Roheim's life: his field trip to Australia and the South Seas between 1929 and 1931.

Although Roheim was a practicing psychoanalyst, he thought of himself primarily as a professional anthropologist. His academic training was in anthropology,[1] and

---

[1] To be precise, Roheim took his major Ph.D. examination in geography and minored in anthropology. Weston La Barre, "Geza Roheim," in *Psychoanalytic Pioneers*, Franz Alexander, Samuel Eisenstein, Martin Grotjahn, eds. (New York, 1966), p. 273.

throughout his career he kept abreast of developments within the discipline. As a result I have been concerned in this chapter both with Roheim's place in the history of the psychoanalytic movement and with the relationship of his thought to the great debates in the history of anthropology—the issues of evolutionism, diffusionism, and functionalism. In particular, I have attempted to show Roheim's debt to the founders of modern anthropology, Sir Edward Burnett Tylor and Sir James Frazer, and at the same time to account for his opposition to the most influential twentieth-century anthropologist, Bronislaw Malinowski. This preoccupation with Roheim's place in the history of anthropology might not appear directly relevant to my more immediate concern with his contribution to the revolutionary psychoanalytic tradition, but in fact it was by way of a critique of contemporary anthropology that Roheim arrived at some of his most radical conclusions.

Roheim, like Reich, was an immensely prolific writer. In contrast to Reich, however, he was above all a scholar. His erudition was in fact staggering. He was of course thoroughly familiar with the intricacies of psychoanalytic theory. At the same time he was the complete master of the standard anthropological literature and a student of ancient history and mythology. He read widely in the major European literary traditions and was a well-informed *amateur* in the field of biblical criticism. He was at home in three European languages and learned at least the rudiments of several primitive languages in order to carry out his field research. His twenty books and several hundred articles were divided more or less evenly among

Hungarian, German, and English.[2] In general he reserved
Hungarian for his more parochial interest in the folklore
of his native land, German for his theoretical contributions to psychoanalysis, and English for his technical
anthropological writings. Roheim's linguistic virtuosity
has been the source of some scholarly anxiety on my part.
I have read the German and English works, but the
writings in Hungarian have remained beyond my competence. As a result, I have been forced to assume that
Roheim took care to present his most important conclusions in the generally more accessible scholarly media of
German and English.

Despite his formidable learnedness, Roheim was not a
pedant. In fact, he was in every respect Reich's peer in
speculative self-indulgence. Likewise, his writings are
equally as difficult to read as Reich's, although for completely different reasons. Roheim's stylistic inadequacies
were those of the overly knowledgeable antiquarian. His
technique was to overwhelm the reader with detailed
descriptions of seemingly endless myths, folk beliefs, and
ritualistic practices. The conclusions he wished to draw
from this mass of evidence often appeared tucked between apparently innocent examples, sometimes without
even the amenity of a separate paragraph. Furthermore,
he obviously wrote at breakneck speed, wasting little time
on the finer points of prose style and organization.[3] Yet

[2] For a complete bibliography of Roheim's works to 1951 cf.
Psychoanalysis and Culture: Essays in Honor of Geza Roheim,
George B. Wilbur and Warner Muensterberger, eds. (New York,
1951), pp. 455–62.
[3] Roheim's publishers were apparently equally hurried; his books
are riddled with printing errors and inconsistencies.

for all the casualness of their execution, Roheim's writings add up to a very impressive achievement. He was capable of sustained theoretical analyses of extreme complexity, and many passages in his works are as tightly argued and economical as anything that Freud wrote. Thus even more than in the case of Reich, I hope to establish that Geza Roheim is an unduly neglected intellectual, a figure of major importance in the history of psychoanalysis, and of perhaps only slightly lesser stature in the general intellectual history of the twentieth century.

I

Psychoanalysis was born in the death throes of the Austro-Hungarian empire. However, the fact that the empire remained intact until 1918 has perhaps been insufficiently emphasized by historians of Freudianism. This neglect has obscured the extent to which Hungarian intellectuals participated in the elaboration of psychoanalytic theory. In fact, it could be argued that psychoanalysis provided Hungarian thinkers with one of their most important means of access to the Western European intellectual community. After Freud (and discounting for the moment such heterodox figures as Jung and Adler), the greatest of the original psychoanalysts was the Hungarian Sandor Ferenczi. It was Ferenczi who founded the Budapest Psycho-Analytic Society in 1913,[4] and who, as the president and most eminent member of the Society,

[4] Ernest Jones, *The Life and Work of Sigmund Freud*, Vol. II (New York, 1955), p. 103.

quickly established Budapest as one of the major psycho-analytic centers of Europe. Many non-Hungarians, among them Melanie Klein,[5] came to Budapest for analysis and training with Ferenczi. However, his chief accomplishment undoubtedly was to draw native Hungarian talent into psychoanalytic studies. Among his most illustrious students were Sandor Rado and Geza Roheim. Roheim remained a close friend and loyal disciple until Ferenczi's death in 1933,[6] and there was more than an accidental similarity between their dogmatic and often extravagant analytic styles.

Roheim was born in Budapest in 1891. He was the only child of a prosperous bourgeois family, a background which at least one acquaintance blamed for "a certain imperiousness and categorical quality of his adult personality."[7] Roheim's early intellectual interests were exclusively literary and historical.[8] Freud had shared similar interests as a young man, but he of course went on to pursue a thoroughgoing scientific education. Roheim's entire professional training, by way of contrast, was in geography and anthropology. In fact, he never received an M.D., although he did obtain clinical training at the Budapest Institute of Psychoanalysis.[9]

---

[5] John Arnold Lindon, "Melanie Klein," in *Psychoanalytic Pioneers*, pp. 361, 363.

[6] La Barre, "Geza Roheim," p. 273.

[7] *Ibid.*, p. 272. Cf. also Geza Roheim, *Psychoanalysis and Anthropology* (New York, 1950), p. 380.

[8] Sandor Lorand, "Introduction" to *Psychoanalysis and Culture*, p. xi.

[9] La Barre, "Geza Roheim," p. 274.

There was no chair of anthropology in prewar Hungary, and as a result Roheim was forced to move to the universities of Leipzig and Berlin in order to pursue the professional training he desired. It was during this stay in Germany that he was introduced to psychoanalysis, and he was easily won over to the Freudian point of view.[10] His conversion, however, did not signify any abandonment of his commitment to anthropology. Instead it led to the creation of a new discipline, which Roheim christened "psychoanalytic anthropology" in 1915.[11] After completing his formal education Roheim made his home in Hungary, and when the Béla Kun government established a chair of anthropology at the University of Budapest in 1919, Roheim became its first occupant.[12]

Roheim's early work was somewhat old-fashioned from the perspective of academic anthropology. Before his field trip of 1929–31, he was an "armchair" anthropologist, both by choice and by necessity. He read extensively in the primary literature on primitive cultures and collected an impressive library of works on European folklore. On the basis of this reading, and in the privacy of his study, he produced psychoanalytic "interpretations" of the beliefs and practices recorded by investigators in the field. These pre-1929 writings can be separated into two groups, a division which reflects the principal tension in all of Roheim's subsequent work. There were, in the first place, his folklore and mythology studies, which involved cross-

[10] Lorand, "Introduction" to *Psychoanalysis and Culture*, p. xi.
[11] Roheim, *The Gates of the Dream* (New York, 1952), p. vii.
[12] La Barre, "Geza Roheim," p. 273; Marthe Robert, *The Psychoanalytic Revolution* (New York, 1966), p. 324.

cultural psychoanalytic interpretations of particular cultural artifacts. Secondly, there was a group of writings devoted to a defense and elaboration of Freud's primal crime theory. Since Roheim's intellectual development could be described as a prolonged effort to resolve the contradictory assumptions underlying these two endeavors, it will be worthwhile to examine his work in each category.

A representative writing of the first type was Roheim's study of "mirror magic" (*Spiegelzauber*), published in 1919.[13] This work undertook to analyze various folk beliefs and customs which involved mirrors, such as the familiar superstition that breaking a mirror will bring seven years' bad luck. The book contained literally hundreds of such items, drawn primarily from European folklore. Roheim grouped these artifacts under several different rubrics, according to their psychoanalytic meanings. The basic conceptual tool which he employed to explain these beliefs and practices was the psychoanalytic theory of narcissism. Thus he interpreted various taboos against looking in mirrors as attempts to repress childish and unsocial narcissistic wishes.[14] Likewise, fortunetellers who employed mirrors to prophesy the future were analyzed as individuals who had never progressed beyond the infantile narcissistic stage of psychic development.[15] The widespread superstitions concerning broken mirrors were interpreted as destructive impulses directed against

[13] The two other major writings in this category were *Drachen und Drachenkämpfer* (1912) and *Mondmythologie und Mondreligion* (1927).

[14] Roheim, *Spiegelzauber* (Leipzig, 1919), pp. 13–14.

[15] *Ibid.*, p. 34.

a loved one, most frequently a member of the family.[16] I have greatly oversimplified the content and argument of *Spiegelzauber*, but the above should be sufficient to illustrate the basic approach Roheim employed in his psychoanalytic folklore studies. Of course, he was not the only (nor the first) psychoanalyst to undertake this type of investigation. Freud had occasionally turned his attention to folklore and mythology, and among the other psychoanalytic pioneers Otto Rank, Ernest Jones, and Carl Jung had done similar work. Nevertheless, Roheim was the first psychoanalyst to make such studies his central, if not exclusive, concern.

In his psychoanalytic folklore studies Roheim made certain psychological and sociological assumptions, and an analysis of these presuppositions serves to highlight the relationship of his work to the major intellectual traditions in the history of anthropology. The most important, and yet perhaps least obvious, assumption was that cultural artifacts could be interpreted in terms of the psychology of the individual. Roheim cavalierly ignored the possibility that the various customs and beliefs he chose to study might have economic, religious, or sociological meanings. In more general terms, he refused to recognize any substantial difference between the delusions of the individual and those of the community. Later in his career he was prepared to admit at least the possibility of nonpsychological interpretations, if only to refute them. In the early years, however, he simply chose to ignore such alternatives.

Roheim was fully conscious of the assumption he had

[16] *Ibid.*, pp. 191, 197.

made concerning the individual psychological basis of shared ideas and behavior.[17] It was an assumption that put him at odds with the then extremely influential Durkheimian school of anthropology (Marcel Mauss, Lucien Lévy-Bruhl, Alfred Radcliffe Brown), which disallowed any attempt to explain collective behavior in terms of individual psychology. In this respect, as in so many others, Roheim belonged to an older, nineteenth-century, tradition in anthropology. He shared the presuppositions of the founders of the discipline, and in particular of Sir Edward Burnett Tylor, who had explained the widespread primitive belief in animism in terms of individual dream psychology.[18] Of course, it is important to point out that Roheim's psychological perspective was that of psychoanalysis; he rejected the naïve attempts of the founding fathers to explain culture in terms of a simpleminded rationalistic psychology. The psychological motives which stood behind a particular belief or practice were always *unconscious* motives. Myths were indeed a reflection of the inner psychic experiences of the individual, but these experiences were unknown to the individual himself. In short, a myth was to be treated very much like the manifest content of a dream.[19]

The second principal assumption of Roheim's folklore studies was the "psychic unity of mankind," and, like his psychological reductionism, this assumption reflected Roheim's intellectual dependence on the nineteenth-century founders of modern anthropology. The history of

---

[17] *Ibid.*, pp. 262–63.
[18] H. R. Hays, *From Ape to Angel* (New York, 1958), pp. 68–69.
[19] *Spiegelzauber*, pp. 227–28.

anthropology could be characterized as an unresolved debate over the origin of cultural similarities. Only the complementary issue of how to account for cultural differences has proved as vexing. The major nineteenth-century anthropological tradition was labeled "evolutionary" precisely because it attempted to resolve the problem of similarities by way of a hypothesis borrowed from Darwin. Tylor, Frazer, and their contemporaries argued that cultural resemblances existed because all cultures went through identical processes of development.[20] Underlying this evolutionary argument was the assumption that human nature (the raw material on which cultures were built) was a historical constant, or, more precisely, the assumption that man evolved (both intellectually and psychologically) according to a single pattern. Thus primitive cultures, the evolutionists suggested, represented a faithful copy of modern civilization at an earlier stage of development.

The twentieth century has witnessed a twofold reaction against the evolutionist doctrine of mankind's psychic unity. The first group of anthropologists to take issue with Tylor and Frazer were the diffusionists. Simply stated, diffusionism was an attempt to explain cultural resemblances in *historical* terms. If the same artifact was found in two separate cultures, it was assumed that at some point in the past one civilization had borrowed the particular artifact from the other—or received it by mediation of a third civilization. In its most extreme form, as expounded by the English anthropologist Elliot Smith

[20] For this reason the Darwinian doctrine is sometimes referred to as "parallelism."

(1871–1937), diffusionism sought to account for *all* cultural achievements in terms of direct or indirect contact with the single birthplace of civilization, the valley of the Nile. The critics of diffusionism were quick to make jocular remarks about the Egyptian origins of the Alaskan igloo, but the diffusionists did confront the problem of similarities head on, even though their solution was somewhat improbable. The same cannot be said of the second, and ultimately much more influential, school which took evolutionism to task—the functionalist school. The functionalists really offered no solution to the problem of resemblances; they simply denied that the problem existed. For Malinowski, the greatest of the functionalists, a given artifact could be understood only in terms of the cultural context in which it was found. It had no cross-cultural significance whatsoever. Indeed, according to the functionalist doctrine of cultural relativism, the very idea of cross-cultural comparisons was strictly taboo.[21]

This brief detour through the history of anthropology[22] should illustrate how firmly Roheim was grounded in the nineteenth-century tradition within the discipline. Since his technique in a work such as *Spiegelzauber* was to compare similar customs and myths in many different

[21] The functionalist position is structurally similar to that of the German historicists (Dilthey, Meinecke, and Troeltsch), who insisted that each national history was unique and not to be fitted into some universal historical schema.

[22] The best historical survey of anthropology continues to be Robert Lowie's *History of Ethnological Theory* (New York, 1937). Two more recent, but certainly less incisive, histories are H. R. Hays's *From Ape to Angel* (New York, 1958) and Abram Kardiner's and Edward Preble's *They Studied Man* (New York, 1961).

cultures, looking at all times for a common denominator, he was forced to assume that a particular type of artifact always had the same psychological meaning, regardless of the cultural context in which it might appear. To be sure, he attempted to incorporate certain diffusionist and functionalist concepts into his work, but his basic assumptions, particularly the assumption of the psychic unity of mankind, clearly united him with the founding fathers and separated him from his contemporaries.

As Roheim grew older he became acutely aware of the gap between himself and his professional colleagues, and he also became more outspoken in his criticism of the reigning anthropological orthodoxy of cultural relativism. Increasingly he stressed his identification with the "fathers of anthropology" and openly celebrated the accomplishments of "the great and glorious nineteenth century."[23] Moreover, he explicitly acknowledged the primary assumption which he shared with the classical evolutionists: "It would seem to me that the psychic unity of mankind is more than a working hypothesis, it is so obvious that it hardly needs proof."[24] Translated into psychoanalytic categories, this meant, at an absolute minimum, that the unconscious was the same for all cultures.[25] Roheim was willing to go even further, however. Like Freud, he maintained that the primary symbols through which the unconscious revealed itself in con-

[23] *Psychoanalysis and Anthropology*, pp. 1, 438; "Introduction," to *Psychoanalysis and the Social Sciences*, Geza Roheim, ed., Vol. I (London, 1947), p. 26.
[24] *Psychoanalysis and Anthropology*, p. 435.
[25] Roheim, *The Origin and Function of Culture* (New York, 1943), pp. 59–60; *Psychoanalysis and Anthropology*, p. 444.

scious life were also identical in all cultures.[26] Roheim
clearly had gone a step beyond the classical evolutionists:
he suggested that the human mind, in its profoundest
depths, remained constant throughout history. At the
level of the primary psychic processes, modern Europeans
did not differ in the slightest from the rudest primitives.[27]
Thus, for the evolutionary doctrine of parallelism, Roheim
substituted the even more radical notion of an eternal,
static human psyche, upon which the similarity of human
institutions and ideas was founded.

The final assumption of Roheim's psychoanalytic folklore studies was that all cultural artifacts have a contemporary relevance. I place this assumption last, since,
as we shall see, Roheim was ambivalent about this matter.
However, the presupposition that myth and ritual have a
contemporary significance was certainly implicit in a
work such as *Spiegelzauber*. This assumption was also one
of the leitmotivs of functionalist anthropology. Malinowski argued that it was pointless to study myth and ritual
for what they could reveal about the history of a people.
It was much more important to show the function that
such artifacts performed in the contemporary life of a
particular culture. He thus established himself as the
foremost critic of the nineteenth-century evolutionary
doctrine of survivals (Tylor), according to which myth
and ritual represented the distorted vestiges of some real
experience in the past.[28] For once, Roheim seems to have

[26] Roheim, *Animism, Magic and the Divine King* (London,
1930), p. 90.
[27] Roheim, *The Riddle of the Sphinx* (London, 1934), p. 56.
[28] Hays, *From Ape to Angel*, pp. 64, 77.

been in step with his contemporaries, although he was to revert to the evolutionary viewpoint in his study of Freud's primal-crime hypothesis. The overall course of his intellectual development, however, witnessed an ever more explicit acceptance of the Malinowskian doctrine, and an extremely painful (and never fully confessed) rejection of the residualist presuppositions of *Totem and Taboo*.

II

The second preoccupation of Roheim's armchair phase, perhaps even more important than the psychoanalytic exploration of myth and folklore, was Freud's primal-crime theory of the origins of civilization. As in the case of any psychoanalytic intellectual, the single most pervasive influence on Roheim's thinking was Freud himself. Roheim's devotion to Freud was in fact unqualified, and it was with the greatest reluctance that he broke with even the most casual of Freud's ideas. What needs to be stressed, however, is the particular aspect of Freud's achievement which sparked Roheim's imagination. Without question it was Freud the speculative philosopher and "amateur" anthropologist, rather than Freud the clinician, who inspired the bulk of his work. Roheim considered *Totem and Taboo* one of the great landmarks in the history of anthropology, comparable only to Tylor's *Primitive Culture* and Frazer's *Golden Bough*.[29] It was, he said, an "epoch-making work—epoch-making not only

[29] Roheim, *Australian Totemism* (London, 1925), p. 15.

in anthropology but in all social sciences."[30] And even as he liberated himself from the dated and untenable assumptions of *Totem and Taboo*, he never ceased to regard it as a classic, the book which had "created" psychoanalytic anthropology.[31]

Freud arrived at his highly dramatic theory of the origins of civilization by way of an analysis of totemism. He singled out four characteristics of this widespread primitive practice as the basis of his investigation. In the first place, he found that the totem animal was considered sacred by the totem clan and consequently was never hunted or harmed in any way. The one exception to this rule was the practice whereby, on ceremonial occasions, the animal was sacrificed and consumed by the entire tribe. Furthermore, Freud argued that the members of the tribe actually traced their ancestry to the totem animal—that is, the animal was considered the primal father of the tribe. Finally, he noted that totemism was always associated with exogamy; an individual could marry no one belonging to the same totem group as himself.

On the basis of these meager facts, Freud constructed a hypothetical history of the origins of totemism. He suggested that originally the tribe was no more than an extended family, in which all the women—that is, the mother and daughters—were monopolized sexually by the father. At a certain historical moment, however, the sexually deprived sons banded together in revolt against the father, slaughtered him, and actually consumed him.

[30] *The Riddle of the Sphinx*, p. 173.
[31] Roheim, "Introduction," to *Psychoanalysis and the Social Sciences*, p. 12; "Freud and Cultural Anthropology," *The Psychoanalytic Quarterly*, IX, 2 (1940), 246.

After the father had been murdered and eaten, something very curious occurred, an event which for Freud marked the beginning of human history: instead of indulging themselves with the liberated women, the brothers abstained from taking the fruits of their victory. In fact, they contracted with one another to outlaw incest, or, as Freud expressed it, they created the first moral law, the incest taboo, which then became the basis of the first society, the brother clan. The tradition of exogamy that Freud found always accompanied totemism was thus traced back to the incest taboo, since in the original tribe, which was actually only an extended family, the prescription to marry outside the family (incest taboo) was in fact identical with the requirement of marrying outside the tribe (exogamy).

Freud gave two motives for the brothers' action in outlawing incest. The first was purely utilitarian: the brothers realized that only in this way could civil war be prevented from breaking out over the spoils of victory. More important, however, was that after murdering their father the brothers discovered that they had in fact loved him; they recalled the tender side of their relation to him. They therefore relinquished their sexual claims on the women out of remorse. This act of sexual denial created the libidinal basis for the subsequent cohesion of the brother clan (society), which, according to Freud's economic conception of psychic life, could be held together only through aim-inhibited, homo-erotic ties. The brothers' sense of guilt also led to the transformation of the dead father into a god, originally in his actual human form, and later under the guise of the totem animal. Thus in the totem religion Freud found residues of both the primal crime itself and the remorse which followed it; the special treatment accorded the totem animal corresponded to the sons' feelings of repentance, and the totem meal marked a reenactment of the original murder.[32]

Roheim presented his defense and elaboration of the primal-crime hypothesis in several articles and books, the most important of which was *Australian Totemism*, an immense tome published in 1925. The bulk of *Australian Totemism* was devoted to culling evidence from Australian mythology, ritual, and social structure in support of Freud's argument. Roheim contended that there was in fact a single "Primeval Australian Horde," in which the epochal drama was acted out.[33] He found vestigial evidence for the original antagonism of father and sons in a specific body of Australian mythology, known as "the conflict myth," which had traditionally been interpreted as the survival of a primeval contest between hostile races.[34] Furthermore, he interpreted the dualism which permeated all Australian life and thought as a reflection of the prehistoric duality of father and sons. In Australia not only was the social structure (moiety system) dualistic, but the entire universe was held to be divided between two antagonistic phratries.[35] There was also no shortage of mythological and ritualistic evidence for the remaining assumptions of Freud's hypothesis—the conception of the

[32] Sigmund Freud, *Totem and Taboo*, in *The Standard Edition of the Complete Psychological Works of Sigmund Freud*, James Strachey, ed. (London, 1953–1966), XIII, *passim*, particularly Part IV.

[33] *Australian Totemism*, p. 86.

[34] *Ibid.*, p. 38.

[35] *Ibid.*, pp. 86–88.

totem animal as the father of the tribe, the derivation
of exogamy from the incest taboo, the deification of the
murdered father, and so on. Roheim was especially preoccupied with marshaling evidence to illuminate the aim-
inhibited, homo-erotic ties which gave cohesion to the
brother clan, and thus to society as a whole. In Australia
he found striking proof for the existence of such bonds in
the widely prevalent "increase ceremonies" (*Intichiuma*).
The manifest function of these rites was to facilitate the
multiplication of the totem animal. But Roheim characteristically interpreted them as "a symbolic repetition of
collective and mutual onanistic actions" which was
"prompted by the intention to strengthen the feeling of
unity between [the] victorious brothers."[36] The increase
ceremonies, he insisted, were in reality a repetition of the
totem-father's mourning feast.[37]

Even when he was most subservient to Freud's ideas,
Roheim remained a highly original, even idiosyncratic,
thinker. He was not content simply with supplying foot-
notes for *Totem and Taboo*, and in fact *Australian Totemism* (along with the articles and reviews which clustered
about it) contained a number of refinements, modifications, and even startling transformations of Freud's original hypothesis.

Like Freud, Roheim considered the primal murder the
line of demarcation between nature and humanity, the
moment in which man differentiated himself from the rest
of the animal kingdom. But the very fact that the event
was transitional meant that it had to be portrayed against

[36] *Ibid.*, pp. 214, 231, 256–57.
[37] *Ibid.*, p. 233.

the background of man's union with nature. Roheim dramatized this perception by arguing that the primal crime occurred during a stage of human evolution in which man's sexuality, like that of the other animals, was still periodic. The Australian increase rites, in which the natives decorated themselves in apparent imitation of the secondary sexual characteristics that animals develop for the rutting season, were, he argued, a survival of the breeding season.[38] It followed that the primal crime itself occurred during the rutting season, since only at such a time would the sire have found it necessary to exclude the sons from the horde.[39] More precisely, Roheim contended that the primal murder marked the end of man's sexual periodicity. The first act of repression led to an internalization of the distinction between oestrum (period devoted to the libido) and anoestrum (period devoted to the ego). Man was able to discard his sexual periodicity because he had learned to cope with the demands of reality by means of repression.[40]

Roheim also attempted to trace the origins of stone culture to the primal crime. In doing so he anticipated one of the perennial concerns of his later work: the reduction of economic revolutions to their psychological motivations. He suggested that the psychic origins of stone culture were to be found in the particular manner in which the father of the horde was murdered by his sons. He was, according to Roheim, stoned to death. When the

[38] *Ibid.*, p. 242. Roheim also considered the European maypole ceremonies survivals of human sexual periodicity. Cf. *Animism, Magic and the Divine King*, pp. 297, 307.

[39] *Australian Totemism*, pp. 243–44.

[40] *Ibid.*, pp. 280–81.

brothers' victory was assured, they covered the father's body with a large boulder or slab. Roheim surmised that the stone mound or slab later became an object of worship for the repentant sons, and the employment of stone for practical purposes (the Stone Age) followed from the symbolic significance attached to this material because of its instrumental role in the primal crime.[41] The notion that the murdered father was buried under a pile of stones, around which the brothers gathered to mourn him, also provided Roheim with a neat solution to the problem of how the father was transformed into an animal in the totem religion. For not only the repentant brothers, but also carnivores, attracted by the smell of the putrefying corpse, assembled round the cairn. The conscience-stricken murderers were naturally inclined to detect the image of the dead man in every inexplicable appearance of life in the environment, and since they half wished that he might rise from the dead, it was quite understandable that they should identify the animals who came to haunt the grave with the resurrected sire.[42]

Perhaps the most remarkable mutation to which Roheim subjected Freud's hypothesis, and again one reflecting a characteristic preoccupation, was his suggestion that the animal consumed in the totem meal was only secondarily a representative of the father. At a more fundamental level, the level of the primary psychic processes, the totem represented the mother, and eating the animal an upward displacement of intercourse with the

[41] *Ibid.*, pp. 348, 355–56, 362–63, 366–69, 378. Roheim did not attempt to explain how the murdered father could be both consumed and buried under the mound of stones.
[42] *Ibid.*, pp. 384–86.

mother.[43] This piece of interpretation introduces one of the enduring themes of Roheim's work: ambisexuality. In all forms of cultural activity, as well as in individual psychology, he found a massive confusion of masculine and feminine elements. Although bisexuality was not an exclusively Freudian discovery, Freud did in fact incorporate this perception into the psychoanalytic corpus in such a fashion that it has come to be associated with his name. I would argue, however, that the central drama in the Freudian schema—the Oedipus complex—had the effect of shoring up the traditional distinction between masculinity and femininity, since it was the biological and psychological *differences* between mother and father which created the dilemma for the child. In Roheim's thought, on the other hand, there was a clear development away from this sharp differentiation between male and female, and a corresponding deemphasis of the Oedipus complex. In this sense Roheim represented a transitional figure between the exaggerated, almost hysterical, heterosexuality of Reich and the outright celebration of androgyny in Norman O. Brown.

The suggestion that the totem animal symbolized both mother and father was only one among Roheim's many ambisexual interpretations. Mythical figures who combined male and female characteristics crop up throughout his writings. The most illustrious of such hermaphrodites was the Sphinx in the Oedipus legend.[44] Roheim also interpreted the figure of Aphrodite as "the woman with a

[43] *Ibid.*, pp. 249, 285; Roheim "Nach dem Tode des Urvaters," *Imago*, IX (1923), 113; *The Eternal Ones of the Dream* (New York, 1945), pp. 225–26.
[44] *The Riddle of the Sphinx*, p. 22.

penis," whose counterpart appeared in the mythology of many different peoples.[45] Aphrodite's "masculine" opposite was, logically, the man with a vagina, and Roheim found just such an epicene significance in the widespread primitive practice of subincision. The subincision hole, he suggested, was in fact a symbolic vagina.[46] This discovery was of considerable importance for the primal-crime hypothesis, since the subincision wound created the physiological basis for the homo-erotic ties which held masculine society together. The purpose of every initiation rite was to separate the sons from their mothers and unite them to the society of fathers. The meaning of the subincision was thus, "Leave your mother and love us, because we, too, have a vagina."[47] In short, the cohesion of society was predicated on the dissolution of sexual differences between mothers and fathers, men and women.

Despite the sometimes daring departures in *Australian Totemism* from the original Freudian hypothesis, the basic psychological and sociological assumptions of the book were still those of *Totem and Taboo*. Most of these assumptions were dated even in 1913, and by 1925, when

[45] Roheim. "Aphrodite, or the Woman with a Penis," *The Psychoanalytic Quarterly*, XIV (1945), 350–90; *Psychoanalysis and Anthropology*, p. 111; "Psycho-Analysis of Primitive Cultural Types," *International Journal of Psycho-Analysis*, XIII (1932), 53.
[46] *The Eternal Ones of the Dream*, pp. 164–65; *The Riddle of the Sphinx*, p. 72.
[47] *The Eternal Ones of the Dream*, pp. 166, 198. Roheim pursued the analogy even further to suggest that the blood from the subincised penis was meant to suggest menstruation (pp. 170, 176), and that consuming the blood was in effect "drinking men's milk" (pp. 233–34).

Roheim's book appeared, they seemed almost quaint. There was, for instance, the presupposition of a collective unconscious, through which the memory of the primal crime was retained after the deaths of the actual murderers.[48] This assumption was in turn supported by Roheim's acceptance of Haeckel's biogenetic law—that ontogeny recapitulates phylogeny. According to this hypothesis, the individual Oedipal crisis was an ontogenetic reenactment of the formative experience of the race, and thus served to reinforce the primal memory.[49] Intimately associated with these two assumptions, which Roheim shared with Freud, was a specific conception of the nature of myth. In contrast to the presuppositions of his own folklore studies, and of twentieth-century anthropology in general, Roheim found it necessary to argue, with Tylor, that "myths are records of the past."[50] To be sure, he

---

[48] *Australian Totemism*, p. 358; *Animism, Magic, and the Divine King*, pp. 222–23.

[49] *Australian Totemism*, p. 391.

[50] *Ibid.*, p. 312. Cf. also p. 117. Roheim neatly skirted the problem of how a myth could possibly contain residues from an era before the development of language: "Our first difficulty concerns the survival of all those myths which we recognize as reflections of the primal battles. Verbal communication is the only vehicle of traditional continuity we know of; but, *ex hypothesi*, the primal-horde epoch must have been over before the development of speech. We have already outlined the escape from this difficulty. There are play battles, excluding the tragic outcome, as well as real battles in the ape horde. The dramatic rites may have developed from these and so have represented the battle and the defeat of the one against the mass. If so, a text and a myth gradually arose out of the emotional noises that first accompanied the action at a time when *homo alalus* was a past stage of development and man had already learnt the rudiments of speech." *The Riddle of the Sphinx*, p. 234.

hedged a little by insisting that "the past" was to be understood in both ontogenetic and phylogenetic terms.[51] But the basic assumption of the historicity of myth remained intact.

In almost every respect, then, Roheim's early work represented an extension of the nineteenth-century evolutionary tradition in anthropology. Only as a result of his experiences in the field between 1929 and 1931, and after years of painful intellectual struggle, was he able to liberate himself from the fetters of historical realism.

III

It seems appropriate that Roheim's liberation from the antiquated assumptions of Darwinian anthropology was initiated by his abandonment of the armchair. The modern anthropologist, at least since the pioneering work of Franz Boas, is first and foremost a field worker. Unfortunately, however, the preoccupation with the techniques of field research has often been accompanied by a theoretical squeamishness. Perhaps the complexities of primitive life as directly observed in the field have led to a certain skepticism about the viability of ambitious theoretical hypotheses. In any case, it is clear that modern anthropologists have felt strongly disinclined to indulge in the kind of bold speculation which characterized the work of Tylor, Bachofen, Maine, and Frazer. Boas himself was a perfect example of this tendency. Although he is universally considered among the most influential of modern

51 *Australian Totemism*, p. 312.

anthropologists and was in fact the teacher of many of the most famous anthropologists active during the middle years of the century, he was never able to write a general anthropology—to bring together the discrete results of his researches into a synoptic theory of culture. Instead, his entire theoretical contribution took the form of criticism; he never tired of issuing caveats, making distinctions, and cautioning against unwarranted generalizations.[52] The great virtue of Roheim's work, I would suggest, is that he managed to incorporate many of the methodological precepts of modern field anthropology, without at the same time giving in to its theoretical faintheartedness. Thus although he honored the Boasian imperative "to live among them," he remained at all times a faithful disciple of Tylor, Frazer, and, of course, Freud.

Early in 1928 Princess George of Greece (Marie Bonaparte) proposed to finance a field trip which would offer Roheim the opportunity to undertake the first psychoanalyses of primitives. Roheim originally planned to spend the entire expedition among the aborigines of central Australia. This prospective itinerary was based on several considerations. For one thing, the Australians were considered the classical representatives of totemism and the hunting mode of life. Moreover, Roheim had already written extensively on Australia and was anxious to test his theories through direct observation.[53] The most important factor influencing this decision, however, was his conviction that the Australians represented the most primitive existent race. The theme of Australian

[52] Lowie, *History of Ethnological Theory*, pp. 128–55, especially pp. 130–31, 146–48, 151–52.
[53] "Psycho-Analysis of Primitive Cultural Types," p. 2.

primitiveness recurs persistently throughout the many books and articles which Roheim devoted to their civilization in the course of his career.[54] "Only my friends of the Central Australian desert can be described as primitives in the true sense of the word. . . . All other 'primitives' whom I know (Somali, Papuo-Melanesians, Yuma Indians) are closer to us psychologically than to the Australians."[55] Roheim never made explicit the reasons for his preoccupation with the primitiveness of the Australians, but it seems obvious that in the back of his mind was the thesis of *Civilization and Its Discontents*. If civilization was based on repression, then it followed that the most primitive culture should also be the most permissive, and its members the healthiest, psychologically, of living men. And as we shall see when we come to discuss the critical implications of Roheim's thought, this is precisely the contention he was to make.

Roheim did not in fact devote the entire field trip to Australia. Other considerations caused him to modify his original plans, most important among them his desire to refute the claims of functionalist anthropology that the Oedipus complex was not universal, and in particular that it was absent in matrilineal cultures. Consequently the itinerary was altered to include a stay in the matrilineal

[54] Besides *Australian Totemism* the entirety or large portions of the following works were devoted to the Australians: "Psycho-Analysis of Primitive Cultural Types" (1932), *The Riddle of the Sphinx* (1934), *The Eternal Ones of the Dream* (1945), and *Psychoanalysis and Anthropology* (1950).

[55] "Psycho-Analysis of Primitive Cultural Types," pp. 4–5. Cf. also *Australian Totemism*, p. 221; *The Riddle of the Sphinx*, p. 226; *Psychoanalysis and Anthropology*, p. 405.

society of Normanby Island.[56] In the end Roheim spent ten months in Australia and an equal period of time in Normanby. These two sojourns were prefaced and concluded by short stays in Somaliland and among the Yuma Indians of Arizona.[57] He was accompanied on the entire trip by his wife, Illna, who looked after photography and the usual domestic chores.[58]

As a psychoanalyst, Roheim pursued his field work in a somewhat different fashion from most anthropologists. To be sure, he made the usual attempt to observe social structure, economic institutions, and public ritual. But by far the largest portion of his time and energy was devoted to an analysis of the individual.[59] To accomplish this task Roheim employed several different techniques. First, he attempted to psychoanalyze individual primitives, which meant, above all else, the interpretation of dreams.[60] Individual analysis was complemented by a general study of the sexual lives of the natives.[61] Finally, Roheim adopted from Melanie Klein the technique of play analysis, which provided an excellent method for observing

---

[56] "Psycho-Analysis of Primitive Cultural Types," p. 2.
[57] *Ibid.*, p. 3; *Psychoanalysis and Anthropology*, p. 157; *The Origin and Function of Culture*, p. 8.
[58] La Barre, "Geza Roheim," p. 280.
[59] Roheim thus set himself in opposition to the Durkheimian assumption of the primacy of society. "In order to understand a society thoroughly, we must study it in its individuals." "Psychoanalysis of Primitive Cultural Types," p. 151.
[60] Roheim, "Dream Analysis and Field Work in Anthropology," in *Psychoanalysis and the Social Sciences*, I, 81–130; "Psycho-Analysis of Primitive Cultural Types," p. 21; *Psychoanalysis and Anthropology*, p. 127.
[61] "Psycho-Analysis of Primitive Cultural Types," p. 21.

the all-important process of childhood personality formation.[62] As an underlying methodological precept, Roheim
insisted that the investigator had to become good friends
with the natives, since only by means of such intimacy
could one establish the affective ties (transference) so
important to the analyst.[63] Quite clearly the techniques
which Roheim employed presupposed not only that the
anthropologist himself had been psychoanalyzed, but that
he was a practicing clinician as well, and characteristically, Roheim was not a bit reticent about insisting on
these prerequisites.[64]

Given Roheim's dogmatic Freudianism, one might
anticipate that the experience in the field would have had
little effect on his well-established interpretive inclinations. And, in fact, the post-armchair writings bear many
of the familiar trademarks of their predecessors. There is
the same interpretive abandon, the same organizational
chaos, and the same unperturbed conviction of the universal appropriateness of psychoanalytic categories. However, a closer reading reveals that the field trip yielded a
very important discovery, one which signaled the begin-
nings of Roheim's liberation from Freud's historical literalism. Roheim formulated this discovery as "the ontogenetic theory of culture," and just as the name implies, it
entailed a shift of emphasis from the history of the race to
the history of the individual.

Roheim claimed that the crucial importance of field
work lay in what it revealed about cultural differences: "I

[62] *Ibid.; Psychoanalysis and Anthropology*, p. 64.
[63] "Psycho-Analysis of Primitive Cultural Types," p. 8.
[64] *Ibid.*, p. 7.

do not mean to say that the only kind of anthropological work is field work. Universals can be investigated without it but not differentials."[65] Indeed, after his return from the South Seas, he continued to produce speculative works about the origin and function of culture as such, but he maintained conscientiously that only direct observation could lead to an understanding of why one culture differed from another. In brief, the ontogenetic theory of culture contended that cultural differences were a product of infantile traumas. In each culture the child experienced a characteristic crisis. This crisis gave rise to the adult personality structure typical of the culture, and the economic, political, and religious institutions of the society were in turn based upon that personality structure.[66] Roheim's ontogenetic theory bore a striking resemblance to Reich's general social theory in its insistence on the definitive significance of child-rearing practices for personality formation, and consequently for social and economic institutions. However, Roheim adamantly refused to take the further step of grounding child-rearing practices in the economic substructure, and, as a result, his theory, although more elegant from a psychoanalytic point of view than Reich's, exhibited loose ends which the latter avoided. It was in effect a theoretical edifice which lacked a ground floor.

Roheim arrived at the ontogenetic theory of culture by way of specific observations made during the field trip, particularly in Australia and Normanby. The most strik-

[65] Roheim, "Society and the Individual," *The Psychoanalytic Quarterly*, IX, 4 (1940), 544.
[66] *The Riddle of the Sphinx*, p. 169.

ing feature of Australian personality structure and culture, he argued, was their hypermasculinity: the males were extremely aggressive, the women were ruthlessly excluded from all social and ceremonial functions, and the representation of the female in myth, dreams, and children's games was curiously masculine—most frequently the woman was portrayed as a phallic demon. All these characteristics suddenly fell into place when Roheim was told by a female native that Australian mothers slept on top of their young children in exactly the same position which the adult males assumed in coitus.[67] Here was the characteristic childhood trauma which would explain the phallic conception of the female (mother), and, by the way of reaction formation, the hypermasculinity of the adult males, as well as the exclusively masculine organization of Australian lineage, ritual, and social structure.[68]

Roheim discovered an analogous trauma in the lives of Melanesian children. On Normanby Island fathers were in the habit of taking the childrens' genitals in their mouths and saying, "I bite, I eat the penis (or vagina)."[69] Roheim argued that the cultural consequence of this typical childhood experience was the famous Melanesian yam culture, in which yams were exchanged compulsively in order to create an anxious sense of obligation. The yams were symbolic representatives of the giver, and the entire complex was based upon a particularly acute fear of (oral) castration: "These people whose fathers have threatened to eat or castrate them, spend their whole lives

[67] "Introduction," to *Psychoanalysis and the Social Sciences*, p. 18.
[68] *The Riddle of the Sphinx*, pp. 162–65.
[69] *Ibid.*, p. 162.

in repaying or repeating this one experience; they continually eat others or are eaten by them."[70] Even the matrilineal organization of Melanesian society, Roheim argued, could be explained as a reaction formation against the "paternal trauma" in the life of the infant.[71]

Thus cultural differences were attributed to characteristic traumas in the experience of the individual; they were *not* the product of a traumatic experience of the race. The ontogenetic theory rendered the assumption of a collective unconscious completely expendable, at least as far as cultural differences were concerned.[72] Likewise, the new theory considerably undermined any preoccupation with phylogenetic or historical explanations of contemporary artifacts. Indeed, Roheim took Freud and Ferenczi to task for their naïve phylogenetic bias: "It seems to me that attempts to derive specific types of culture from the past vicissitudes of different peoples are merely idle speculations, open to anyone in the study but quite incapable of being weighed scientifically."[73] Realizing the decisive step he had taken in the direction of functionalism, with its radical antihistorical bias, but not yet fully prepared to accept the logical consequences of this about-face, Roheim was quick to add that his strictures did not apply to the primal-horde hypothesis.[74] To a certain extent, of course, this loophole was legitimate, since Freud's theory was designed to explain not cultural

[70] *Ibid.*
[71] *The Origin and Function of Culture*, p. 39.
[72] *The Riddle of the Sphinx*, p. 281.
[73] "Psycho-Analysis of Primitive Cultural Types," p. 198; *The Riddle of the Sphinx*, pp. 166–67.
[74] "Psycho-Analysis of Primitive Cultural Types," p. 198.

differences but the origin of culture as such, and as I have already noted, Roheim maintained that cultural universals were the proper domain of armchair speculation. Nevertheless, the shift from a historical to a contemporary perspective was a decisive one. After 1932 Roheim was never again to take up the hypothesis of *Totem and Taboo* with the enthusiasm he had when writing *Australian Totemism*.

Roheim was aware that the ontogenetic theory of culture suffered from a major shortcoming, but his anti-Marxian bias prevented him from confronting this difficulty in a satisfactory manner. It might in fact be true that cultural patterns were based on characteristic infantile traumas, but what accounted for the fact that the infant was subjected to a particular form of child-rearing in any given culture? Roheim simply moved around in a circle when he argued that the peculiarities of child-rearing practices were explicable in terms of the unsatisfied libidinal tendencies of parents, which were directed toward children.[75] For adult libidinal organization was, of course, itself the product of childhood experience. Roheim ridiculed the idea, originally derived from Montesquieu, that behavioral and cultural differences could be traced to environmental differences.[76] Yet, when pressed he fell back on an equally unsatisfactory explanation. Perhaps, he surmised, the appearance of a particular infantile trauma was based upon some "obscure constitutional factor."[77] The hypothesis that cultural differences

[75] *The Riddle of the Sphinx,* pp. 165, 281.
[76] *The Origin and Function of Culture,* pp. 9–10.
[77] "Psycho-Analysis of Primitive Cultural Types," p. 198.

were at bottom grounded in biological differences never fully satisfied Roheim, as is evident from the diffident manner in which he expounded it. He toyed with other possible explanations, at one time suggesting that the child's observation of the primal scene provided the transition to the various specific traumata,[78] at another time that differences in erotic play activities laid the foundation of cultural variations.[79] But neither of these hypotheses was explained or elaborated. In the end one is left with the feeling that Roheim simply had no ultimate answer to the question of how cultural differences arose.

IV

I have already suggested that the empirical lessons of Roheim's field trip were not so overwhelming as to seriously inhibit his theoretical daring. Indeed, Roheim's principal preoccupation during the decade following his return from the South Pacific was the elaboration of a *general* theory of the origin and function of culture. Nevertheless, the ontogenetic theory of cultural differences—the most significant intellectual gain of his experiences in the field—clearly left its mark on the speculative works of the 1930's and 1940's. I feel that these speculative writings constitute Roheim's most impressive accomplishment as a social theorist, and consequently I want to discuss them in greater detail than his earlier work. I ask the reader to bear with me in this endeavor, for the material is admittedly both abstract and difficult. Yet the

[78] *Ibid.*, p. 196.
[79] *The Riddle of the Sphinx*, p. 235.

total vision is, I think, of sufficient grandeur and incisiveness to make the effort well worthwhile.

The very fact that Roheim continued to be fascinated by the problem of origins indicates the strength of his ties to the nineteenth-century anthropological tradition. But within this general framework he went a long way toward softening the historical literalism that vitiated the hypothesis of *Totem and Taboo*. To begin with, he argued that Freud had never intended the theory of the primal crime to be understood as a literal presentation of the facts. Freud had suggested that although the murder of the primal father was a historical reality, it happened many times over in the course of human history. Only the cumulative effect of thousands of such murders added up to civilization—to the creation of permanent human communities.[80] Roheim underscored this perception by

[80] There is a problem here as to who influenced whom. In *Group Psychology and the Analysis of the Ego* (1921), which predated Roheim's various attempts to reinterpret *Totem and Taboo*, Freud had in fact asserted that the primal-crime hypothesis was not to be understood as a simple statement of fact: "This is only a hypothesis, like so many others with which archaeologists endeavour to lighten the darkness of prehistoric times—a 'Just-So Story', as it was amusingly called by a not unkind English critic; but I think it is creditable to such a hypothesis if it proves able to bring coherence and understanding into more and more new regions." (*Group Psychology, The Standard Edition* . . . , XVIII, p. 122.) However, Freud's most explicit disavowal of historical literalism came only after Roheim's work of reconstruction, in *Moses and Monotheism* (1934–38): "The story is told in an enormously condensed form, as though it had happened on a single occasion, while in fact it covered thousands of years and was repeated countless times during that long period." (*Moses and Monotheism, The Standard Edition* . . . , XXIII, p. 81.)

stretching the primal event out over an immense span of time. Malinowski had complained that it was impossible to believe in the murder if the primal horde was composed of men, and equally impossible to believe in the sons' repentance if the horde was composed of animals.[81] This objection, according to Roheim, ignored Freud's intention in *Totem and Taboo* of presenting a highly compressed and dramatic condensation of the facts. In reality "the father" represented generations of fathers, and "the brothers" generations of brothers.[82] Time and again the horde of brothers would murder the powerful leader and take possession of the women. Only very gradually did a sense of uneasiness begin to inhibit the pleasure of this sexual conquest: "For every father killed there was more of grief and less of triumph than for his predecessor."[83] This response was hardly a satisfactory rebuttal to Malinowski's critique, since at some point in the evolutionary process we still must confront a generation of brothers who were at once murderous and yet remorseful enough to forgo sexual intercourse with the women. Nevertheless, Roheim's modification of the original argument was a revealing reflection of his struggle to escape the historical literalism of *Totem and Taboo*.

The ontogenetic theory of cultural differences suggested a more interesting line of attack. Roheim reasoned that if the unique characteristics of a given culture were dependent on a peculiar infantile experience, it followed

[81] Bronislaw Malinowski, *Sex and Repression in Savage Society* (New York, 1959), pp. 133–52. Roheim, *The Riddle of the Sphinx*, pp. 202–03.
[82] *The Riddle of the Sphinx*, pp. 202–3.
[83] *Australian Totemism*, p. 380.

that culture in general must be the result of an infantile trauma common to all mankind.[84] In effect he admitted that Freud's explanation of the transition from the primal horde to human society in terms of the inadequate satisfaction of the victors and their postponed obedience to the slain father was not totally persuasive. There was no reason to assume that satisfaction would necessarily diminish with each succeeding generation of brothers. The trouble was that Freud had been insufficiently Freudian in his analysis. He had attempted to account for the transition from ape to man in terms of the experiences of only two actors, the father and the horde of brothers. Thus the great change occurred, according to Freud, in the minds of the adult brothers. But as Roheim pointed out, this contention was completely at odds with the psychoanalytic doctrine that real changes occur only in the minds of children. Roheim therefore suggested that there were in fact three actors in the great primeval drama: the father, the brothers, and the children—that is, the members of the horde who, because of their immaturity, were merely witnesses to the murder.[85] The child who observed the violent assault on the father and the subsequent sexual violation of the mother could conceivably experience a trauma of sufficient intensity to initiate the process of sexual repression which marked the origins of civilization.

Roheim argued that Solly Zuckerman's firsthand observations of primate behavior (*The Social Life of Apes and Monkeys*, 1932) confirmed this hypothesis.[86] Young

[84] *The Riddle of the Sphinx*, pp. 173, 216.
[85] *Ibid.*, p. 282.
[86] *Ibid.*, p. 192.

apes, clinging to their mothers' bodies, were often crushed during the battles between the younger males and their older counterparts. If the the infants survived the scrape, they then witnessed the sexual abuse to which their mothers were subjected by the victorious horde—indeed, they were often themselves the objects of sexual stimulation and exploitation. Here, Roheim argued, was a situation in which realistic and erotic anxieties might well lead to a repression of sexuality. The infant pre-man would attempt to cope with the very real dangers to his life, and particularly with the accompanying libidinal stimulation (which was beyond his mastery and thus a threat to the integration of the ego), by way of a denial of sexuality.[87] The process of repression initiated in infancy thus laid the groundwork for the feelings of dissatisfaction and remorse which the adult brothers were to feel with ever increasing intensity.

Roheim was left with the problem of explaining why observation of the primal crime and primal rape led to repression in the case of man and not in the case of the other animals. For a solution he was forced to delve into the realm of biology. Man was distinguished from the other animals by his delayed infancy; he remained depen-

---

[87] *Ibid.,* pp. 282–83. For this argument Roheim drew on one of Reich's findings: "The undeveloped human being is not yet capable of end-pleasure. Therefore he is unable to absorb the libido quantities that arise from his association with grown-up people (parents) and must react to them with repression and other defense mechanisms. The sexual traumata give rise to phobias, as Reich has shown, and these in their turn to character traits ('*Über kindliche Phobie und Characterbildung*')." *The Riddle of the Sphinx,* pp. 205–6.

dent on his parents for an exorbitantly long period of time. The sheer length of this period of dependency was, for Roheim, sufficient to explain why observation of the primal drama would lead to repression in man. "The longer the period of intimate association between parents and children the greater will be the dynamic effects of the traumata to be controlled."[88] But besides this purely quantitative factor there was a qualitative difference in the manner in which men and animals matured. Roheim drew upon the research of the German physiologist Ludwig Bolk to support this latter contention. Bolk had shown that man was characterized by a retarded physical development. His adult physiological characteristics bore a striking resemblance to those of an ape fetus at a certain stage in its development. Furthermore, this physiological infantilization was progressive. It was, of course, precisely the fact of retardation which made man's prolonged childhood necessary. But more important for Roheim's argument was Bolk's discovery that soma and germ plasma reacted differently to the retarding influences. Man's body was much *more* retarded than his sexuality, and as a result the human child was faced with the dilemma of being sexually mature (capable of sexual stimulation) long before he was physiologically mature (capable of procreation). Man was sexually precocious—indeed, much more so than any other animal. Consequently he was subjected to sexual stimuli at an age when he was unable to deal with them satisfactorily. Repression was the defense mechanism he had developed to meet this crisis. In fact, repression might be thought of as an artifi-

---

[88] *Ibid.*, p. 213; cf. also pp. 282–83.

cial retarding device, a psychological means of eliminating the disequilibrium between man's physical and sexual development.[89] The implication of this argument was that repression was in a sense an organic necessity. Roheim admitted as much,[90] although he was never willing to embrace the conservative conclusions to which the argument seemingly led. With Freud (and against Reich), he accepted the inevitability of repression, but he maintained intransigently that civilization had overplayed its hand: it demanded far more repression than was in fact necessary to meet the requirements of man's curiously uneven maturation.

Roheim had arrived at a reinterpretation of Freud's primal-crime hypothesis which enabled him to circumvent the naïve assumptions of the original argument, but at the same time to retain its basic motif. Civilization originated in, and fed upon, the Oedipus complex; it developed out of the ambivalent emotions unique to the family arrangement dictated by man's prolonged infancy. But Roheim no longer found it necessary to postulate the existence of a group mind or collective memory.[91] To be sure, "the primal horde really existed,"[92] but it was not imperative to make it responsible for the human psyche in general. The universal fact of man's delayed infancy provided civilization with a mechanism which was at once

[89] Ibid., pp. 246–56; The Origin and Function of Culture, pp. 17–25.
[90] The Riddle of the Sphinx, pp. 250–51.
[91] Ibid., pp. 234–35.
[92] Roheim, "Primitive High Gods," Supplement to The Psychoanalytic Quarterly, III (1934), 121; "Society and the Individual," pp. 533–34.

historical (since retardation was an ongoing process) and contemporary. Roheim had at last arrived at the twentieth century, and he had done so without abandoning the intellectual baggage of his youth.

In what was perhaps his most important work, *The Origin and Function of Culture* (1943), Roheim brought to a successful culmination the task of elaborating a psychoanalytic interpretation of culture which was thoroughly modern in both its substantive and methodological assumptions. This uncharacteristically brief masterpiece marked his unqualified acceptance of the contemporary point of view (the primal crime was not mentioned), and it also contained his most general statement of the psychological dynamics of civilization. In the works that preceded *The Origin and Function of Culture* ("Psychoanalysis of Primitive Cultural Types," 1932; "Primitive High Gods," 1933; and particularly *The Riddle of the Sphinx*, 1934), Roheim's analysis of culture had been couched in uncomfortably clinical rhetoric. He did not completely abandon this technical vocabulary in *The Origin and Function of Culture*, but there was an undeniable effort to find a language more appropriate to the philosophical issues to which he addressed himself. The principal themes of the book were not such familiar clinical items as the Oedipus complex, object cathexis, or repression, but rather love, death, and, most important, separation.

Roheim's point of departure in *The Origin and Function of Culture* was again man's delayed infancy and prolonged dependency. But instead of examining this situation from the Oedipal point of view as he had in his previous theoretical forays, that is, from the perspective which stressed the erotic and aggressive anxieties which were part of every child's experience, Roheim chose to emphasize a much more obvious (and much less explicitly psychoanalytic) infantile dilemma. The child began his life in what Roheim termed the "dual unity" situation: he was at once a separate entity and a part of his mother. This was most obviously the case while the child was still in his mother's womb. But, unlike any other animal, the child experienced an abnormal prolongation of the dual-unity situation because of his delayed infancy. The process of growing up, which was in effect the process of separation from the mother, was therefore much more painful in the case of the human infant. Indeed, Roheim suggested that the inevitable experience of separation was almost too much for the child to bear.

In the light of this analysis, Roheim went on to argue that civilization could best be understood as a colossal effort on the part of the aging child to protect himself against object loss. In all his cultural enterprises man sought substitutes for his lost mother.[93] These enterprises, according to Roheim, had one feature in common: "They unite one human being to the other, they are cunning devices adopted by man, the infant, against being left alone."[94] Thus, whereas Freud interpreted culture as a prolonged act of expiation arising out of the sense of guilt which the sons felt for having murdered their father, Roheim conceived of the civilizing process as an effort to compensate for the sense of loss experienced by the child separated from his mother. Roheim had in effect illumi-

[93] *The Origin and Function of Culture*, pp. 36–39, 76–77, 81–82; *The Eternal Ones of the Dream*, p. 202.
[94] *The Origin and Function of Culture*, pp. 83–84.

nated the specific mechanism through which Eros accomplished its eternal task of uniting men into ever larger groups. Freud had written of this "work of love" in the spectacular concluding pages of *Civilization and Its Discontents*, but he was apparently satisfied to express himself in vague metaphorical language. Roheim brought the analysis down to earth, as it were, by arguing that the child's constant search for a substitute mother provided the civilizing process with its momentum.[95] The paradox of civilization was that man became civilized only in order to remain an infant.[96]

Roheim's interpretation of civilization as a grandiose effort to overcome separation through the formation of group ties was a thoroughly original piece of analysis. But the theory was not conceived in a vacuum, and it is possible to identify certain of its intellectual forebears. *The Origin and Function of Culture* was most obviously indebted to Otto Rank and Sandor Ferenczi. The theme of separation shifted the focus of attention from the Oedipus complex to the birth trauma, for although man shares the experience of birth with all animals, it nevertheless remains the archetypal "separating" experience. For polemical reasons Roheim never admitted that this shift of focus had taken place. Perhaps for personal reasons, he was equally unwilling to acknowledge the extent to which his theory of culture depended on the work of Otto Rank, whose name is most intimately associated with the theory of the birth trauma.[97] Acknowledged or not, the influence

[95] *Ibid.*, pp. v, 98–100.
[96] *Ibid.*, p. 31; *The Riddle of the Sphinx*, p. 214.
[97] Roheim always maintained that it was Freud, not Rank, who first established the connection between birth and anxiety. Cf. *The*

of Rank on *The Origin and Function of Culture* seems undeniable.

On the other hand, Roheim was quite ready to give credit to Rank's sometime collaborator Sandor Ferenczi for his contribution to the separation-anxiety hypothesis. The psychological corollary of Rank's birth trauma was Ferenczi's concept of uterine regression. In his most important work, *Thalassa* (*Versuch einer Genitaltheorie*), Ferenczi had interpreted sexual intercourse as an attempt to reverse the process of being born. In the sexual act a man identified himself with his penis, which, quite literally, returned to the womb. Furthermore, it was because the penis was the sole means by which reunion with the mother could be achieved that the child experienced castration anxiety.[98] Roheim in a sense projected Ferenczi's analysis of the psychological foundations of sexual intercourse into a general theory of culture. All of man's civilized endeavors, he suggested, were in reality cleverly disguised attempts to return to the womb.

Roheim intended this analysis to be taken quite seriously. Two years after completing *The Origin and Function of Culture* he published his last monograph on Australian culture (*The Eternal Ones of the Dream*), in which nearly every artifact which he had earlier analyzed as a residual product of the primal crime was reinterpreted in the light of the theory of separation anxiety. In

---

Origin and Function of Culture, p. 19 n., and *The Eternal Ones of the Dream*, p. 77.

[98] Sandor Ferenczi, *Versuch einer Genitaltheorie* (Leipzig, 1924), pp. 37–38.

particular, the initiation ceremonies, which constitute the central ritual institution of so many primitive cultures, were interpreted as efforts to negotiate the final separation of the child from his mother and to offer incorporation into the society of males as a substitute gratification. The dualism which permeated Australian ideology and social organization was no longer to be understood as the vestigial remains of the primal antagonism of father and sons, but as a reflection of the duality of mother and child.[99] Roheim stuck with this interpretation until the end of his life. In his last papers he pursued the theme of separation into an analysis of such universal primitive phenomena as magic and animism, and he even employed it to explain the clinical phenomenon of schizophrenia.[100]

Roheim's investigation of the role of separation anxiety in individual and mass psychology brought him to the verge of an important hypothesis about the psychological meaning of death. There is a rich Western literary tradition which contends that love and death are in reality one, and more specifically (as in *Tristan und Isolde*) that sexual intercourse is in fact a form of dying. Roheim expressed this same insight in the vivid clinical language of psychoanalysis: he argued, echoing Freud, that sexual intercourse was the psychological equivalent of castration. "From the libidinal point of view [sexual intercourse] is the goal of our strivings but from the point of the narcis-

[99] *The Eternal Ones of the Dream*, pp. 64–67, 117, 136–38, 222–23, 237–38, 243, 249–50.
[100] Roheim, *Magic and Schizophrenia* (Bloomington, Indiana, 1955), pp. 109–10, 117–18, 194–95, 223–24.

sistic retention in the ego, coitus is death or castration."[101]
For the most part Roheim was concerned in this analysis
of the psychology of death with explaining the fear of
dying, and he argued that at the level of the primary
processes anxiety about death was in reality anxiety about
castration.[102] However, he felt somewhat uneasy about
this interpretation, particularly in view of Freud's assertion of a primary death instinct, and in a footnote to
Animism, Magic and the Divine King (1930), he admitted that the entire complex might be "rooted in a still
deeper layer, i.e. in the death impulse itself."[103]

This was as far as Roheim got in his analysis. After he
had discovered the primary importance of separation anxiety in the 1940's, he was willing to argue that the fear of
death was perhaps the final manifestation of man's horror
of being left alone in the dark.[104] But he was never able
to invert the formula in order to explain why it might be
that men *desire* death, as Freud's hypothesis implied.
Nevertheless, all the ingredients for such an explanation
were present. If "death is coitus and coitus is death,"[105]
then surely death is a desideratum because it signifies
eternal reunion with the mother. It represents the ulti-

[101] *Animism, Magic and the Divine King*, p. 247. Roheim's
argument displayed the typical masculine bias of psychoanalysis.
We can well understand why Tristan dies, if sexual intercourse is in
fact a form of castration. But why does Isolde die? Roheim suggested, rather lamely, that the feminine equivalent of castration
was childbirth. *Animism, Magic and the Divine King*, p. 82.
[102] *Ibid.*, p. 190.
[103] *Ibid.*, p. 191 n.
[104] *The Origin and Function of Culture*, pp. 85, 91; *Psychoanalysis and Anthropology*, p. 137.
[105] *Animism, Magic and the Divine King*, p. 233.

mate solution to the problem of separation. However, Roheim never arrived at this formulation; he never explicitly reversed his earlier contention (1930) that the symbolism of uterine regression so prevalent in the funereal rites of all cultures was anything more than "a consolation to overlay the dread of castration."[106] For a synoptic psychoanalytic investigation of the psychology of death we must await the speculations of Herbert Marcuse and Norman O. Brown.

V

I began this chapter by claiming that Roheim was not a political thinker, and that, as a result, his radicalism did not take the form of explicit political criticism, such as we find in Reich and Marcuse. I would now like to qualify this statement. Although there was nothing in Roheim's writings so obviously political as there was in the writings of the other members of the Freudian Left, his work did contain at least the rudiments of a political theory, as well as some very pointed observations on economics. Roheim apparently intended these latter remarks at least as a critique of historical materialism, but his own position was, if anything, more radical than the Marxists'. In all of his observations on politics and economics, he indulged in a ruthless psychological reductionism,[107] and it was pre-

106 *Ibid.*, p. 56.
107 *Psychoanalysis and Anthropology,* p. 452: "A psychoanalytic view of culture is necessarily reductionist (reducing culture to psychology and even to biology) . . ."

cisely this quality that endowed his analysis with its abrasive polemical thrust.

For Roheim, politics was a kind of black magic. The political leader, far from being descended from the gods (as in traditional hierarchical theory), had risen from the depths of hell. The politician was the modern descendant of the sorcerer, and political science, therefore, was most accurately treated as a branch of demonology. In primitive societies, Roheim argued, the extraordinary influence of the sorcerer derived from his role as symbolic castrator. His political authority followed from his psychological authority as the focal point of primitive man's unconscious fear of and desire for castration. The sorcerer's magic staff, so important in primitive medical practice, was a castrating penis, and the sorcerer himself was an individual who suffered from particularly acute castration anxiety, and who coped with this problem by castrating others rather than being castrated himself.[108]

This interpretation of the psychological origins of sorcery was in itself a rather imaginative piece of analysis. But Roheim was not satisfied to end his interpretation at this point. He went on to project the phallic-castration theory of sorcery into a theory of the origins of kingship, and, ultimately, into a general interpretation of the psychological foundations of all political authority. In this endeavor he was following in the footsteps of Sir James Frazer, who had, in Roheim's own words, "demonstrated in masterly fashion the origins of kingship among the social class of magicians."[109] But of course Roheim's

[108] *Animism, Magic and the Divine King*, pp. 58, 68–69, 104, 135, 154, 163, 175, 381–82.
[109] *Spiegelzauber*, p. 82.

Freudian explanation of the psychic mechanism of kingship was entirely new, and indeed quite foreign to Frazer's style of analysis.

Roheim found considerable evidence in the lore and ritual of royalty to substantiate Frazer's contention that the king was in fact little more than a glorified medicine man, and he postulated that the same psychic mechanism which accounted for the authority of the medicine man was responsible for the king's authority as well. Like the medicine man, the king was both the sender and the healer of disease[110]—an aspect of monarchy which Marc Bloch had elaborated in *Les rois thaumaturges*. Similarly, the king, like the sorcerer, was a rainmaker.[111] Most importantly, the king shared the phallic characteristics of the sorcerer. The royal scepter was clearly heir to the sorcerer's staff, and the king's elaborate headgear could be interpreted either as the secondary sexual characteristics of the male animal during the rutting season, or as a vagina, in which case the king's head represented the phallus, and the head in the crown corresponded to the penis in the vagina.[112] In short, the king was the castrating phallus around which society was organized.

Roheim's interpretation of the phallic nature of political authority must be seen against the background of Freud's great book on politics, *Group Psychology and the Analysis of the Ego*. In fact, Roheim's *Animism, Magic and the Divine King* was basically an attempt to spell out in concrete terms the nature of the political ties which

[110] *Animism, Magic and the Divine King*, pp. 204–5.
[111] *Ibid.*, pp. 88, 249.
[112] *Ibid.*, p. 230. Cf. also pp. 227, 231, 247, 258, 296.

Freud had outlined in *Group Psychology*. For Freud, the very existence of communal life constituted a problem. It seemed to him almost impossible that men, who hate each other, could come together to form cohesive groups. The utilitarian gain made possible by such union was, in Freud's mind, of insufficient importance to offset the innate hostility which held men apart.[113] The existence of groups could be explained only in terms of aim-inhibited libidinal ties which counteracted the hateful emotions separating men. Moreover, such ties could come into being only by way of a common love object—a common ego ideal—which all men in the group would share. Thus arose the political leader who by virtue of being loved by all forged a community out of disparate individuals.[114]

Roheim extended this line of reasoning by arguing that the adored leader must be thought of as a symbolic penis.[115] The body politic was inconceivable without a political phallus. Roheim intended that the imagery of the body be taken most seriously. Adopting Ferenczi's hypothesis concerning the rhythm of libidinal life—according to which each person experiences a constant flux and reflux of sexual energy, concentrated in the genitals in the moment of sexual union and diffused throughout the body during the intervals of sexual inactivity—he argued that the history of man's communal life followed a pattern in which periods of authoritarianism (erection) alternated

[113] Freud, *Civilization and Its Discontents, The Standard Edition* . . . , XXI, 112.
[114] Freud, *Group Psychology, passim*.
[115] *Animism, Magic and the Divine King*, pp. 194, 309–10, 384–86.

with periods of democratic anarchy.[116] With characteristic polemical enthusiasm Roheim exposed the erotic
reality hidden beneath the traditional political pieties. In
effect, he translated the thesis of *Civilization and Its
Discontents* into the colorful rhetoric of genitality. The
genital type of society, the society which was stabilized
under the aegis of the phallic leader, evolved at the
expense of individual genital character formation.[117]

Thus, like Freud, Roheim arrived at the pessimistic
conclusion that democracy was, at best, highly problem-
atic from a libidinal point of view. Similarly, individual
genital primacy could be achieved only at a tremendous
social cost. "Liberty has always been more a fiction than a
reality, and the history of mankind appears to be a series
of hardly successful attempts to attain genital primacy."[118]
However, in contrast to Freud, Roheim was never able
to accept these unhappy conclusions with equanimity. He
bristled with indignation at the demands which society
made upon the individual. Smoldering anger rather than
Olympian resignation was his characteristic mood.

Roheim carried his psychological reductionism to the
study of political conflict with the same sublime confidence that he brought to the analysis of political
consensus. War was another manifestation of man's
communal experience which could be adequately understood only by means of psychological analysis. Utilitarian
theories which attempted to explain group conflicts in
terms of the struggle for existence simply did not fit the

[116] *Ibid.*, pp. 309–10, 385.
[117] *Ibid.*, pp. 385–86.
[118] *Ibid.*, p. 386.

facts. In this instance Roheim aimed his barbs at the
English theorist M. R. Davie, whose *Evolution of War*
was published in 1929, but his strictures could as easily be
applied to Robert Ardrey's recent explanation of war in
terms of innate "territoriality." Roheim argued that the
Australian example ruled out the Darwinian hypothesis
from the start. In Australia there were simply no wars of
conquest. When conflict did appear, it arose "as a result of
a blood feud due to the killing of a member of one local
group by a member of another local group, nearly always
by magical means."[119]

Roheim believed that Freud had laid the foundations of
an adequate psychological theory of war when he posited
the existence of an innate biological urge to destroy.[120]
But Roheim also saw the need for a more specific mechanism to explain how aggression achieved social expression. He found it in his hypothesis concerning the dual-
unity character of group life. According to the argument
of *The Origin and Function of Culture,* one's sense of
union with the group (the nation) was a projection of the
unity of mother and child. Everything outside this pleasurable union was a source of frustration and thus inevitably conceived as "bad." The first "other" was of course
the father, who came to play a crucial role in separating
the child from his mother. In social life, Roheim argued,
the image of the bad father was projected onto all those
outside the group. National hatred was merely an "adult"
version of the hatred of the child for the separating father.
"War and international relationships are specifically based

119 Roheim, "War, Crime and the Covenant," *Journal of Criminal
Psychopathology,* IV, V (1943, 1944), 842–43.
120 *Ibid.,* p. 840.

on the Oedipus situation, the father is the first stranger in the infant's life and the stranger is always the father."[121] Thus war, like society itself, was a product of man's infantilism. Man fought, as he loved, because he was unable to bear the inevitable burden of separation.

One of the themes of this study has been the attempt on the part of various thinkers to work out an intellectual reconciliation between Marx and Freud. Wilhelm Reich, as we have seen, struggled for years to achieve this synthesis, in both his thought and his life, and the same endeavor was a major preoccupation of the theorist yet to be investigated, Herbert Marcuse. Roheim, on the contrary, was if anything more hostile to Marxism than was Freud himself.

The mutual antagonism of psychoanalysis and revolutionary socialism is one of the as yet inadequately explained mysteries of twentieth-century intellectual history. Certainly it has mystified modern conservatives, who regard both movements as almost satanic threats to the established political and moral order. Undoubtedly a good portion of the distrust which Marxists and Freudians have felt toward one another must be attributed to the psychological naïveté and rigidity of the Marxists. As political activists, they were perhaps legitimately fearful that the introspective posture dictated by psychoanalysis might undermine revolutionary ardor. But they failed to recognize the extent to which psychoanalysis exposed yet another dimension of repression and alienation, and thereby established itself as a major vehicle for cultural

[121] *Ibid.*, p. 844.

criticism. On the other hand, one must admit that Freud's own bourgeois sensibilities, along with his inordinate proprietory fear of any "impure" exploitation of his new science, led to an exaggerated fastidiousness about political movements on his part.

In any event, Roheim was too loyal a disciple to break with Freud on this matter. Furthermore, within his own chosen discipline he was confronted with the unhappy fact that those anthropologists with psychoanalytic leanings who based their analyses on Marx often did so by watering down Freud's ideas to the point of rendering them unrecognizable. Thus Roheim's bout with Marxism took the form of an acrimonious debate with the neo-Freudians, particularly with the anthropologist Abram Kardiner,[122] a most unfortunate state of affairs since it kept Roheim from the much more serious task of reading and digesting Marx himself. The result was an ever more rigid reliance on psychological reductionism, although, as I have already suggested, this self-consciously anti-Marxian stance often led to no less radical conclusions.

Roheim had long maintained that economic or environmental explanations of basic cultural and psychological patterns were grossly inadequate. The Australian experience had thoroughly substantiated this perception. Here was a people who, because of the arid soil and erratic climate of their homeland, lived at all times on the verge of starvation. Yet they had no fear of famine; on the contrary, they were extremely happy and secure. From Roheim's perspective the disparity between the real pre-

[122] Cf. Roheim, "Society and the Individual," pp. 526–45; "Introduction," to *Psychoanalysis and the Social Sciences*, p. 29; *Psychoanalysis and Anthropology*, pp. 255–56, 260–61, 423–24.

cariousness of the Australians' situation and their psychic composure could only be explained psychologically. "These children of the desert have been given so much security at the outset of life by their mothers that the real difficulties of the environment can never make them insecure afterwards."[123] However, Roheim was not satisfied to limit the application of psychological reasoning to situations where such incongruities existed. He was a much bolder Freudian than that. Even when he recognized very substantial realistic reasons for a particular psychological structure or economic practice, he insisted that infantile motivations provided the foundations upon which the "rational" superstructure was built. Thus he proceeded to review all of the major economic revolutions of human history, in order to point out their irrational and childish origins. Inherent in this endeavor was a marked (if perhaps only partially conscious) polemical undercurrent. The Marxists had dissected the exploitative character of man's economic institutions, but even they had tacitly admitted the rationality of these institutions, at least from the standpoint of the exploiters. Roheim went a step further to show that even the most reasonable economic practices were grounded in infantile fears and fantasies.[124]

The first great economic revolution of human history was the change from food-gathering to herding societies. For Roheim the basic motive behind the domestication of animals was not economic but libidinal. Animals were objects of affection before they were beasts of burden, and their incorporation into the economic structure was sim-

[123] *Psychoanalysis and Anthropology*, p. 62.
[124] *The Origin and Function of Culture*, p. 40.

ply another manifestation of man's search for substitute love objects, or, in more philosophical terms, of Eros' eternal task of creating larger and larger unities, joining "one man to the other and man to the animal world."[125] "Cattle-breeding tribes are cattle-loving tribes. . . . The bovine herd is a reduplication of human society based on the Oedipus complex and the reverence paid to cattle is due to Father Bull and Mother Cow."[126] Likewise, the second great economic transformation, the agrarian revolution, was reduced to its erotic essentials. Agriculture meant incest with Mother Earth,[127] and the principal implement of the agrarian revolution, the plow, was evidently a symbolic phallus.[128] Roheim interpreted the harvest—the extraction of the agricultural product from the earth—in the light of Melanie Klein's theory of infantile body-destruction fantasies. Just as the frustrated child fantasied himself pulling the "good body contents" out of the weaning mother, so the gardener angrily uprooted the nourishing tuber from Mother Earth.[129]

Roheim subjected the origins of the commercial revolution to a similar psychological analysis. We have already seen how he portrayed the development of the first profession—the medicine man or sorcerer—in terms of a

---

[125] *Ibid.*, p. 64. As evidence for this hypothesis Roheim noted that young mothers in primitive societies were frequently observed suckling pups and other young domestic animals. *Spiegelzauber*, pp. 155–56; *The Origin and Function of Culture*, pp. 62–63.

[126] *The Origin and Function of Culture*, pp. 65–67.

[127] *Animism, Magic and the Divine King*, p. 252.

[128] *The Origin and Function of Culture*, p. 62.

[129] *Ibid.*, pp. 57–59.

phallic-castration complex.[130] The second profession, according to Roheim, was that of trader, and trade partners were in reality recreating the mother-child situation through an exchange of body contents.[131] Furthermore, the commodities exchanged (and thus invested with "value") could easily be shown to be feces—as Freud had already suggested.[132] Thus the trader, like the shepherd, the farmer, and the doctor, was merely acting out a childhood fantasy.[133] Roheim did not contend that the realistic gain inherent in the great economic revolutions of human history was inconsequential. In fact he was willing to concede that the practical benefit garnered from the invention of farming and commerce could well account for the *survival* of these institutions. But the original motives were in every case libidinal.[134] Furthermore, it made perfect sense that the goals of the id would in these instances correspond to those of the ego, since each revolution represented an attempt to recreate the dual-unity situation in which the infant obtained both pleasure and nourishment at the mother's breast. It was man's nature to master reality on a libidinal basis.[135]

Roheim had entered the enemy's homeland and come

[130] *Ibid.*, pp. 50–51.

[131] *Ibid.*, pp. 52–53. "Trade partners are united by the umbilical cord, they are mutually in a mother-child situation."

[132] Roheim, "The Evolution of Culture," *International Journal of Psycho-Analysis*, XV (1934), 388, 401–2; "Heiliges Geld in Melanesien," *Internationale Zeitschrift für Psychoanalyse*, IX (1923), 384–401.

[133] *The Origin and Function of Culture*, p. 72.

[134] *Psychoanalysis and Anthropology*, pp. 405, 418.

[135] *The Origin and Function of Culture*, pp. 80–81.

away unscathed. Even those cultural achievements which were apparently most remote from the unconscious, most thoroughly grounded in reality, had been successfully subjected to psychoanalytic scrutiny and dissection. In his work, as in his religion and mythmaking, man remained essentially an overgrown child. Roheim's critical vision reduced politics to penis worship, warfare to the tantrums of a frustrated infant, and economics to a ritualistic exchange of feces. Yet we have only begun to explore the radical implications of his thought. I wish now to turn to Roheim's confrontation with the dominant tradition of contemporary anthropology, functionalism, and his explicit assaults on the conservative intellectual establishment.

VI

Roheim emigrated to America in 1938. One biographer has commented that when he left Hungary "it was a toss-up whether he was in greater danger from the Communists or from the Fascists."[136] In any case, the emigration marked no important milestone in Roheim's intellectual biography, although direct exposure to American academic anthropology, which at the time was dominated by the ideas of Boas and Malinowski, certainly precipitated his in-depth critique of functionalism. After working a short while as a clinician at the Worcester State Hospital, Roheim settled in New York City in the early 1940's and remained there, except for short trips to the field (most

[136] La Barre, "Geza Roheim," p. 280.

notably to the site of Clyde Kluckhohn's research among the Navahos), until his death in 1953.[137]

The most important of Roheim's last writings was undoubtedly *Psychoanalysis and Anthropology* (1950), in which he subjected his professional colleagues to an unmerciful tongue-lashing for their intellectual cowardice. The book was a prolonged attack on the functionalist dogma of cultural relativism (which, ironically, has become a kind of academic absolutism) and a reassertion of the psychic unity of mankind. It represents the most readable of Roheim's many writings and a highly spirited recapitulation of his life's work.

"Functionalism" has come to represent two related (and often inadequately distinguished) intellectual attitudes. In the most general sense, indeed so general that I sometimes wonder if it can legitimately be designated as a distinct intellectual position, functionalism suggests that all ideas and institutions serve a purpose. As a matter of intellectual history, however, only certain types of ideas and institutions have, in the twentieth century, been subjected to functionalist analysis, namely those which traditional Liberal ideology dismissed as meaningless or positively reprehensible. Thus Durkheimian functionalists have demonstrated the constructive role which religion (in Liberal ideology, *"l'infame"*) plays in achieving social integration, while functional anthropologists like Malinowski have argued that magic, traditionally regarded as a manifestation of primitive irrationality, represents a

[137] Roheim, *Magic and Schizophrenia*, p. 93; *Psychoanalysis and Anthropology*, pp. 324, 343; Sandor Lorand, "Preface," to *Magic and Schizophrenia*, p. vii.

legitimate prescientific means of mastering reality. The dominant tradition in American social science, with which Roheim came into direct contact as a result of his emigration, has remained within this general intellectual framework—much to the dismay of radicals like C. Wright Mills.[138]

Roheim was not necessarily unsympathetic to the functionalist enterprise, understood in this sense, although he was aware of its conservative bias. Indeed, as he grew older he often adopted the functionalist point of view quite self-consciously. His changing ideas about the nature and purpose of magic are a case in point. In *Animism, Magic, and the Divine King* (1930) he interpreted magic completely negatively: magical procedures were a manifestation of castration anxiety. In the case of sympathetic magic, for example, the sorcerer achieved his objective by obtaining some separated part of the victim's body (hair, excrement, etc.), and in Roheim's mind the affect associated with the separated part was clearly a form of castration anxiety.[139] However, in a later work, the posthumously published *Magic and Schizophrenia*, Roheim completely reversed himself on this matter. Here his interpretation of magic was very much in the functionalist vein. Like Malinowski, he attempted to show that magic represented a constructive tool for mastering the environment. His argument was complex and sophisticated, but in essence he maintained that the magical endeavor to control reality through thought (Freud's *Allmacht der Gedanken*) was a necessary prerequisite to

138 Cf. especially *The Sociological Imagination* (New York, 1959).
139 *Animism, Magic, and the Divine King*, pp. 1–5, 15, 74, 95–96.

mastering it in fact.[140] Similarly, as I have already re-
marked, Roheim arrived at a qualified acceptance of the
theory of myth implicit in the functionalist point of view;
myths were functional in that they reflected contemporary realities rather than forgotten historical experiences.[141]
However, the term "functionalism," particularly as used
to characterize a specific intellectual tradition within anthropology, has taken on a second, more parochial, meaning. Functionalism in this sense is used to designate the
Malinowskian doctrine that cultural artifacts can be
understood only in terms of the total context of the
particular culture in which they appear. This meaning of
functionalism amounts to a radical cultural relativism; it
rules out all cross-cultural comparisons, as well as any
statements about culture in the abstract. It was against
this brand of functionalism that Roheim directed his
broadsides in *Psychoanalysis and Anthropology*.[142]
Unfortunately, Roheim weakened his critique of cultural relativism by involving himself in a pointless debate
over the universality of the Oedipus complex.[143] In this

[140] *Magic and Schizophrenia*, pp. 3, 10–11, 46, 82–85, 226–27.
[141] Cf. Roheim's remarks on Kardiner and Malinowski in "Introduction," to *Psychoanalysis and the Social Sciences*, pp. 17–18,
32.
[142] The origins of Roheim's critique, however, can be traced back
to the early 1930's. Cf. "Psycho-Analysis of Primitive Cultural
Types," pp. 20–21: "All the publications of this school, be they on
canoes or marriages, magic or trade, seem to come to the same
conclusion, viz. that the phenomenon in question is part of a whole,
has a well-defined function in the social organism, is correlated to
other social phenomena. We shall hardly be satisfied by truisms of
this kind."
[143] *Psychoanalysis and Anthropology*, pp. 424–26.

effort he was arguing against the archfunctionalist Malinowski, who had claimed that the Trobriand Islanders
suffered no such psychic trauma. Roheim apparently felt
it necessary to confront the enemy directly on this issue,
because it had become a popular rallying point for all
critics of psychoanalysis. Thus he contended that Malinowski had seriously misinterpreted the Trobriand situation when he suggested that an "avuncular complex"
appeared in place of the "European" Oedipus complex.
Indeed, he went so far as to call Malinowski's analysis
absurd, since even in the Trobriand Islands the child lived
with his father and mother for the first five to ten years of
his life, and was only then turned over to his maternal
uncle.[144] The "avuncular complex" might in fact exist,
but it was, in Roheim's mind, clearly derivative from the
earlier, and psychologically more fundamental, Oedipus
complex.[145]

In similar fashion, Roheim took up, one by one, each of
the cultures in which various anthropologists or psychol-
ogists claimed to have found no indication of an Oedipus
complex, and he proceeded to unearth the wanted evidence.[146] This undertaking, which frequently found
Roheim straining to make the facts fit the theory, constituted a tactical mistake on his part. It suited very badly
his own inclination to deemphasize the Oedipus complex

[144] Malinowski, *The Sexual Life of Savages* (New York, 1929),
pp. 201–22.
[145] *Psychoanalysis and Anthropology*, p. 167; "Society and the
Individual," p. 542.
[146] *Psychoanalysis and Anthropology*, pp. 264–65, 302, 311–12,
316–17, 322, 339.

in his later writings, where separation anxiety was seen as the most basic trait of human psychology. Furthermore, he was able to make his case against cultural relativism more effectively by relying on a general analysis of cultural universals, and his insistence on the Oedipus complex introduced an unnecessary and inappropriate note of specificity into the argument.

At the time of its enunciation, the doctrine of cultural relativism had performed an important critical service, as Roheim was well aware.[147] In the writings of a thinker like Boas, it had been aimed at the misuse of the nineteenth-century evolutionary doctrines by political imperialists. If cultures were truly incomparable, then it was impossible to justify the exploitation of the "underdeveloped" peoples of the globe in terms of their moral and cultural inferiority. African and Asian cultures were indeed different from European culture, but they could not therefore be judged better or worse. In their desire to defend the primitives, however, the functionalists had, in Roheim's mind, overstated the case. While it was perfectly legitimate to focus on cultural differences, it was no less reasonable to pursue the study of cultural universals.[148] After all, Roheim pointed out, men share the same basic biological and instinctual traits, they all confront similar environmental problems, and, most important from the psychoanalytic point of view, they all experience a prolonged period of infantile dependence.[149] Furthermore, there was overwhelming empirical evi-

[147] *Ibid.*, p. 394.
[148] *Ibid.*, pp. 1–2, 363.
[149] *Ibid.*, pp. 63, 409.

dence to support the thesis of mankind's psychic unity—the evidence of dreams, symbols, ritual, and magic.[150]

To Roheim, the intransigent hostility of the functionalists to cross-cultural comparisons and abstract generalizations about the nature and function of culture could only be explained psychoanalytically. Thus he pursued the familiar *ad hominem* tactic so dear to Freud. The functionalists chose to disregard the "clear evidence" for the universality of the Oedipus complex because they did not want to acknowledge their own Oedipal strivings. Moreover, Roheim was so brazen as to suggest that the functionalists, for all their overt cosmopolitanism, were in fact secret nationalists: "The idea that all nations are completely different from each other and that the goal of anthropology is simply to find how different they are is a thinly veiled manifestation of nationalism, the democratic counterpart of the Nazi racial doctrine. . . . 'You are completely different, but I forgive you' is what it amounts to."[151]

Whether or not Roheim's analysis of the psychological bias of functionalism was justified, he was, in my opinion, completely correct in sensing a conservative undertone in the dogmatic cultural relativism of the functionalists. Conservatism depends for its survival on the denial of abstraction, just as radicalism relies heavily on the legitimacy of categorical statement. This is as true of Edmund Burke's critique of the universalism of the *philosophes* as it is of the historicists' opposition to the universal history of the Hegelians. The established order can be defended

150 *Ibid.*, pp. 5, 13, 15, 22, 24–27, 38–39.
151 *Ibid.*, p. 362.

only if it is exempted from the strictures of abstract rationality and from comparison with normative conceptions of human health or the good society. Roheim, as we shall see, wished to indulge in precisely such a critique of modern civilization. In view of this conscious polemical purpose, his hostility to functionalist cultural relativism made perfect sense.

VII

I have stated many times in the course of this chapter that Roheim's thought was basically critical—in the revolutionary sense that Marx's was critical, and as opposed to the diffident and fundamentally conservative criticism of an anthropologist like Boas. I must admit, however, that Roheim, unlike Reich or Marcuse, never completely liberated himself from the pessimistic assumptions of Freud's cultural philosophy. His criticism remained at all times within the conservative conceptual framework of *Civilization and Its Discontents*. That is, Roheim accepted Freud's equation of civilization and repression.[152] He agreed with Ernst Cassirer that man was a symbol-making animal, and by definition a symbol was the aim-inhibited (cultural) transformation of a libidinal impulse, taking the place of actual gratification by sublimating instinct into metaphor (language, ritual, economic activity, social structure, politics).[153]

[152] *The Riddle of the Sphinx*, pp. 232, 236, 276; *Australian Totemism*, pp. 426–27.
[153] *Australian Totemism*, pp. 251–52.

To be sure, there were hints in Roheim's writings that the civilization/repression formula might not be invariable. Being of a post-Victorian generation, he recognized, as Freud did not, that twentieth-century developments seemed to undermine the general validity of the hypothesis. The tendency of European and American civilization since 1900 to liberalize its sexual mores and child-rearing techniques posed difficulties for those who, like Roheim, looked for a correlation between cultural complexity and sexual repression. In order to remain loyal to the thesis of *Civilization and Its Discontents,* Roheim found it necessary to argue that we moderns were experiencing a kind of neoprimitivism: "The liberating tendencies of the French Revolution and of modern culture are to be conceived as backslidings towards the primitive (Rousseau); they do not form the essence of the process that determines human history and that, as a progressive humanization, we call culture."[154] Thus Roheim was left in the curious position of having to maintain that the Middle Ages represented the high-water mark of the civilizing process.[155] Clearly he felt somewhat uneasy about Freud's general formula, but he stuck by it nonetheless. One even comes across passages in his work which echo Freud's appreciation of the achievements of civilization, albeit these statements don't carry much conviction. Civilization, he argued, was a neurosis, but it was not without a secondary *Krankheitsgewinn* (advantage of disease).[156]

Having acknowledged the limits within which Roheim

[154] *The Riddle of the Sphinx,* p. 284. Cf. also p. 243.
[155] *Ibid.,* pp. 242–43; *Animism, Magic and the Divine King,* p. 94.
[156] *The Riddle of the Sphinx,* pp. 279–80; *The Origin and Function of Culture,* pp. 24–25.

chose to frame his cultural criticism, I want now to stress the conviction and passion with which he pursued that criticism. On almost every page of his writings he sought to establish the psychological superiority of primitive culture and to contrast primitive health with modern sickness. And, like all the Freudian radicals, he found the key to the primitives' well-being in the general permissiveness of their culture.

One of the characteristic preoccupations of modern anthropology, and of functionalism in particular, has been its insistence on primitive morality. In their desire to counteract the imperialists' equation of the primitive with subhuman life, the functionalists set about demonstrating the severity of primitive ethical and religious codes. To a great extent Freud's anthropological writings supported this point of view. He found that the primitive experienced a much more intense horror of incest than did modern man, and that consequently he established extraordinarily stringent incest taboos, backed by the severest sanctions. Indeed, Freud went so far as to compare the primitives' horror of incest with modern obsessional neuroses.[157]

Strictly speaking, Roheim did not deviate from Freud on this matter. He too compared primitive ideas and practices with modern neuroses,[158] and he emphasized perhaps even more than Freud the strength of primitive incest taboos.[159] Primitives, after all, were men, and repression was the price of becoming human. But Roheim insisted that among true primitives (that is, among the

[157] Freud, *Totem and Taboo*, pp. 26–29.
[158] *Australian Totemism*, pp. 98, 189.
[159] *Ibid.*, p. 151.

Australians), the scope of repression was strictly limited to the incest taboo. In all other dimensions of human activity, they enjoyed an almost total permissiveness. It was as if the repressiveness which is diffused throughout modern life were concentrated upon a single prohibition among the primitives. The Australian child was guaranteed complete oral gratification by his mother: "Children are never weaned and the mother never refuses them her breasts."[160] Excretory functions were subjected to none of the characteristic modern controls: "The child is indeed told to defecate out of doors, but this rule is not taken very seriously."[161] Likewise, there were none of the modern sexual prohibitions, the one exception being that children were not allowed to observe their parents in sexual intercourse.[162] Indeed, Roheim even argued that there was no such thing as a latency period in Australia, no period in which the natives did not "make more or less successful attempts at coitus."[163] In short, the Australians had extremely weak superegos; with one notable exception—the incest taboo—they simply acted out their instincts.[164]

The significance of Australian permissiveness was summed up by Roheim in a single sentence: "The Aranda is a happy man."[165] Instinctual fulfillment resulted in psychic health. Roheim's observations on the Australians in effect substantiated Reich's basic contention about the

---

[160] *The Riddle of the Sphinx*, p. 30; *Psychoanalysis and Anthropology*, p. 55.
[161] *The Riddle of the Sphinx*, p. 30.
[162] *Ibid.*, pp. 30, 115.
[163] "Psycho-Analysis of Primitive Cultural Types," p. 91.
[164] *Ibid.*, p. 120.
[165] *Ibid.*, p. 119.

relationship of sexuality and happiness. As a result of the almost complete absence of prohibitions, the Australians developed healthy "genital" character structures.[166] Roheim found no evidence among the primitives of impotence or frigidity and only a few "doubtful symptoms" of sadomasochistic perversions.[167] The Australians were eminently rational, apparently incapable of the tyranny and intolerance so prevalent in modern civilization.[168] They were "a singularly pleasant people, easy to get on with, helpful to those . . . in distress, and as unneurotic and free of anxiety as any human being could be."[169]

Roheim was thus heir to a long tradition of primitivism in European thought. But unlike his great forebear Rousseau, he explicitly designated sexual permissiveness as the measure and source of primitive happiness. The central message of Roheim's work was that we have paid too high a price for civilization. The primitive, despite the obvious hardships he faced, had solved the problem of communal life in a much more satisfactory manner than his civilized brother.[170] Modern civilization, with its "insane" methods of education, its repression of sexuality, and its "sphincter morality," had made man sick.[171] Culture was

[166] *Ibid.*, p. 94; *Psychoanalysis and Anthropology*, p. 150; *The Riddle of the Sphinx*, p. 237.
[167] *Psychoanalysis and Anthropology*, p. 113; *The Riddle of the Sphinx*, p. 237.
[168] *The Riddle of the Sphinx*, pp. 241–42; *Psychoanalysis and Anthropology*, p. 34.
[169] *Psychoanalysis and Anthropology*, p. 57. Reprinted by permission of the Hogarth Press Ltd.
[170] *The Riddle of the Sphinx*, pp. 237, 278–79.
[171] *Ibid.*, pp. 244, 284.

a neurosis, and individual neuroses "a super-culture, an exaggeration of what is specifically human."[172] It was the function of psychoanalysis to diagnose that neurosis. Roheim was admittedly rather pessimistic about the possibilities of cultural therapy.[173] In this respect he was closer to Freud than to Reich or Marcuse. But he insisted that it was the duty of the analyst to protest loudly against the pathology of culture and to expose those intellectual formulas, such as functionalism, which would have us believe that this is the best of all possible worlds:

> Our opponents are apt to complain that analysis is hostile to culture. We should not, I believe, protest too violently against this complaint. . . . Culture involves neurosis, which we try to cure. Culture involves super-ego, which we seek to weaken. Culture involves the retention of the infantile situation, from which we endeavor to free our patients."[174]

From this it should be clear why Roheim objected so strongly to the attempts of revisionists and ego-psychologists to add a "cultural" dimension to psychoanalysis. In doing so they inevitably became apologists for the established cultural order, adepts of sublimation and adjustment.[175] Erik Erikson's analysis of the Yurok was a case in point.[176] Roheim objected strenuously to Erikson's

[172] *Ibid.*, pp. 235–36.
[173] *Ibid.*, p. 254.
[174] *Ibid.*, pp. 235–36. Cf. also pp. 214, 254–55.
[175] *Ibid.*, p. 245; *Psychoanalysis and Anthropology*, p. 287.
[176] Erik Erikson, "Observations on the Yurok; Childhood and World Image," *University of California Publications in American Anthropology, Archeology, and Ethnology*, Vol. 35 (Berkeley, 1943).

softening of Freud's critical terminology. Instead of calling the Yurok anal, which they were, Erikson preferred to speak of "retentiveness," and worse yet, he even praised the Yurok for this quality.[177] But his most unforgivable transgression was to endorse the repression of adolescent sexuality among the Yurok, arguing that it prepared the young to take on the values and life styles of adult Yurok civilization. "Some anthropologists and evidently also Erikson seem to think that whatever a 'culture' demands must be 'good' and the main thing is 'cultural synthesis.'"[178] To Roheim, however, Yurok civilization stood condemned; no culture with such a pronounced antigenital attitude could possibly be considered healthy.[179]

Without question Roheim's dogmatic refusal to adopt the comfortable conservatism of his fellow anthropologists and analysts contributed to his intellectual isolation. He was well aware that his work had had little impact on academic anthropology or psychology.[180] Among the leading American anthropologists, only Margaret Mead and Clyde Kluckhohn seemed to be at all responsive to his

[177] *Psychoanalysis and Anthropology*, pp. 272, 286.
[178] *Ibid.*, p. 287. It was this same willingness to give in to culture which Roheim found so objectionable in functionalism. The functionalists concluded from the mere fact that a culture existed that it was integrated and functioned harmoniously. They would thus "scotomize" all of those psychoanalytic facts which drew attention to the terrible price we pay for civilization: the Oedipus complex, the superego, the castration complex, and anal character formation. Cf. *Psychoanalysis and Anthropology*, p. 455; "Introduction" to *Psychoanalysis and the Social Sciences*, p. 32.
[179] *Psychoanalysis and Anthropology*, p. 288.
[180] "Introduction" to *Psychoanalysis and the Social Sciences*, pp. 13–14.

particular genius, and even their enthusiasm was highly qualified.[181] Nevertheless, Roheim himself remained quietly confident that his accomplishment would one day be recognized and that psychoanalytic anthropology would be "the only anthropology of the future."[182] From our vantage point, however, Roheim does not appear so isolated a figure as he felt himself to be. He clearly belongs in that on-going tradition of post-Freudians who have interpreted Freud's work as an indictment of contemporary civilization and a call to arms. Although the highly speculative philosophical essays of Herbert Marcuse and Norman O. Brown are hardly the legacy that Roheim might have anticipated, it is clear that they are the thinkers who have inherited his critical task.

[181] Cf. Clyde Kluckhohn, "Some Notes on Navaho Dreams," in *Psychoanalysis and Culture: Essays in Honor of Geza Roheim,* pp. 120–21; La Barre, "Geza Roheim," pp. 274–75, 277.

[182] "Psycho-Analysis of Primitive Cultural Types," p. 6.

HERBERT MARCUSE

———————◆———————

THE RADICAL tradition in psychoanalysis has represented a
distinctly minority school of interpretation, operating on
the periphery of the conservative Freudian establishment.
Reich was officially excluded from the International Psychoanalytic Association, and Roheim, although he remained loyal to Freud, was able to pursue his radical
criticism only in the allied discipline of anthropology. By
the 1940's, when psychoanalysis had lost its shocking
novelty, the European and American intellectual community had reached substantial agreement on the fundamentally conservative character of Freudian theory.
Furthermore, this consensus was justified in view of the
timid and exclusively clinical direction in which the psychoanalytic movement had developed. Psychoanalysis
had become a branch of the medical profession, and the
typical practicing psychoanalyst carefully distinguished
the discrete precepts and techniques of his therapeutic

science from the ambitious metahistorical adventures in which Freud had indulged.

Critics and apologists outside the psychoanalytic movement, whether on the left or the right, seemed to confirm the prevailing interpretation of Freud as conservative. The neo-Freudians broke away from psychoanalytic orthodoxy precisely because of the purported conservative bias of Freudian theory. Erich Fromm and his associates argued that Freud's pansexualism, his psychic determinism (focusing exclusively on early infancy), his concept of the death instinct, and his explicit denial of the meaningfulness of social and political reform all served the interests of political reaction.[1] Dissenters like Fromm on the left found their assessment of Freud confirmed, ironically, by sympathetic interpreters on the right. One can take Philip Rieff as the most erudite and forceful representative of this second school of interpretation. In *Freud: The Mind of the Moralist* Rieff portrayed Freud as heir to the tradition of Montaigne, Burton, Hobbes, and La Rochefoucauld, a man deeply impressed by the limitations of the intellect and the obstinacy of the passions. According to Rieff, Freud was the advocate of psychic compromise, urging men to make the best of an inevitably unhappy fate. Moreover, Rieff obviously admired Freud's sober realism; he became annoyed only when Freud abandoned his Olympian skepticism to assume the role of strident critic, as in *The Future of an Illusion.*[2]

In the 1950's three books appeared which brought the

[1] Erich Fromm, *Fear of Freedom* (London, 1960), pp. 1–18, 239–53.
[2] Philip Rieff, *Freud: The Mind of the Moralist* (New York, 1961), pp. 281 ff.

prevailing interpretation of Freud into question: Lionel Trilling's *Freud and the Crisis of Our Culture,* Herbert Marcuse's *Eros and Civilization,* and Norman O. Brown's *Life Against Death.* Trilling's essay was a lightweight contribution beside those of Brown and Marcuse, but it shared with them the conviction that Freud's great accomplishment was to remind us of the high price we have paid for our civilization.[3] All three authors were in agreement that the critical element in Freud was to be found in his late metahistorical forays, that is, in precisely those works which the orthodox considered unscientific and which the neo-Freudians condemned as reactionary. Brown and Marcuse undertook a systematic analysis of psychoanalytic theory in order to reveal its critical, even revolutionary, implications. Both went far beyond Reich or Roheim in probing the dialectical subtleties of Freud's thought, and both reached conclusions which were more extreme, more "utopian," than those to be found in either of Freud's earlier left-wing exegetes.

I have chosen in this chapter to examine the revolutionary Freudian criticism of Herbert Marcuse, devoting only a short section to Norman O. Brown. I had originally planned to give equal attention to both men, but I have become convinced that Marcuse is definitely the finer of the two theorists. He has written more extensively than Brown, and his treatment of Freud in *Eros and Civilization* now appears to me more substantial than Brown's comparable excursion in *Life Against Death.* As with Reich and Roheim, I have attempted to trace the logic of

[3] Lionel Trilling, *Freud and the Crisis of Our Culture* (Boston, 1955), *passim.*

Marcuse's evolution as a Freudian radical. This effort has often led me far afield from psychoanalysis. Marcuse came to Freud rather late in life; before 1955 his work was largely in the tradition of Hegelian philosophy and Marxian social criticism. Since the principal justification for including Marcuse in a study of this sort rests on his contribution to Freudian radicalism, I will be preoccupied in my treatment of his early work with underlining anticipations of his later psychological interests. At the same time, I plan to take note of those tendencies in his pre-Freudian writings which militated against any serious involvement with psychoanalytic theory and which therefore had to be overcome or held in abeyance when he came to write *Eros and Civilization.* The examination of Marcuse's early work will enable me to distinguish the characteristic features of his intellectual style, which has remained remarkably consistent from his first writings on Hegel down through *One-Dimensional Man.*

I

Herbert Marcuse's scholarly career can be divided into two distinct phases. During the Second World War and for several years thereafter he served in the Office of Strategic Services and the Office of Intelligence Research. While working for the government Marcuse apparently found little time for scholarly pursuits; he published only one article between 1942 and 1950.[4] The 1940's thus

[4] For a complete bibliography of Marcuse's writings to 1967, see *The Critical Spirit,* K. H. Wolff and B. Moore, Jr., eds. (Boston, 1967), pp. 427–33.

constitute a natural divide in his intellectual development. During the 1930's Marcuse was a member of the
Institute for Social Research, located in Frankfurt am
Main until the Nazi takeover forced its transplantation
first to Geneva and then to New York City, where from
1934 to 1950 it was housed in a building made available
by Columbia University.[5] The Institute had been established in 1923 as an affiliate of the University of Frankfurt. Its avowed purpose was the interdisciplinary study
of problems in social theory, with a view toward integrat-
ing the social sciences "into a comprehensive theory of
society."[6] When Marcuse joined the Frankfurt Institute in
the early 1930's, its small but distinguished faculty included Max Horkheimer, Frederick Pollock, Leo Lowen-
thal, Erich Fromm, Theodor Adorno, and (after 1936)
Franz Neumann,[7]

The young Marcuse, who was the Institute's resident
expert on philosophy and political theory, was clearly
influenced by the general theoretical perspective
espoused by his associates. The intellectual climate of the
Institute was thoroughly Marxian, although not dogmati-
cally so, and Marcuse's early work can also be characterized, in a rather loose sense, as Marxian. Moreover, the
problems to which the Institute devoted particular atten-

[5] *International Institute of Social Research; A Report on Its History,
Aims and Activities, 1933–1938* (New York, no date), pp. 6–7.
[6] *Ibid.*, p. 5. Cf. also Max Horkheimer's inaugural address (1931)
in *Institut für Sozialforschung an der Johann Wolfgang Goethe-
Universität Frankfurt am Main; Ein Bericht über die Feier seiner
Wiedereröffnung, seine Geschichte und seine Arbeiten* (Frankfurt
am Main, 1952), p. 10.
[7] *International Institute of Social Research*, pp. 4, 6.

tion, in both its individual and its collective researches, to a great extent defined the concerns of Marcuse's own writings in the 1930's. Erich Fromm and Franz Neumann were the authors of two of the classic studies of Nazism, *Escape from Freedom* and *Behemoth,* and Marcuse likewise devoted considerable attention to the ideological origins of Fascism. He shared in particular Neumann's interest in the intellectual, cultural, and political significance of monopoly capitalism, which he, along with Neumann, considered the characteristic economic vehicle of Fascism.

The major collective project of the Institute during the 1930's was a study of the political function of the European family, the results of which were published in an immense monograph entitled *Studien über Autorität und Familie. Autorität und Familie* was in fact a preparatory study for the more famous *The Authoritarian Personality* (1950), also sponsored by the Institute (long after Marcuse had left its active ranks) and edited by Marcuse's one-time colleague Theodor Adorno. *Autorität und Familie,* to which Marcuse dutifully contributed a chapter on the history of the family in European thought, prefigured *The Authoritarian Personality* in both method and content. Methodologically it incorporated the strengths of Anglo-Saxon empirical research (including the use of questionnaires, statistical analysis, etc.) and of continental European theoretical sophistication, which meant in particular a healthy dose of Marxism. In substantive terms the study was concerned with the psychological foundations of authority. It was aimed at explaining the triumph of authoritarian politics in Europe in the 1930's, just as *The Authoritarian Personality* concerned itself with the psychological underpinnings of what its authors considered the American variants of Fascist anti-Semitism and ethnocentrism.[8] Marcuse's relationship to this undertaking was somewhat ambivalent. He endorsed its general methodological assumptions, which avoided the pitfalls of uncritical empiricism on the one hand and metaphysical abstraction on the other. However, he took no part in the actual empirical research, thus setting a kind of negative precedent for all of his subsequent social criticism. Nor was he particularly taken with his colleagues' interest in the family and its relation to authority. Again his indifference was to be chronic; even when he himself turned to psychological matters in *Eros and Civilization,* he avoided any significant analysis of the family. Thus although Marcuse shared many of his colleagues' interests, and sympathized with their general theoretical perspective, he was very much an independent thinker, thoroughly convinced of the legitimacy of his own exclusively theoretical approach to those historical problems which preoccupied him no less than his associates.

Marcuse's work during the period before he served in the OSS was encompassed in two books, *Hegels Ontologie und die Grundlegung einer Theorie der Geschichtlichkeit* (1932) and *Reason and Revolution* (1941), as well as in a number of long articles, most of which appeared in the Institute's journal, the *Zeitschrift für Sozialforschung.* Two figures dominated these writings—Hegel and Marx—and

[8] *Ibid.,* pp. 10–13; *Studien über Autorität und Familie: Forschungsberichte aus dem Institut für Sozialforschung* (Paris, 1936), pp. 899–907. Cf. T. W. Adorno *et al., The Authoritarian Personality* (New York, 1964), I, v–xii, 1–27.

I will be concerned in the early portion of this chapter with Marcuse's analysis of the historical fate of Hegelian philosophy and Marxian social criticism.

Marcuse was trained as a professional philosopher at the Universities of Berlin and Freiburg.[9] His first book, *Hegels Ontologie,* was a highly competent philosophical exercise, written apparently with an audience of Hegel scholars and students of philosophy in mind. The book presented a carefully circumscribed thesis concerning the meaning of certain Hegelian conceptions, especially those of the *Logik.*[10] The most remarkable feature of *Hegels Ontologie* was the manner in which it differed, in scope and intention, from the bulk of Marcuse's subsequent writings on Hegel. There was nothing in the book about the critical import of Hegel's ontological categories, no attempt to argue that Hegel and Marx were kindred spirits.[11] Indeed, Marcuse hardly mentioned Hegel's political philosophy. The tone of the book was characteristically friendly to Hegel, and, as in all of Marcuse's writings, it is extremely difficult to distinguish between simple exposition and analysis on the one hand and critical approval on the other. But those aspects of Hegel's thought which Marcuse singled out for special commendation were the usual ones cited by historians of philosophy: his attempt to overcome the traditional dichotomies

[9] Herbert Marcuse, *Kultur und Gesellschaft I* (Frankfurt am Main, 1965), p. 2.

[10] Marcuse, *Hegels Ontologie und die Grundlegung einer Theorie der Geschichtlichkeit* (Frankfurt am Main, 1932), pp. 3–4.

[11] Marcuse was more concerned with the connection between Hegel and Dilthey than that between Hegel and Marx. *Hegels Ontologie* . . . , 2–3.

of subject and object, mind and body, reason and sensuousness; and his insistence on a conception of reality as movement, process, or development.[12] Thus although *Hegels Ontologie* exhibited great technical expertise, it gave no promise of the originality or forcefulness of Marcuse's major contribution to Hegel scholarship in *Reason and Revolution.* The book demonstrated only that the young professional philosopher felt perfectly at ease with the most abstract philosophical vocabulary.

Reason and Revolution, published almost a decade after *Hegels Ontologie,* marked the culmination of Marcuse's association with the Institute for Social Research. Marcuse characterized the book as a popularization, aimed at introducing Hegel to English and American intellectuals.[13] But *Reason and Revolution* was much more than a general introduction to Hegel. It was in fact a highly polemical tract, setting forth the argument that Hegel was a revolutionary.

Like Freud, Hegel is one of those intellectuals who are very difficult to locate ideologically. In fact the major debate in the history of Hegel scholarship has concerned whether he is to be treated as a radical or a reactionary. The debate originated in the nineteenth century itself, with the splitting of the Hegelian camp into left wing (Young Hegelian) and right wing (Old Hegelian) contingents. In the twentieth century the controversy has been renewed as a result of the rise of Fascism. Karl Popper has taken perhaps the most hostile position, arguing that there is a direct line of development from Hegel to Hitler.

[12] *Hegels Ontologie* . . . , pp. 5–7.
[13] Marcuse, *Reason and Revolution* (Boston, 1960), pp. xv–xvi.

In *Reason and Revolution* Marcuse undertook to refute this allegation and to establish Hegel's revolutionary credentials.[14] The book was thus in purpose and structure remarkably similar to *Eros and Civilization*. In the case of both Hegel and Freud, Marcuse sought to rescue a major European intellectual from the grips of interpreters who, whether friendly or hostile, argued that the great innovator was fundamentally a conservative (and in Hegel's case even a proto-Fascist). In his efforts to salvage the revolutionary reputations of Freud and Hegel, Marcuse followed the same basic tactic. With both he attempted to make his case by disregarding their explicit political pronouncements and turning instead to an analysis of their basic philosophical or psychological conceptions. In each case Marcuse found a revolutionary message, which remained intact despite all overt concessions to historical pessimism, authoritarianism, the status quo, or the inevitability of violence. And in both instances the result was to uncover beneath an apparently conservative veneer the same critical impetus which achieved explicit formulation in the writings of Karl Marx.[15]

[14] Obviously Marcuse's apology was not aimed at Popper himself, since the latter's attack on Hegel (in *The Open Society and Its Enemies*) postdated *Reason and Revolution* by nine years. In *Reason and Revolution* the Hegel-as-totalitarian thesis was represented by L. T. Hobhouse, who set forth the argument (in a less virulent form than Popper) in his *Metaphysical Theory of the State* (1918). *Reason and Revolution*, pp. 389–90.

[15] The remarkable similarity of *Reason and Revolution* and *Eros and Civilization* extends even to their parallel critiques of the supposedly positive-minded opponents of the original doctrines: in the case of Hegel, the mid-nineteenth-century positivists; in the case of Freud, the mid-twentieth-century revisionists.

Marcuse's case for Hegel as revolutionary depended heavily on his analysis of Hegel's concept of reason—thus the title of the book. He argued that Hegel conceived of reason as a historical force which dissolves the established reality; reason undermines the existing historical order in so far as that order is irrational: "Hegel's concept of reason . . . has a distinctly critical and polemical character. It is opposed to all ready acceptance of the given state of affairs. It denies the hegemony of every prevailing form of existence by demonstrating the antagonisms that dissolve it into other forms."[16] Furthermore, Marcuse insisted that the famous Hegelian dictum "the rational is the real and the real the rational" was not intended as a vindication of the established order. The unity of reason and reality was rather a projection of human and historical potentialities; instead of sanctioning the existing order as rational, the famous dictum was in fact intended as a political and moral imperative. It suggested that so long as there was any gap between what is and what might be, "the former must be acted upon and changed until it is brought into line with reason."[17]

Marcuse supported this thesis by pointing to Hegel's distinction between reality and actuality, the former representing what in fact exists, the latter a reality which has overcome the discrepancy between the possible and the existent.[18] Moreover, Marcuse insisted that Hegel's revo-

[16] *Reason and Revolution*, p. 11.
[17] *Ibid.*
[18] *Ibid.*, p. 153. A note of ambiguity persists, nevertheless, since the famous equation of the real and the rational would lead one to anticipate Hegel's designating "actuality" rather than "reality" as

lutionary reason did not pertain merely to the domain of thought. Admittedly, the driving force in this historical development was Mind or Spirit,[19] but the rationalizing process was not confined to the realm of mind. Hegel opposed the manner in which Kant and Fichte had relegated freedom to pure thought, "attributing to the autonomous person all the freedom that is lacking in the external world."[20] In Hegel's conception the entire spatiotemporal world, including human society, was incorporated into the rationalizing process.[21] In short, Marcuse contended that Hegel's concept of reason was eminently political.

The major difficulty with Hegel's philosophy of history is that it seems to leave little significant space for the concrete interaction of revolutionary and counterrevolutionary movements.[22] Marcuse, however, refused to ad-

---

the imperfect embodiment of the rational. However, he does just the opposite.

[19] *Reason and Revolution*, p. 227.

[20] *Ibid.*, p. 47.

[21] *Ibid.*, pp. 5, 10.

[22] This difficulty suggests an important difference between the Hegelian conception of rationalization and that expounded by Max Weber. Weber also characterized the history of the world (or at least the Western world) as the history of the progress of rationality. But Weber's analysis was offered only as a description of the historical facts, or, more precisely, as a way of looking at and organizing the historical experience of the West—an ambitious ideal type. Consequently, Weber did not run the risk of nullifying the reality or meaningfulness of the efforts of the great rationalizers, whether men or movements. At the same time, Weber could offer no explanation for the rationalizing process; indeed, his fictionalist manner of approaching the problem suggested that the history of

mit that Hegel conceived of the inevitable progress toward a higher rationality as occurring independently of the historical efforts of mankind; he argued that Hegel identified the rationalizing process with the actual historical activities of revolutionaries. In some sense the revolutionary historical process was nothing more than the history of revolutions.

To substantiate this thesis Marcuse turned to Hegel's statements on the European revolutionary tradition. He put great emphasis on the enthusiasm with which even the mature Hegel, heir to Fichte's philosophical chair at the University of Berlin and the "official" philosopher of the Prussian state, had endorsed the accomplishments of the French Revolution. According to Marcuse, Hegel approved of the Revolution precisely because it represented an important step forward in man's effort to rationalize his world:

> In Hegel's view, the decisive turn that history took with the French Revolution was that man came to rely on his mind and dared to submit the given reality to the standards of reason. . . . Man . . . set out to organize reality according to the demands of his free rational thinking instead of simply accommodating his thoughts to the existing order and the prevailing values.[23]

---

the West was the history of rationality only if, and so long as, one chose to look at it that way. In Hegel's conception we encounter no such diffidence or epistemological coyness; for Hegel history was rational because transcendental reason ruled the world. See Reinhard Bendix, *Max Weber: An Intellectual Portrait* (Garden City, New York, 1962), especially Chapters Three and Twelve.

[23] *Reason and Revolution*, pp. 5–6. Reprinted by permission of Humanities Press, Inc., and Routledge & Kegan Paul Ltd.

As for Hegel's opposition to the critics of the German Restoration, Marcuse undertook to show that the liberal credentials of these reformers were highly suspect. He cited in particular the case of the Students' Associations (*Burschenschaften*), whose libertarian views were thoroughly compromised by an incipient racism.[24] Thus Hegel's hostility to the German left of the early nineteenth century was, in Marcuse's mind, perfectly consistent with his sympathy for the French Revolution.

In marshaling further evidence for his conception of Hegel as the philosopher of the French Revolution, Marcuse turned to the unlikely domain of Hegel's pronouncements on the state. The "deification" of the state in Hegel's political writings has traditionally been taken as unmistakable evidence of his conservatism and authoritarianism. Marcuse's rebuttal of this accusation took two forms, one theoretical, the other historical. At the level of theory, he noted that Hegel's state was always conceived as a state of law (*Rechtsstaat*).[25] Therefore Hegel could endorse no "power state" which did not enhance the freedom and power of its individual citizens. More important was the fact that in its historical context, Hegel's conception of the strong state served a progressive function. In early nineteenth-century Europe, to be an exponent of a strong centralized state meant to be on the side of the Revolution, for the state, as even Marx acknowledged, was the inveterate opponent of the reactionary feudal social order.[26] Furthermore, Marcuse contended that in

[24] *Ibid.*, pp. 179–80.
[25] *Ibid.*, p. 83; cf. also pp. 178, 181.
[26] *Ibid.*, pp. 54, 61.

the context of the German Restoration, Hegel's enthusiasm for a strong state was directed against a very particular group of reactionary, or potentially reactionary, social forces, notably the pseudodemocratic *Burshenschaften* and the fanatical enthusiasts of the religious revival.[27]

Marcuse's portrayal of Hegel as revolutionary did not end with establishing his commitment to the bourgeois revolution of the eighteenth century. In Marcuse's mind it was not enough simply to show that Hegel was a latter-day *philosophe;* that would perhaps suffice to refute the charge of conservatism, but it would hardly establish Hegel as an original and radical thinker in the context of post-Revolutionary Europe. Thus much of *Reason and Revolution* was devoted to the thesis that Hegel had anticipated a fundamentally Marxian critique of modern civilization. Marcuse was not interested in belaboring the obvious methodological or structural similarities in Marx and Hegel—the issue of the dialectic. Rather he contended that Hegel's writings contained many of the substantive insights which were to become the central precepts of Marxism. This effort to discover Marx in Hegel was in effect a corollary to Marcuse's simultaneous attempt to reinterpret Marx's own social criticism. Marcuse was significantly influenced by the rediscovery of Marx's early manuscripts in the 1930's and was thus preoccupied with Marx's role as social philosopher in the

[27] *Ibid.,* pp. 180, 220. Marcuse all but ignored the argument that Hegel was himself a religious, even a Christian, philosopher. It was sufficient for him that Hegel treated all moral or religious concepts in terms of their immanent significance, thus denying the existence of any transcendent reality. Cf. p. 137 and p. 167 of *Reason and Revolution.*

larger sense. His analysis of Hegel as a revolutionary
social critic was an analogue to his analysis of Marx as
philosopher. The composite result of these parallel endeavors was to reduce substantially the ideological distance between the two thinkers.

Marcuse focused on three Marxian themes in Hegel's
philosophy: alienation, conflict, and labor. He argued that
the term "alienation" in Hegel's writings bore precisely
the same meaning as it did in the Marxian corpus. Marx
did not need to translate any putative idealistic perception into materialistic terms, since for Hegel the concept
already signified the transformation of the world of objects, the products of human labor, into independent en-
tities "governed by uncontrolled forces and laws in which
man no longer recognizes his own self."[28] Moreover, for
Hegel as for Marx, the historical fact of alienation was
directly linked to the institution of private property. In
the *Philosophy of Right* Hegel had expounded in thoroughly Marxian fashion the connection between capital
accumulation and the growing impoverishment of the
workers, culminating in the rise of "a vast industrial
army."[29] Marcuse was able to argue, therefore, that
Hegel conceived of history not merely as a dialectical
struggle between competing ideological systems, but as a
very real struggle between antagonistic social forces.

Marcuse also contended that for Hegel, as for Marx, the
system of conflicting social forces had its origins in the
mode of social labor. He emphasized especially that
Hegel had developed the concept of "abstract labor" (the

[28] *Ibid.*, p. 23.
[29] *Ibid.*, pp. 205–6; cf. pp. 34–35.

notion that under capitalism the individual's labor loses its particularity, becomes general), which played a crucial role in Marx's analysis of surplus value in *Capital*. Marcuse quoted Hegel to the effect that the quantification of labor forces men " 'into a state of utmost barbarism,' " especially that portion of the population which " 'is subjected to mechanical labor in the factories.' "[30] It followed that Hegel's conception of the rationalization of reality included some notion of transcending the existing (contradictory) social order. The analysis of alienation and abstract labor pointed toward a transformation of social reality which would reconcile men to each other and to the world of nature.[31] Thus Marcuse concluded his case for Hegel as Marxist, having shown that the central categories of revolutionary social theory as well as the transcendence of those categories had already been adumbrated, if only in rudimentary form, in the Hegelian corpus.

Once Marcuse had established Hegel's revolutionary credentials, it was relatively easy to exonerate him from the charge that he paved the way for Nazism. It was Hegel's theory of the state which left him most vulnerable to this accusation, and, as I have already indicated, Marcuse turned the tables on Hegel's critics by arguing that his statism actually performed a critical function. Marcuse went on to claim that the Fascist state represented the rule of special interests over the whole—the very situation which Hegel's *Rechtsstaat* aimed to prevent.[32]

[30] *Ibid.*, pp. 57–58, 77–79, 148.
[31] *Ibid.*, pp. 113, 148.
[32] *Ibid.*, p. 216.

Furthermore, he argued that the Fascist conception of the state was in fact heir to the organicist tradition in political theory, and Hegel, as an advocate of a rationalist theory of the state, had written polemically against one of the earliest and most influential organicist theoreticians, K. L. von Haller.[33] Finally, there was the critical judgment of the Fascist theorists themselves, and here Marcuse very effectively pointed out that the Nazis had been unanimous in their rejection of Hegel's political theory on the grounds of its "rational humanitarianism."[34]

Marcuse's concern with defending Hegel against the charge of Fascism was related to his general preoccupation in the 1930's with the ideological origins of the radical right. In exonerating Hegel he did not want to suggest that Nazism was an isolated twentieth-century aberration. On the contrary, he was convinced that Nazism had its roots deep in the nineteenth century.[35] He did not seek those roots in peripheral or eccentric nineteenth-century thinkers, as have recent German intellectual historians like Fritz Stern and George Mosse.[36] Instead he propounded the paradoxical thesis that Nazism grew out of the central nineteenth-century ideological tradition which on the surface seemed most hostile to totalitarianism, namely Liberalism.[37] Of course Marcuse

---

[33] *Ibid.*, p. 181; "Theoretische Entwürfe über Autorität und Familie," *Studien über Autorität und Familie*, p. 220.

[34] *Reason and Revolution*, pp. 390, 411, 413.

[35] "Vorwort," *Kultur und Gesellschaft I*, pp. 7–8.

[36] Fritz Stern, *The Politics of Cultural Despair* (Berkeley, 1963); George Mosse, *The Crisis of German Ideology* (New York, 1964).

[37] Marcuse, "Vorwort," *Kultur und Gesellschaft I*, p. 8; *Soviet Marxism* (New York, 1958), p. 221.

was prepared to admit that other intellectual traditions contributed to the mélange of doctrines and attitudes which characterized European Fascism. In particular he pointed an accusing finger at the existentialists and their precursors, including Kierkegaard, who espoused a philosophy of activism without content—activity for its own sake rather than as a means to some rational end.[38] There was likewise a hostile bow to Comtean Positivism, with its pseudoreligious posturing and undisguised authoritarianism.[39] However, most of Marcuse's critical energies were reserved for an analysis of the Fascist undercurrents in the Liberal tradition.

Presupposed in this endeavor was Franz Neumann's demonstration of the interdependence of advanced capitalism and Fascism, which Marcuse saw reflected at the ideological level in the Fascist concept of heroic self-denial. The Fascist insistence on duty, sacrifice, and dedication served nicely to reconcile the masses to their unhappy fate as the hard-working servants of the capitalist machine.[40] But Marcuse was not willing to limit his critique of the Liberal tradition to a formal analogy which portrayed Fascism as serving the ideological needs of monopoly capitalism in the same manner as classical

[38] Marcuse, "Der Kampf gegen den Liberalismus in der totalitären Staatsauffassung," *Kultur und Gesellschaft I*, pp. 43–44, 47; *Reason and Revolution*, pp. 264, 267. Nietzsche, however, was explicitly excepted from this stricture; Marcuse was thus guilty of no awkward about-face when in *Eros and Civilization* he included Nietzsche in his pantheon of critical philosophers. Cf. "Der Kampf gegen den Liberalismus . . . ," pp. 18–19.
[39] *Reason and Revolution*, pp. 342–43, 350–51.
[40] "Der Kampf gegen den Liberalismus . . . ," pp. 33 ff, 40, 43.

Liberalism had served those of the individualistic capitalism of the Early Modern era. He did not doubt that Fascism had ousted Liberalism as the official capitalist ideology precisely because it better served the purposes of the new monolithic economy, in particular the need for a strong state to mobilize the full productive powers of the population.[41] But it was not a question of an old ideology being replaced by an entirely new one better suited to the contemporary economic situation. The old ideology already contained the seeds of the new.

Marcuse focused in particular on two characteristic Liberal shibboleths: naturalism and empiricism, both of which were to remain favorite objects of abuse throughout his career as social and philosophical critic. While admitting that both doctrines undoubtedly served an important critical function during the Enlightenment, and thus contributed to the rationalization of European society, he insisted that their ultimate significance was to abandon the historical process to forces beyond the province of reason. That is, although the Liberal theorists had endorsed the rationalizing enterprise of the individual entrepreneur, they had relegated the rationality of the whole to the "laws of nature." The economic apparatus, they felt, would "naturally" develop its own rational and harmonious balance. Thus Marcuse found a soft, irrational foundation under the Liberal edifice, which served to legitimize the most inhumane and unreasonable economic arrangements as "natural." Fascist irrationalism grew out of Liberal irrationalism, and the doctrine of

[41] *Ibid.*, pp. 22, 32.

natural law itself allowed of easy translation into the *Blut und Boden* naturalism of the Nazis.[42] Marcuse argued that dogmatic Liberal empiricism implied an analogous submission to irrationality. In this instance reason fell victim, not to nature, but to an uncritical worship of matters of fact. When "the facts" were raised to the level of absolute authority, it was impossible to distinguish between good and bad facts, and the established economic order was exempted from rational criticism simply because it existed.[43]

Marcuse's critique of Liberalism was clearly a corollary to his championing of Hegelianism. Hegel was an attractive figure for Marcuse because he opposed the uncritical empiricism and naturalism of Liberal ideology. However, I should point out that Marcuse's attitude toward Hegel was not entirely apologetic. He was able to recognize the limits of the case for Hegel as revolutionary. He admitted, for example, that Hegel's commitment to the rationalization of the world of people and things was constantly threatened by his absolute idealism. At the end of the *Phenomenology of Mind* "absolute knowledge" seemed to displace the rational organization of society as the fulfillment of history; as Marcuse put it, "The self-certainty of philosophy comprehending the world triumphs over the practice that changes it."[44] Moreover, Marcuse confessed that the critical traits contained in Hegel's philosophy of the state were "dwarfed by the oppressive trends inherent

[42] *Ibid.*, pp. 25–26, 31, 39; *Reason and Revolution*, p. 341.
[43] "Der Kampf gegen den Liberalismus . . . ," pp. 27–30; *Reason and Revolution*, pp. 20–21.
[44] *Reason and Revolution*, pp. 120, 92–93, 161.

in all authoritarianism."[45] Marcuse was most offended by
Hegel's notion that war was the inevitable and legitimate
test of sovereignty and by his arrogant disregard for the
sufferings and sacrifices of human history. Indeed, Marcuse called Hegel's vision of inevitable and harmonious
progress toward a higher rationality "preposterous."[46]
Nevertheless, these critical remarks, judiciously sprinkled
throughout *Reason and Revolution,* offered only a gentle
corrective to the central portrait of Hegel as loyal son of
the Enlightenment and proto-Marxian critic of the European social order.

I don't want to dispute Marcuse's characterization of
Hegel as critical philosopher; in general I find it quite
persuasive. Nor do I think it worthwhile to quibble with
his portrayal of the German left at the beginning of the
nineteenth century. Marcuse's case rested primarily on his
dissection of Hegel's concept of reason, and he could very
well have admitted that Hegel's explicit political pronouncements were reactionary without jeopardizing his
analysis of the critical impetus inherent in the theory
itself. On the other hand, I do think it important to note
that Marcuse's polemical intent to a considerable extent
inhibited an accurate assessment of Hegel's place in European intellectual history. In making his case for Hegel as
revolutionary, Marcuse chose to ignore Hegel's theoretical
debt to European conservatism. However, it is one thing
to argue that Hegel was not himself a conservative—or
that the implications of his philosophizing were distinctly
revolutionary—and quite another to disregard the manner

[45] *Ibid.,* p. 221; cf. "Theoretische Entwürfe über Autorität und
Familie," pp. 182–83.
[46] *Reason and Revolution,* p. 246; cf. p. 221.

in which he was clearly influenced by conservative theorists.

We can understand how Hegel's revolutionary philosophy differed from that of his eighteenth-century predecessors only when we recognize that the new ingredient in this philosophy was a conception of history borrowed, more or less self-consciously, from conservative thinkers such as Burke and Herder. Hegel attempted to bridge the gap between the Enlightenment and its nineteenth-century critics. In general the Enlightenment believed that history was to be judged by reason. The laws, institutions, attitudes, and customs which were the historical legacy of European society were subjected to a rigorous critical perusal, and when they fell short of the dictates of reason, they were judged unworthy of further sustenance, no matter how hallowed. The French Revolution can be regarded as an acting out of this critical attitude toward the past; its underlying assumption was that man could reconstruct society according to a rational formula, or, more modestly put, that man could eliminate those institutions which were sustained, in spite of their irrationality, simply on the basis of tradition. The thinkers of the first post-Revolutionary generation, as is well known, opposed the claims of reason with those of history. For both Burke and de Maistre, for example, history and historically evolved society sat in judgment of any supposedly "ideal" society that pure reason might concoct. Traditional institutions, by virtue of their very historicity, had a claim on the present—and the future; they could not be dissolved in accordance with the dictates of some abstract theory about the good society.

It was Hegel's genius, I believe, to have synthesized the

opposing claims of reason and history and to have elaborated a theoretical position which transcended the debate
between the Enlightenment and its critics. He did this
quite simply by identifying reason with history. He
thereby set himself apart both from the *philosophes,* who
regarded rationality as an accident of individual consciousness which was brought to bear on the passive data
of history, and from the conservatives, who recognized
the organic character of history, but failed to assess properly its rational content. It was of course Hegel's identification of reason with history which Marcuse set about to
demonstrate in *Reason and Revolution,* but without pay-
ing adequate historical tribute to the conservative
thinkers who made this synthesis possible. Apparently he
felt that such a concession to the opposition would have
undermined the effectiveness of his case.

II

Karl Marx, as I have already suggested, was the second
focal point of Marcuse's early intellectual enterprises.
Marcuse's inquiry into Marxism represented one manifestation of a general reevaluation of historical materialism which was prompted by the discovery of Marx's
economic and philosophical manuscripts. This was in fact
the second major reinterpretation to which Marx had
been subjected, coming approximately three decades
after the great revisionist controversy of the turn of the
century. In both of these episodes, the same issues were
raised: the questions of materialism, revolution, and determinism. Because of historical developments and tem-

peramental inclinations, both generations of scholars were disillusioned with the rigid sociological reductionism and historical determinism of orthodox Marxists. They were confronted in the first instance with a revolution which had failed to materialize as predicted, and secondly with a gross insensitivity to psychological and moral issues on the part of Marx's official interpreters. Eduard Bernstein's solution had been to abandon Marx completely, denying both the historical dialectic and the primacy of material over intellectual and moral forces in the historical process. His critics, in particular Lenin, tried to salvage Marx's vision of the inevitable collapse of capitalism by introducing a new economic factor, the theory of imperialism. Thus the split between revisionists and antirevisionists at the beginning of the twentieth century left one with the choice between an ahistorical moralism, loyal to the Enlightenment tradition of free will and ethical commitment, and a rather crude, but thoroughly historical, economic determinism.[47]

The discovery of the early manuscripts offered the neo-Marxians of the 1930's a much more attractive middle road between these two alternatives. The manuscripts indicated quite clearly that Marx's social criticism had grown out of a prolonged struggle with Hegelian philosophy. For some of the reinterpreters, this meant that at bottom Marx was still an idealist philosopher, a free spirit concerned with the problems of ethical choice and psychological fulfillment.[48] Marcuse went out of his way to disso-

---

[47] For a clear account of the first revisionist controversy, see Peter Gay, *The Dilemma of Democratic Socialism* (New York, 1952).
[48] Cf., for example, Erich Fromm, *Marx's Concept of Man* (New York, 1961).

ciate himself from this school of interpretation. He was not interested in Marx the poet, or even Marx the philosopher. Instead, he used Marx's Hegelian musings as evidence for the thesis that Marx's economic criticism was the direct product, indeed the only legitimate extension, of the critical tendencies in Hegel's own thought.[49] It was incorrect, he argued, to conclude from the early manuscripts that Marx was a frustrated philosopher posing as an economist. The central concepts of even these early writings were already economic concepts, if not in the narrow sense of technical economic theory. They represented a translation into economic terms of the critical tendencies previously expressed in a more or less exclusively philosophical vocabulary. This was true even where Marx retained the traditional philosophical (i.e., Hegelian) terminology: "All the philosophical concepts of Marxian theory are social and economic categories. . . . Even Marx's early writings are not philosophical. They express the negation of philosophy, though they still do so in philosophical language."[50] At the same time Marcuse insisted that Marx's basic economic concepts contained *within* them a critique of the human situation under capitalism in its totality.[51]

Like his fellow neo-Marxians Georg Lukács and Antonio Gramsci, Marcuse focused on three notions elaborated in the early manuscripts. The first of these, and perhaps the most important, was alienation. Marcuse

[49] *Reason and Revolution*, p. 252; "Der Kampf gegen den Liberalismus . . . ," p. 55.
[50] *Reason and Revolution*, p. 258.
[51] Marcuse, "Philosophie und kritische Theorie," *Kultur und Gesellschaft I*, p. 102.

showed that the concept of alienation contained within it a general psychological critique of the human condition under capitalism. As an economic concept alienation signified the separation of the working class from the means of production under the system of private property. But in Marx's hands the concept further denoted the total frustration of human faculties. In particular, alienation signified the massive and perverse contraction of individual talents into the performance of a single, monotonous task. The problem was no longer a philosophical one, since the dilemma of alienation could be solved only by abolishing "the prevailing mode of labor."[52] Thus while it was clear that Marx was heir to the humanitarian impulses of the Enlightenment, he translated the Enlightenment's concern for human fulfillment into exclusively economic categories. In Marcuse's reading of Marx, the traditional problem of human freedom had become an economic problem.

The concept of consciousness provided the second focus of Marcuse's analysis. Here he was struggling with the problem of determinism. In purely philosophical terms it was the question of whether Marx's historical dialectic left any significant space for human intervention, and thus for the meaningful exercise of human freedom. In historical terms, Marcuse was addressing himself once again to the issue which had split the ranks of Marxism at the turn of the century: the unrealized revolution. Marx's *Capital* seemed to suggest that the development of European society from capitalism to socialism was a matter of simple economic logic. The capitalist system contained

[52] *Reason and Revolution*, p. 275; cf. pp. 273–78, 281–82.

within it certain purely economic mechanisms—overproduction, the declining rate of profit, inevitable crises—which led to its downfall. If it had been Marx's intent to propound such a thesis, then there was apparently no place for human freedom in his conception of history. It also followed that the proper tactic to pursue in attempting to explain the failure of the revolution was that adopted by the antirevisionists, who introduced yet another economic fact (imperialism) and tried to illustrate how this new fact interfered with the economic logic Marx himself had delineated.

Marcuse, however, drew attention to the central role of consciousness in the Marxian historical dialectic.[53] He did not abandon the notion of an objective economic dynamism, as had Bernstein's generation of revisionists, but he argued that Marx never conceived of the historical process as functioning according to automatic economic laws. The revolution did depend on the "totality of objective conditions,"[54] but these conditions provided only the general context for free initiative. The key to the success or failure of the revolution, indeed to the historical dialectic in its entirety, was consciousness. Thus Marcuse shifted the emphasis of his analysis away from the purely economic mechanisms of the dialectic (overproduction, falling rate of profit, etc.) and insisted on the central importance of revolutionary awareness. Economic logic might well create the material conditions for revolution,

[53] In this matter, as in much of his reinterpretation, Marcuse was following the lead of Georg Lukács, whose *Geschichte und Klassenbewusstsein* (Berlin, 1923) anticipated many of the revelations of *The Economic and Philosophical Manuscripts*.

[54] *Reason and Revolution*, p. 318.

but these conditions became revolutionary "only if seized upon and directed by a conscious activity that has in mind the socialist goal."[55] From this analysis it was clear that Marxism, properly understood, was incompatible with "fatalistic determinism."[56]

Marcuse's insistence on the central role of consciousness in Marx's thought also accounted for his complete lack of interest in Marxian sociological reductionism. In the traditional interpretation of Marx, the concept of an inevitable economic dialectic was linked to a materialist sociology which denied the autonomy, and therefore the historical importance, of ideological, religious, and philosophical factors. Marx himself had laid the theoretical groundwork for such a sociology in *The German Ideology*, and he had been among the most expert practitioners of the reductionist art. But I can recall not a single instance in Marcuse's writings where he demonstrated the *causal* dependence of a particular ideological tradition on objective economic forces. He did not argue that such endeavors were illegitimate or un-Marxian, but his discovery of the central role of consciousness in Marx led him to pursue exactly the opposite tack. All of his attention was directed to the historical impact of ideological forces, particularly those which bore on the crystallizing or muting of revolutionary consciousness. Apparently he felt that the orthodox Marxians and the sociologists of knowledge had fairly well exhausted the possibilities of sociological reductionism. It was their proper task to demonstrate what was false and heteronomous in the history of

[55] *Ibid.*
[56] *Ibid.*, p. 319.

thought. The philosopher, on the other hand, was concerned with the truth—albeit the truth about man and society—contained in the speculative endeavors of the past.[57]

Finally, along with the new perspective on Marx suggested by the notions of alienation and consciousness, the early manuscripts also introduced a new understanding of communism. Marcuse felt that the official interpreters of Marx, preoccupied as they were with economic mechanisms, had made a fetish of the abolition of private property and the socialization of the means of production.[58] Since economic categories always denoted a more fundamental human reality for Marx, the specific economic arrangements he envisioned were only means to some more basic human goal. The early manuscripts announced this goal as the abolition of labor. If the basic irrationality of the capitalist order was alienated labor—which, as we have seen, Marcuse interpreted as the total frustration of human potentialities—then it followed that the meaningful overthrow of capitalism involved eliminating its central perversion: "The abolition of the proletariat also amounts to the abolition of labor as such."[59] The question of private property became important only because "alienation has taken its most universal form in the institution of private property."[60] Marcuse was in effect arguing that Marx's conception of communism was even more

---

[57] "Philosophie und kritische Theorie," pp. 115–16.

[58] *Reason and Revolution*, p. 294.

[59] *Ibid.*, p. 292. "Marx . . . envisioned the future mode of labor to be so different from the prevailing one that he hesitated to use the same term 'labor' to designate alike the material process of capitalist and of communist society" (p. 293).

[60] *Ibid.*, p. 282.

radical than his epigones had imagined. It signified a great deal more than a rearrangement of property relations. Communism meant "not only a new and different economic system, but a different system of life, . . . a new form of individualism."[61]

I think it important to emphasize how Marcuse's understanding of Marx differed both from the traditional interpretation, with its rigid determinism, sociological reductionism, and exclusively economic focus, and from the unhistorical and soft-minded reevaluations propounded by some of his fellow revisionists. If we take George Lichtheim's recent study of Marxism as a symptomatic résumé of what many Western scholars have made of the early Marx, we discover immediately that Marcuse's brand of Marxism was still quite tough-minded and revolutionary by comparison. Marcuse insisted that a correct understanding of Marx could not rest exclusively, or even primarily, on the early manuscripts, writing off later developments as aberrations or tactical maneuvers, as Lichtheim often does.[62] And in fact Marcuse substantiated his interpretation of alienated labor and consciousness through a discriminating reading of Marx's mature writings, in particular *Capital*. Furthermore, unlike Lichtheim, Marcuse did not attempt to blame Engels for all those items in the Marxian credo which did not fit well with the portrait of Marx as humanist and democrat (the violent revolution, the dictatorship of the proletariat, the economic determinism). Indeed, he hardly mentioned Engels at all. Most important, for all his emphasis on the role of consciousness and his insistence on Marx's concern

[61] *Ibid.*, p. 286.
[62] *Ibid.*, p. 295; George Lichtheim, *Marxism* (New York, 1961), pp. 54, 105.

for the human situation in its totality, he vigorously disputed the suggestion that Marx was anything but a revolutionary. For Marcuse, Marx was not the prophet of a more humane capitalism or even a democratic socialism, which could be achieved through gradual constitutional reform. Here he distinguished himself from those revisionists of both his own and Bernstein's generation who shied away from the revolutionary implications of the Marxian dialectic.[63] Marcuse was clearly not interested in diluting Marx to make him more attractive to Western liberals.

Having claimed that Marcuse portrayed Marx as a revolutionary, I have now to explain Marcuse's own relation to the revolutionary cause. Before entering upon his scholarly career he had been active in the Spartacist movement, particularly during the political upheavals which swept Germany in 1918 and 1919. Moreover, it is clear from a number of his comments that he and his associates in the Institute for Social Research remained moderately sanguine about the fate of the revolution well into the 1930's.[64] Perhaps it would be more accurate to state that it was not yet clear to them whether the European working class would accomplish its historical mission or succumb to the administrative and military pressures of Fascism. In 1934, for example, Marcuse wrote, "today the fate of the workers' movement . . . lies in uncertainty."[65] Final disillusionment came with the

[63] *Reason and Revolution*, pp. 398–99; Lichtheim, *Marxism*, pp. 58–62, 99, 234–58.
[64] See, for example, "Zur Kritik des Hedonismus," *Kultur und Gesellschaft I*, pp. 159–60.
[65] Marcuse, "Der Kampf gegen den Liberalismus . . . ," p. 55; "Vorwort," *Kultur und Gesellschaft I*, p. 7.

Spanish Civil War and the Moscow trials.[66] It was at this time, according to his own account, that Marcuse turned to an in-depth reading of Freud.[67] He did not lose faith in the correctness or the relevance of Marxian theory, but the historical failure of the forces to which Marx had entrusted the revolution convinced him that European society had reached a stage where even more radical critical concepts were needed. Marxism had proved inadequate not because it was overly abstract and revolutionary, but precisely because it was not revolutionary enough. The social criticism of the future, Marcuse felt, would have to be both more negative and more utopian than even Marxism. In the era of monopoly capitalism and totalitarianism, only the most radical of Marx's conceptions retained their full critical force. In particular, Marcuse pointed to Marx's notion of the abolition of labor. This concept, enunciated in the early manuscripts and discarded by the more sober theorist of the mature writings, still retained a meaningful promise of a humane existence beyond the bounds of advanced industrial capitalism and totalitarianism.[68]

III

Before turning to Marcuse's confrontation with Freud, I want to comment on several characteristic attitudes and

[66] "Vorwort," p. 11.

[67] Marcuse gave me this information at a private interview on November 15, 1965, in Cambridge, Massachusetts.

[68] "Vorwort," pp. 12, 14–16.

intellectual prejudices which pervaded his early writings and became permanent fixtures of his mature thought. In my discussion of Marcuse's critique of Liberalism, I touched on his hostility to philosophical empiricism. However, this antagonism was so basic to his entire philosophical and political outlook, and was articulated with such conviction, that it deserves more expansive treatment.

Marcuse's critique of empiricism and its characteristic by-products, in particular scientism and relativism, was based on a single perception: that empiricism raised to the dignity of a philosophical doctrine an attitude toward reality which was essentially conservative. In *Reason and Revolution* he presented this argument through an analysis of English empiricism, particularly the philosophy of David Hume. If experience and custom were taken to be the sole guides to truth, then, according to Marcuse, man was robbed of the one faculty—reason—which enabled him to act in accordance with ideas and principles that transcended the established order. The end product of the Humean attitude was thus not merely skepticism but also conformism. The empiricists' critique of metaphysics was in reality "an attack upon the conditions of human freedom, for the right of reason to guide experience was a proper part of these conditions."[69]

Marcuse argued that the conservative implications of this philosophy were made explicit in the most influential nineteenth-century variety of empiricism: positivism. By positivism Marcuse meant the attempt to discover through empirical research a system of inexorable social

[69] *Reason and Revolution*, pp. 20–21.

laws, analogous to those of natural science. As propounded by Auguste Comte in France and Friedrich
Julius Stahl in Germany, the positivist repudiation of
metaphysics was accompanied by an explicit denial of
man's right to reorganize his society in accordance with
the dictates of reason: "The protagonists of this positivism
took great pains to stress the conservative and affirmative
attitude of their philosophy: it induces thought to be
satisfied with the facts, to renounce any transgression
beyond them, and to bow to the given state of affairs."[70]
In Marcuse's analysis, then, positivism appeared as direct
heir to the tradition of Burke and de Maistre. Moreover,
he pointed out that positivism had arisen, particularly in
Germany, in response to the negative or critical tendencies of Hegelian idealism.[71] In other words, Marcuse
found in the historical antagonism of positivism to
Hegelianism a concrete illustration of the alliance of empiricism and conservatism against the critical forces of
reason.

Closely related to Marcuse's opposition to philosophical
empiricism was his critique of relativism. In this instance
also he focused on the mid-nineteenth-century positivists,
who had insisted that a scientific theory of society was
necessarily value-neutral. Marcuse quoted Comte to the
effect that positivist sociology " 'neither admires nor con-
demns political facts but looks upon them . . . as simple
objects of observation.' "[72] Marcuse considered all of
modern sociology, with its insistence on the neutrality of

[70] *Ibid.*, pp. 27, 343–44, 348–49.
[71] *Ibid.*, pp. 326–28.
[72] *Ibid.*, p. 354.

scientific research, the victim of positivist relativism.[73] The notion that relativism was inherently conservative was of course precisely the conclusion which Geza Roheim had reached in his struggles with the functionalist tradition in anthropology. But Marcuse went beyond Roheim in pursuing this implicit conservatism to its origin in the basic assumptions of the Western scientific enterprise—a matter to which he was to return with a vengeance in *One-Dimensional Man*. In the scientific *Weltanschauung* he found not merely that uncritical submission to the facts which achieved philosophical formulation in English empiricism, but also a preoccupation with a neutral mode of abstraction, i.e., mathematics, to the exclusion of other, potentially critical, modes. In the dominant intellectual tradition of the modern period, a blind worship of "the facts" had combined with "mathematical formalism" to inhibit any genuinely critical understanding of the world we experience.[74]

If Marcuse charged the Anglo-Saxon philosophical tradition with empirical acquiescence, he considered Continental philosophy utterly compromised by its persistent dualism. Here again his basic complaint was political: the mind-body dualism which permeated much of European philosophy relegated freedom and self-realization to an inner world of the spirit, while the "external" world of material culture and social relations was judged irrelevant to human fulfillment, a realm of inevitability and misery. In his contribution to *Autorität und Familie*, Marcuse traced the history of this philosophical tradition from

[73] *Ibid.*, pp. 375–76.
[74] *Ibid.*, p. 145.

Luther to Kant, showing the connection between dualism on the one hand and political conservatism and authoritarianism on the other.[75] Hegel was one of the few European philosophers who attempted to overcome this opposition of subject and object—which provided yet another justification for Marcuse's portrait of Hegel as revolutionary.[76]

Marcuse found the same political motives at work in the famous German distinction between culture and civilization. He coined the phrase "affirmative culture" to characterize the notion of an inner cultivation which stands in opposition to any "mere" physical well-being. Affirmative culture represented a world of beauty, freedom, and happiness which was entirely separate from the workaday world of civilization, and thus accessible to every individual, regardless of the ugliness, misery, and toil of his material existence. In other words, the doctrine of a beautiful and free spirit within an enslaved body served to perpetuate the established economic order.[77]

Marcuse's dissection of the repressive function of culture fitted rather badly with another basic theme of his early writings: the critical function of art. We are dealing here with an ambiguity which was in fact intensified in Marcuse's Freudian writings of the 1950's and 1960's, and which exactly mirrors a parallel ambivalence in Freud's attitude toward art. In his analysis of affirmative culture, Marcuse treated art as another aspect of that internal

[75] Marcuse, "Theoretische Entwürfe über Autorität und Familie," pp. 137, 140–46, 172.
[76] Hegels Ontologie . . . , pp. 13, 15.
[77] Marcuse, "Über den affirmativen Charakter der Kultur," Kultur und Gesellschaft I, pp. 63, 66, 77.

culture which serves to reconcile the individual to an exploitative economic order: "Since art shows the beautiful as present, it pacifies revolutionary desire. Together with the other cultural artifacts it has contributed to the larger educational task of this culture: to discipline the liberated individual . . . so that he can bear the unfreedom of societal existence."[78] This antagonism to art strikes me as perfectly consistent with the general distrust of culture exhibited throughout Marcuse's early writings. It is comparable to the Freudian treatment of art as sublimation—i.e., as a substitute for some more basic bodily satisfaction.

But like Freud, Marcuse was unable to maintain a consistently hostile attitude toward the artistic endeavor. Indeed, he more frequently argued that art represented an asylum for revolutionary truth; it was the handmaid of radical social theory. Even when philosophy and religion had betrayed their critical function, art remained steadfastly committed to the promise of a better future.[79] Marcuse thus argued that the essence of art was criticism, and he even suggested that the final realization of a rational society would mean the end of art as we know it. Once the critical task was completed, life would take on the reality now preserved in the work of art, and art itself would become "objectless."[80]

Throughout his writings Marcuse employed the antithesis negative-positive, or affirmative-destructive, in an ironical fashion. To be positive, affirmative, glibly opti-

---

[78] *Ibid.*, p. 89.
[79] *Ibid.*, p. 85; "Philosophie und kritische Theorie," p. 123.
[80] "Über den affirmativen Charakter der Kultur," p. 99.

mistic, whether in the sense of Auguste Comte or Norman Vincent Peale, implied a fundamentally conservative point of view. The truly progressive attitude was one of negation. I feel that Marcuse's obviously self-conscious choice of this paradoxical vocabulary tells us a great deal about his intellectual and psychological makeup. In the most immediate sense, it reveals a rather playful quality of mind, a philosophical cleverness—as when he announced that he had written *Reason and Revolution* in order to revive "the power of negative thinking."[81] At the same time the repeated honorific use of "negation" and "destruction" suggests a barely concealed and fierce anger, reflecting the extent of Marcuse's alienation from the established order.

Marcuse's fascination with negation was in some degree responsible for his predilection for certain thinkers and concepts. It defined, for example, the measure of his identification with Hegel. In *Soviet Marxism* Marcuse made very clear that he did not accept the Hegelian notion of a metaphysical or spiritual Reason which moves history toward a predetermined end.[82] Thus in a strict sense he was not, I suppose, a Hegelian. What Marcuse shared with Hegel, beyond a commitment to the legitimacy of an uninhibitedly abstract philosophical perspective, was a firm belief in the progressive function of negative thinking. He cited with approval Hegel's contention that dialectics had a "negative" character, and he endorsed the verdict of European positivism that Hegelianism was a "negative philosophy."[83] Hegel's philosophy

---

[81] *Reason and Revolution,* p. vii.
[82] *Soviet Marxism,* pp. 1–5.
[83] *Reason and Revolution,* pp. 123, 325.

was "motivated by the conviction that the given facts that appear to common sense as the positive index of truth are in reality the negation of truth, so that truth can only be established by their destruction."[84]

This apotheosis of negation and destruction, which stood at the heart of Marcuse's Hegelianism, manifested itself in his willingness to entertain seriously the most negative and violent intellectual constructions, in particular Freud's death instinct. It also accounted for his annoyance at the easy optimism of both anti-Hegelian positivists and neo-Freudian revisionists. Admittedly, Marcuse plunged into the depths of negation only in order to ascend to a more lofty vision of human affirmation. He insisted, for example, that although Hegel's philosophy "begins with the negation of the given and retains this negativity throughout," it "concludes with the declaration that history has achieved the reality of reason."[85] Similarly, as we shall see, he adopted Freud's notion of the death instinct with a view to affirming the ultimate triumph of Life over Death. Nevertheless, I think it important to emphasize the extent of Marcuse's alienation from the existing intellectual and material culture. Only intense anger could have given rise to such enthusiasm for negation and death.

My portrait of the young Herbert Marcuse will be incomplete without an evaluation of those tendencies in his early work which anticipated his later interest in Freud. On the surface of things, many of Marcuse's intellectual predilections seemed to inhibit any serious in-

[84] *Ibid.*, pp. 26–27.
[85] *Ibid.*, p. 27.

volvement with psychoanalysis. His enthusiasm for Hegelian rationalism, for instance, implied a certain insensitivity to the seamy side of the human mind—its immense capacity for irrationality which Freud so systematically investigated. It further implied a rather casual attitude toward the body in general, and sexuality in particular. Marcuse insisted of course that in Hegel's thought the antithesis of mind and body had been overcome. But it is impossible to deny that there is little sense of bodily concreteness in the heady atmosphere of the *Phenomenology of Mind*, where reality constantly threatens to dissolve into pure self-consciousness.[86]

Marcuse was himself not above mouthing the ancient (and repressive) wisdom of the Christian-rationalist tradition, which singled out man's capacity for thought as the ultimate measure of his dignity.[87] In the same vein was his negative appraisal of those philosophical traditions, such as utilitarianism and hedonism, which seem to share a good deal in common with psychoanalysis. Marcuse considered both utilitarianism and hedonism inherently conservative, since both offered exclusively individualistic solutions to the problem of happiness, and neither was able to distinguish between true and false needs.[88]

Finally, there was Marcuse's general aversion to psychological modes of reasoning. In this context I should perhaps again mention his ambivalent participation in the psychopolitical project of the Institute for Social Research. When the results of the project were published in

[86] Cf. *Hegels Ontologie* . . . , p. 29.
[87] "Der Kampf gegen den Liberalismus . . . ," p. 53.
[88] "Zur Kritik des Hedonismus," pp. 136–37, 160; "Über den affirmativen Charakter der Kultur," p. 98.

Studien über Autorität und Familie, Marcuse was assigned the task of writing a history of European thought on the subject. The resulting essay was remarkable for the manner in which it managed to avoid almost any mention of the family. The few remarks Marcuse did address to this topic were unoriginal and perfunctory,[89] and he devoted most of his energy to an analysis of the interrelationship of philosophical dualism and authoritarianism. In an appended essay entitled "Authority and Family in German Sociology to 1933," Marcuse as much as confessed that the family was hardly of paramount historical significance; it was not the bulwark of authoritarianism, because beside the bourgeois family there was the proletarian family, "raising its children with full consciousness of the proletarian class morale."[90] Thus Marcuse did not share even the modest Freudian enthusiasms of his closest associates.

Nevertheless, I want to argue that there were in fact elements in Marcuse's early work which clearly pointed in the direction of *Eros and Civilization.* Several of his early essays contained bits of analysis which were already thoroughly Freudian, sometimes even Reichian, in spirit. Even in the 1930's Marcuse considered bodily repression, and in particular sexual repression, one of the most important attributes of the exploitative social order. He was more sensitive to the sexual dimension of repression than either his orthodox Marxist forebears or his revisionist contemporaries. Thus his critique of Western dualism

[89] "Theoretische Entwürfe über Autorität und Familie," pp. 156–57, 159–60, 184, 197, 216–17.

[90] Marcuse, "Autorität und Familie in der deutschen Soziologie bis 1933," *Studien über Autorität und Familie,* p. 752.

emphasized not only the economic misery but also the sexual misery perpetuated and rationalized by dualistic metaphysics.[91] At the same time he softened his critique of the individualistic excesses of hedonism and eighteenth-century materialism by praising their insistence on man's right to physical pleasure without guilt and shame.[92]

A similar preoccupation with sexual repression was evident in Marcuse's critical analysis of the bourgeois concept of love. Under the capitalist order, Marcuse argued, sexual love was stripped of its playfulness and spontaneity (qualities which were still preserved, if only vicariously, in the physical artistry one encounters in circus and variety shows).[93] Love became a matter of duty and habit, carefully circumscribed by the ideology of monogamic fidelity. Its sole function, beyond perpetuating the species, was the hygienic one of maintaining the physical and mental health necessary to the continued functioning of the economic apparatus.[94] Among the workers sexuality was strictly limited to the brief period of free time allotted for relaxation and recuperation, and Marcuse suggested that a blunting of sensuality was the inevitable by-product of industrial labor, which resulted in the atrophy and coarsening of the body's organs.[95]

Marcuse did not raise the question of sexual repression merely as an aside. Sexual repression was more than "just

[91] "Über den affirmativen Charakter der Kultur," p. 58.
[92] *Ibid.*, pp. 68–69; "Zur Kritik des Hedonismus," pp. 130–31; *Reason and Revolution*, p. 270.
[93] "Über den affirmativen Charakter der Kultur," p. 84.
[94] "Zur Kritik des Hedonismus," p. 155.
[95] *Ibid.*, pp. 153–56; "Über den affirmativen Charakter der Kultur," pp. 79–80.

another" evil of capitalism. In Reichian fashion he argued that the repression of sexuality contributed significantly to maintaining the general order of repression. It was a political as well as a psychological fact. Marcuse's analysis of the political function of sexual repression was quite ingenious. He argued that in a society where all value is based on labor, pleasure was necessarily devalued: "If abstract labor alone creates the value according to which the fairness of exchange is regulated, then pleasure may not be a value. Were it such, then the fairness of the society would be brought into question; indeed, it would reveal itself as striking unfairness."[96] Even more important, any increase in pleasure would endanger the discipline and regimentation so necessary to the continued functioning of the machinery of capitalism:

> The unsublimated, unrationalized release of sexual relations would mean the most emphatic release of pleasure as such and the total devaluation of work for work's sake. The tension between the innate value of work and the freedom of pleasure could not be tolerated by the individual: the hopelessness and injustice of working conditions would strikingly penetrate the consciousness of individuals and render impossible their peaceable regimentation [*Einordnung*] in the social system of the bourgeois world.[97]

Precisely because the dominant classes were consciously or subliminally aware of the revolutionary potential of sexuality, they had insisted on a puritanical, even Manichaean, sexual ethic. At the same time they had devised

[96] "Zur Kritik des Hedonismus," p. 153.
[97] *Ibid.*, p. 156; cf. also p. 152.

clever substitute gratifications, which channeled sexual energies into harmless pursuits such as sports and popular entertainment.

Finally, anticipating one of the central themes of *Eros and Civilization,* Marcuse suggested that there was a direct connection between the repression of sexuality and the eruption of aggression in the form of sadistic terror and masochistic submission.[98] Here also, as in his analysis of the political function of sexual repression, Marcuse was in substantial agreement with Reich. The rational organization of society would mean an end both to repressive sexual morality and to the psychological distortions it introduced. If Marcuse was less sanguine than Reich concerning the possibilities of human perfection ("There will still be invalids, neurotics and criminals"[99]), and considerably more vague concerning the limits of sexual permissiveness, he nevertheless insisted on the real possibility of a world substantially free of guilt, misery, and injustice, a world in which the internalization and sublimation of sexuality would give way to a heightening of pleasure.[100]

IV

Marcuse's employment by the United States government during the 1940's afforded him what Erik Erikson

[98] *Ibid.,* pp. 153–54, 157–58.
[99] *Ibid.,* p. 161; cf. also "Über den affirmativen Charakter der Kultur," p. 100.
[100] "Zur Kritik des Hedonismus," pp. 161–62, 166–67.

has called a "moratorium," a period in which to reassess
the intellectual skirmishes of his youth and to chart the
course of future ventures.[101] Marxism had provided a
useful but insufficiently radical tool of analysis, and it was
clearly in need of some major modifications if it were to
serve Marcuse's critical purposes in the post-Fascist era. I
have already mentioned that Marcuse read extensively in
Freud during the late 1930's. But before he cast his lot
with psychoanalysis, he apparently entertained alternative possibilities. Clearly the intellectual tradition which
most attracted him was existentialism. In the writings of
Jean-Paul Sartre, existentialism had achieved that union
of metaphysics and critical politics which Marcuse found
so irresistible in Hegel. And in terms of Marcuse's interest
in existentialism, it was significant that the existentialists
were among the most avid students of Hegelianism. In his
first book on Hegel, Marcuse had praised Heidegger for
his contributions to Hegel scholarship—[102] an encomium
which he probably regretted after Heidegger had shown
his political colors following the Nazi takeover. Sartre on
the other hand had impeccable political credentials, and
Marcuse took a long, close look at the French philosopher's work. In fact, Marcuse's only substantial publication during his years at the State Department was a
lengthy review of *L'Être et le néant,* published in *Philosophy and Phenomenological Research* in 1948. This
article documented the sources of his interest in and
ultimate disillusionment with Sartre's brand of radicalism.
Its most revealing feature was the enthusiasm it exhibited

[101] Erik Erikson, *Young Man Luther* (New York, 1958), p. 43.
[102] *Hegels Ontologie* . . . , p. 8.

for certain themes in Sartre's work which suggested the possibility of a more erotic organization of reality. Freud was obviously lurking in the wings, and Marcuse's flirtation with existentialism can be seen in retrospect as a brief detour on the road to *Eros and Civilization*. Marcuse's critique of Sartre will sound familiar to those acquainted with his earlier philosophical endeavors. Sartre was charged with promulgating an illusory brand of radicalism, which in reality perpetuated the old dualistic metaphysics of inner freedom and outer enslavement: "The essential freedom of man, as Sartre sees it, remains the same before, during, and after the totalitarian enslavement of man. For freedom is the very structure of human being and cannot be annihilated even by the most adverse conditions: man is free even in the hands of the executioner."[103] Thus Sartre's leftist politics were, in Marcuse's mind, completely extrinsic to his metaphysics, which implied logically a kind of political quietism.[104]

The most famous theme in *Being and Nothingness* was Sartre's distinction between *pour-soi*, being for itself, and *en-soi*, being in itself, a distinction which corresponds roughly to the difference between human existence and

[103] Marcuse, "Existentialism: Remarks on Jean-Paul Sartre's *L'Être et le néant*," *Philosophy and Phenomenological Research*, VIII, 3 (March, 1948), 311.

[104] *Ibid.*, pp. 335–36. The German translation of Marcuse's review, published in 1965, contained a new final paragraph in which he acknowledged that his negative evaluation of Sartre in 1948 had been premature. Evidently the *Critique of Dialectical Reason*, as well as Sartre's personal commitment to "radical opposition," prompted Marcuse to second thoughts about *Being and Nothingness*. Cf. *Kultur und Gesellschaft II* (Frankfurt am Main, 1965), pp. 83–84.

the existence of things. Sartre urged man to embrace the *pour-soi* character of his existence, his capacity for action, decision, and consciousness, and to resist the strong inclination to fall back into the passive, semiconscious existence characteristic of things. Marcuse did not at all care for this line of argument, because it served to rationalize the compulsive need to perform, to be productive, which capitalism had instilled in modern man. He noted, however, that in the passages of *Being and Nothingness* dealing with sexuality, Sartre presented an analysis which contradicted the conformist implications of the *pour-soi/en-soi* distinction. According to Sartre, in sexual desire one becomes very much like a thing; consciousness is dulled and the ego abandons its incessant "projects" and performances in order to give in passively to pleasure. Marcuse seized on this piece of analysis as a portent of the revolutionary force of sexuality. The sexual act and the attitudes associated with it subverted the entire psychological structure of capitalism:

> The *"desire sexuel"* reveals its object as stripped of all the attitudes, gestures, and affiliations which make it a standardized instrument, reveals the "body as flesh" and thereby "as fascinating revelation of facticity." Enslavement and repression are cancelled, not in the sphere of purposeful "projective" activity, but in the "body lived as flesh," in the "web of inertia."[105]

Marcuse was well aware that in arguing for the revolutionary significance of sexual passivity, he had in effect sanctioned a kind of reification. Both human happiness, as a purely psychological problem, and the undoing of the

[105] *Ibid.*, p. 327.

established economic order seemed to be linked to man's capacity to be "thinglike." Marcuse candidly admitted that this was in fact reification, but of a liberating variety: "Reification no longer serves to perpetuate exploitation and toil but is in its entirety determined by the 'pleasure principle.' "[106] This suggestion was not further elaborated in the article of 1948, but the notion of a passivity or purposelessness which is good was to reappear in *Eros and Civilization*. And, obviously, the use of the Freudian category "pleasure principle" in the critique of *Being and Nothingness* was a clear indication of the direction in which Marcuse was moving.

V

It is of course Marcuse the author of *Eros and Civilization* who must be the principal subject of analysis in this study of the Freudian Left. Neither the works which preceded *Eros and Civilization* nor those which followed it were in any sense sufficiently explicit in their Freudianism to qualify Marcuse as a major representative of the radical tradition in psychoanalysis. Marcuse's purpose in *Eros and Civilization* was to demonstrate that beneath the apparent pessimism and conservatism of Freud's thought was an underlying critical tendency—Marcuse called it "the hidden trend in psychoanalysis"[107]—which contained both a crushing indictment of the established civili-

[106] *Ibid.*, p. 328.
[107] Marcuse, *Eros and Civilization* (2nd ed.; Boston, 1966), pp. 11, 20.

zation and a promise of ultimate liberation. He proposed to reverse the prevailing interpretation of Freud which took as the central message of psychoanalysis the notion that civilization was necessarily repressive. Marcuse was fully aware that the neo-Freudians claimed to have already accomplished this task—to have rescued Freud from his own pessimistic and unhistorical presuppositions. He thus set out to distinguish his own reinterpretation of Freud from the revisions propounded by Erich Fromm and his associates. Although his critique of neo-Freudianism appeared as an "Epilogue" to *Eros and Civilization*, it had been published earlier in article form,[108] and in terms of the evolution of Marcuse's thinking about Freud, the critique of revisionism should more logically have appeared as a "Prologue."

Marcuse was (and still is) extremely effective as a critic. Nowhere was this more apparent than in his dissection of neo-Freudianism. The critique was unrelenting and utterly devastating. By comparison Erich Fromm's attempts to defend himself and his fellow neo-Freudians in the columns of *Dissent* were rather feeble.[109] Marcuse showed that the revisionists had arrived at their ameliorative conclusions by abandoning the hard, unpleasant facts of Freud's depth psychology: the preponderant role of sexuality in human psychology, the function of the unconscious, the primacy of childhood, the death instinct, and

---

[108] Marcuse, "The Social Implications of Freudian 'Revisionism,'" *Dissent*, II, 3 (Summer, 1955), 221–40.
[109] Erich Fromm, "The Human Implications of Instinctual 'Radicalism,'" *Dissent*, II, 4 (Autumn, 1955), 342–49. Cf. also Marcuse, "A Reply to Erich Fromm," *Dissent*, III, 1 (Winter, 1956), 79–81; Fromm, "A Counter-Rebuttal," *ibid.*, pp. 81–83.

the theory of the primal crime. They were thus guilty of
both intellectual cowardice and theoretical shallowness.
The systematic philosopher in Marcuse reacted violently
against the eclectic or additive character of neo-Freudian
theory, the refusal to treat theoretical issues with the rigor
he felt such matters deserved. He had no tolerance for the
revisionists' putative common sense, nor for their inveterate pluralism—what might be called the "yes but" character of neo-Freudian theory: "There is . . . the laboring of
the obvious, of everyday wisdom. . . . Freud was right;
life is bad, repressive, destructive—but it isn't *so* bad,
repressive, destructive. There are also the constructive,
productive aspects. Society is not only this, but also that;
man is not only against himself but also for himself."[110]
In particular Marcuse objected to the revisionists' claim to
have "added" a sociological dimension to Freud's psychology; he objected both because of their apparent igno-
rance of the profoundly sociological character of Freud's
thought, and because of their unsystematic notion that a
social dimension could be tacked on an individual psychology. In Freud's theory, he insisted, the sociological
dimension was included and developed in the basic categories, whereas in revisionist Freudianism it appeared
under the guise of "sociological aspects"—as "incompre-
hended, external factors." In general, then, Marcuse regretted the "decline of theory" in the revisionist schools.[111]

Marcuse argued that in abandoning the critical concepts of Freud's psychology, the revisionists had also
implied that the problem of human unhappiness was a

[110] *Eros and Civilization,* p. 250.
[111] *Ibid.*

great deal less serious than it had appeared to Freud, and consequently that it admitted of a fairly easy solution. If sexuality, for example, did not play the central constitutional role attributed to it by Freud, then obviously the conflict between the individual's pursuit of pleasure and society's demand for useful productivity (Freud would say sublimation) was easily minimized. The revisionists' insistence on psychoanalyzing the "whole personality," rather than the mere "biological" facts of sexuality, achieved precisely such a minimalization of the conflict between individual and society.[112] For Marcuse it was another example of the repressive spiritualization of human freedom and happiness characteristic of Western thought in general. Freud, on the contrary, was at one with the materialistic refusal to translate bodily deprivation into a moral or mental problem.[113]

Marcuse argued that the neo-Freudians had further obscured the dimensions of human alienation by shifting the focus of their psychology away from Freud's nearly exclusive emphasis on early childhood. For Marcuse Freud's stress on early childhood underlined the superficial character of the individual and societal diversities emphasized by the revisionists, infancy being "the formative period of the universal fate of the individual."[114] Actually, Freud's focus on childhood did not lead him to minimize individual differences, but he certainly was preoccupied with the necessarily repressed character of all civilized men; as Marcuse expressed it: "Behind all the

[112] *Ibid.*, pp. 247–48, 251, 267.
[113] *Ibid.*, pp. 265, 268–70; "Existentialism . . . ," pp. 332–33.
[114] *Eros and Civilization*, pp. 253–54.

differences among the historical forms of society, Freud saw the basic inhumanity common to all of them, and the repressive controls which perpetuate, in the instinctual structure itself, the domination of man by man."[115]

Thus the revisionists' apparently progressive demand for a "dynamic" conception of society, one sensitive to the variations among cultures, was in fact reactionary. It ignored the repressive common denominators uniting all societies. Indeed, the revisionists' very stylish insistence on the influence of "social conditions" in the formation of personality was, in Marcuse's mind, "sociologically and psychologically far more inconsequential than Freud's 'neglect' of these conditions."[116] It drew attention to the superficial differences in personality which resulted from varying social conditions, while ignoring the profoundly repressive impact of all historical forms of society. Similarly, in discarding the death instinct, the revisionists had once again opted for a comfortable optimism, avoiding the critical thrust of Freud's concept, which "revealed the hidden unconscious tie which binds the oppressed to their oppressors."[117]

Having shown that the neo-Freudians were guilty of theoretical sloppiness and of stripping Freud's theory of its critical bite, Marcuse concluded his critique by demonstrating that the political and social radicalism of the revisionists was thoroughly illusory. At a deeper level neo-Freudian theory, such as it was, remained committed to the repressive values of the capitalist order. Marcuse argued that despite their criticism of specific institutional

[115] *Ibid.*, p. 257.
[116] *Ibid.*, p. 265.
[117] *Ibid.*, p. 270.

arrangements and patterns of behavior, the revisionists continued to espouse the idealistic values which rationalized the exploitation and alienation characteristic of capitalism. This was reprehensible first of all because it was utterly arbitrary from a theoretical point of view—another example of the theoretical shabbiness of revisionism.[118] Moreover, the specific content of revisionist ethics was the old roster of Protestant-capitalist virtues: productivity, achievement, responsibility, respect for one's fellowmen, inner strength, and integrity. "Fromm revives all the time-honored values of idealistic ethics as if nobody had ever demonstrated their conformist and repressive features."[119] Revisionist social criticism was, in the last analysis, directed only at surface phenomena of the market economy, leaving the basic ideological and psychological premises of the criticized society virtually untouched.

In contrast to the neo-Freudians, then, Marcuse proposed to undertake a genuinely radical reinterpretation of Freud. He would neither avoid the unpleasant psychological facts discovered by Freud nor espouse any easy solution to the problems posed by those facts. In true Hegelian fashion, Marcuse's reinterpretation was thor-

---

[118] *Ibid.*, p. 250: "There is . . . the distinction between good and bad, constructive and destructive (according to Fromm: productive and unproductive, positive and negative), which is not derived from any theoretical principle but simply taken from the prevalent ideology. For this reason, the distinction is merely eclectic, extraneous to theory, and tantamount to the conformist slogan 'Accentuate the positive.' "

[119] *Ibid.*, pp. 258, 260–62, 265.

oughly dialectical. He began by accepting Freud's most extreme, and apparently most pessimistic, psychological assumptions: the unparalleled importance of sexuality, the primary significance of the unconscious and repression, and, finally, the hypothesis of a death instinct. He even employed, although not always consistently or in the sense intended by Freud, such unpopular notions as the primal crime, the ontogenetic/phylogenetic parallel, and the hydraulic conception of libidinal energy. Yet he managed to reach conclusions which were even more "positive" than those imagined by the revisionists. It is this sense of the dialectical emergence of human fulfillment out of the depths of depravity and oppression which gives *Eros and Civilization* its uncanny dramatic impact, a quality which in my reading is to be encountered in equal degree only in Marx's *Capital.*

The mention of Marx is intended as more than an idle comparison. He was clearly the unacknowledged hero of *Eros and Civilization.* That Marcuse never mentioned Marx's name in the book was an extraordinary feat of legerdemain. It is my contention that the underlying tactic of *Eros and Civilization* was to bring Freudian theory into line with the categories of Marxism. This endeavor did not result in the reduction of Freud to Marx; Marcuse honestly felt that psychoanalysis opened up dimensions of criticism unanticipated in Marxian theory. But as one reads and rereads *Eros and Civilization,* one is inevitably impressed by the systematic fashion in which Marcuse translated the unhistorical, psychological categories of Freud's thought into the eminently historical and political categories of Marxism. It is precisely this synthesis of Freud and Marx which I intend to emphasize in the following pages.

In defending Freud against his neo-Freudian critics, Marcuse argued that Freud's theory was "in its very substance 'sociological,'" and that it required "no new cultural or sociological orientation . . . to reveal this substance."[120] This claim was somewhat misleading, because Marcuse's own reinterpretation of psychoanalytic theory in fact depended on the introduction of several important historical and sociological distinctions. Marcuse implied that these distinctions were introduced only to reinforce the essentially historical character of Freud's own hypotheses. However, Marcuse's distinctions had the effect of transforming what I believe were thoroughly unhistorical perceptions—the notion, for example, that civilization was always and inevitably repressive—into historical ones, thereby enabling Marcuse to correlate psychoanalytic theory with the presuppositions of Marxism.

The two most important concepts which Marcuse elaborated in *Eros and Civilization* were surplus repression and the performance principle. The notion of surplus repression was meant to introduce a historical dimension into Freud's general equation of civilization and repression. Surplus repression denoted the *quantitative* restrictions on sexuality which resulted from economic and political domination.[121] This concept in effect united Freud's hydraulic theory of psychic energy with an essentially Reichian notion of the sexual component of political

[120] *Ibid.*, pp. 5, 16.
[121] *Ibid.*, pp. 35, 37.

and economic rule. Moreover, Marcuse's terminology clearly revealed that surplus repression was meant to be identified with Marx's surplus value—that is, the *quantitative* measure of human exploitation under capitalism. While admitting that Freud was correct in recognizing a certain minimal amount of repression as the necessary concomitant of civilization, Marcuse argued that a good deal of sexual repression was made necessary by the particular historical form of civilization. Indeed, Marcuse insisted that the *larger* portion of sexual repression in modern civilization was in fact surplus repression, repression in the service of domination.[122] The crucial significance of Marcuse's distinction between basic repression and surplus repression was that it opened up, at the theoretical level at least, a way out of Freud's unhappy equation of civilization with repression. In theory, modern society might be relieved of its repressive character without at the same time falling back into barbarism and chaos—without dissolving the libidinal cement which holds society together.

Marcuse traversed this same theoretical ground, now from a *qualitative* point of view, with his distinction between the reality principle and the performance principle. Freud's own distinction between the two principles of mental functioning, the pleasure principle and the reality principle, corresponded roughly to the difference between unrepressed behavior on the one hand and repressed, civilized behavior on the other. The reality principle was thus the rubric under which civilization

[122] *Ibid.*, p. 155.

emerged.[123] Marcuse admitted the legitimacy of Freud's distinction, but he argued that in the modern period, under capitalist domination, the reality principle had assumed a particular form which demanded greater or, to be precise, more varied repression than was in fact necessary for the continued survival of civilization per se.[124] The performance principle was the name which Marcuse gave to this specific historical variant of the reality principle.

Like surplus repression, which could be correlated with Marx's essentially quantitative notion of surplus value, the performance principle, Marcuse implied, corresponded to Marx's *qualitative* characterization of existence under capitalism, namely the notions of alienation and reification: "Under the rule of the performance principle, body and mind are made into instruments of alienated labor; they can function as such instruments only if they renounce the freedom of the libidinal subject-object which the human organism primarily is and desires."[125] To be sure, Marcuse's performance principle was a more inclusive concept than either alienation or reification. It incorporated elements of Weber's Protestant ethic (the irrational psychological need to perform, to work for work's own sake) as well as the salient features of modern mass society analysis (the technique of mass manipulation and the organization of leisure by the communica-

---

[123] Freud, "Formulations on the Two Principles of Mental Functioning," in *The Standard Edition of the Complete Psychological Works of Sigmund Freud*, James Strachey, ed. (London, 1953–1966), XII, 218–26.
[124] *Eros and Civilization*, p. 124.
[125] *Ibid.*, p. 46.

tions and entertainment industries).[126] But at the heart of the concept was Marx's notion of the transformation of men into things, alienated from the products of their labor, from the labor process itself, and from their fellowmen.[127]

The distinction between quantity and quality was carried over into the analysis of sexuality as well. I have already noted that Marcuse introduced the concept of surplus repression to designate a quantitative dimension of sexual repression made necessary by the interests of domination. In this instance his argument was identical to Reich's. The qualitative notion of the performance principle was correlated with a qualitative analysis of the sexual repression made necessary by political and economic domination. Here Marcuse clearly went beyond Reich. Indeed, it was this qualitative analysis of sexuality under capitalism which represented the most original moment in Marcuse's book.

The performance principle involved not merely an unnecessary repression of sexuality per se, but of a particular type of sexuality, namely the secondary or partial sexual drives. Freud had argued that sexuality originated in a generalized bodily eroticism. For the infant the entire body was a source of sexual pleasure. However, in the first five years of life, this generalized eroticism was concentrated in or organized about particular bodily organs: the mouth, the anus, and finally the genitals. Freud seemed to imply that there was a kind of biological logic which accounted for the progression of sexual organizations

[126] *Ibid.*, pp. 46–48.
[127] Marx, "Alienated Labor," in Fromm, *Marx's Concept of Man*, pp. 93–109.

from the generalized eroticism of earliest infancy to the genital sexuality of adolescence and adulthood.[128] Marcuse did not deny the underlying biological rationale of this progression (and in this point his analysis was less radical than Norman O. Brown's), but he insisted that the progression was accentuated and perverted by the performance principle.[129] The performance principle led to the nearly complete desexualization of the pregenital erotogenic zones, indeed of the body in general, and reinforced the total genitalization of sexuality. This desexualization of the body resulted in a radical reduction of man's potential for pleasure. Marcuse explained the historical connection between "genital tyranny" and the performance principle in an extraordinarily ingenious piece of reasoning: libido became concentrated in one part of the body, namely the genitals, in order to leave the rest of the body free for use as an instrument of labor: "The normal progress to genitality has been organized in such a way that the partial impulses and their 'zones' were all but desexualized in order to conform to the requirements of a specific social organization of the human existence."[130]

[128] Freud, *Three Essays on the Theory of Sexuality, The Standard Edition* . . . , VII, especially the second essay.

[129] *Eros and Civilization*, pp. 38–41.

[130] *Ibid.*, pp. 38, 48. Marcuse presented several other arguments to explain the connection between desexualization and the performance principle. For example: "Smell and taste give, as it were, unsublimated pleasure *per se* (and unrepressed disgust). They relate (and separate) individuals immediately, without the generalized and conventionalized forms of consciousness, morality, aesthetics. Such immediacy is incompatible with the effectiveness of organized *domination*, with a society which 'tends to isolate people, to put distance between them, and to prevent spontaneous relation-

The obvious conclusion to be drawn from this analysis of the fate of sexuality under capitalist domination was that resexualization of the body was the goal of human fulfillment. Mankind longed to return to a state of "polymorphous perversity," in which the entire body would once again become a source of sexual pleasure.[131] Marcuse thus criticized Reich, although in a sympathetic fashion, for assuming that the object of human happiness was an intensification of genital sexuality.[132] Such a notion was sexually reactionary, because it left the body essentially desexualized and susceptible to further economic and political exploitation. Only the resexualized body, the polymorphously perverse body, resisted transformation into an instrument of labor. In accordance with this line of reasoning, Marcuse argued that sexual perversion needed to be regarded in an entirely new fashion. He did not defend homosexuality in the sentimental and patronizing manner of liberal ideology. Instead he emphasized the critical function of sexual perversion: "The perversions . . . express rebellion against the subjugation of sexuality under the order of procreation, and against the institutions which guarantee this order."[133] Sexual devi-

---

ships and the "natural" animal-like expressions of such relations.' The pleasure of the proximity senses plays on the erotogenic zones of the body—and does so only for the sake of pleasure. Their unrepressed development would eroticize the organism to such an extent that it would counteract the desexualization of the organism required by its social utilization as an instrument of labor" (p. 39).

[131] *Ibid.*, p. 49.

[132] *Ibid.*, p. 239.

[133] *Ibid.*, p. 49; cf. pp. 49–51, 109, 171, 252–53.

ance represented in particular a protest against genital tyranny. In a certain sense, then, the social function of the homosexual was analogous to that of the critical philosopher.

I find further evidence of Marcuse's attempt to synthesize Freudian and Marxian categories in his reinterpretation of Freud's primal-crime hypothesis. He stated without qualification that he intended to use Freud's hypothesis for its symbolic value only, making no pretense to competence in anthropological matters.[134] In Marcuse's hands the primal crime became a kind of capitalist allegory. Although he did not state so explicitly, he obviously transformed Freud's primal father into the capitalist entrepreneur, and the band of brothers into the European proletariat. The most significant result of this transmutation of Freud's theory was that it moved the focal point of the drama away from the revolt of the brothers, which marked the beginning of civilization for Freud, and back to the establishment of the paternal dictatorship. For Marcuse civilization began not with the revolt against paternal tyranny, but with the founding of the father's rule over his sons. This was the historical moment at which the reality principle (or, more accurately, the performance principle) replaced the pleasure principle.[135]

Marcuse did not ignore the brothers' revolt altogether. It became for him a symbol of the unsuccessful proletarian revolution, and he suggested that the guilt felt by the brothers following the murder was a product not

[134] *Ibid.*, p. 60.
[135] *Ibid.*, p. 15.

merely of their love for the father, but also of their sense of having betrayed the revolution in reinstating the paternal tyranny and the paternal morality under the guise of the totem religion. The brothers' guilt was the guilt which the proletariat bore for its inability to carry the revolution through to a successful culmination.[136] This analogy also suggested that the historical failure of the proletarian revolution was as much a matter of psychology as of political and economic power. Because the proletariat still bore the psychological scars of the paternal-capitalist order, it cooperated in the reestablishment of the system of domination. Even in the moment of revolution, it continued to identify with the power against which it revolted.[137]

Marcuse agreed with Freud that the most important result of the primal dictatorship was to exclude the sons from sexual access to the sisters and the mother. And he stated explicitly that the economic corollary of this sexual isolation was that the sons bore the burden of work within the primal horde. Excluded from sexual pleasure, they were "free" to channel their instinctual energy into unpleasurable but necessary activities.[138] Thus the matter of sexual repression was clearly linked to economic subordination—and therefore to the rise of capitalism. But Marcuse was unable to explain whether the father established his economic domination *because* he succeeded in excluding the sons from the supreme pleasure (as Reich

[136] *Ibid.*, pp. 66–67.
[137] *Ibid.*, pp. 90–91.
[138] *Ibid.*, pp. 61–62.

would have it), or whether sexual repression followed from economic subordination.[139] Furthermore, he was not able to connect his analysis of the primal crime with his notion of the repression of secondary sexual impulses. The sexual suppression initiated by the primal father pertained apparently to genital sexuality alone, and in fact Freud's suggestion that the brother clan was held together by homosexual ties implied that only the secondary drives survived the paternal revolution. Marcuse could thus use Freud's hypothesis to substantiate only the quantitative restraints imposed on sexuality by the interests of domination, and not the qualitative dimension of repression, which had been the most original feature of his analysis of the performance principle.

I think it important to remark at this point that in the entire analysis of the interrelation of sexual repression and political domination, Marcuse made practically no mention of the family. Even the primal family was treated as a symbolic representation of sociological forces. In this respect, as in his treatment of the partial drives, his analysis diverged sharply from Reich's. For Reich the patriarchal family was the specific mechanism through which the repressive features of the social order were transmitted to the individual. Marcuse, on the contrary, felt that the peculiar development of European and American civilization in the twentieth century had effectively eliminated the family as a vehicle of repression. In the overadministered civilization of the 1950's, the repressive society acted directly on the individual. The repressive father had been edged out by the bureaucracy and the mass

139 *Ibid.*, p. 61.

media.[140] And with the "decline of the social function of the family"[141] came a comparable diminution of the psychological significance of the Oedipus complex. The Oedipus complex stood at the heart of Freud's individual psychology and of his social psychology as well; civilization began with a historical dramatization of the eternal triangle of father, mother, and child. By way of contrast, Marcuse hardly mentioned the Oedipus complex in *Eros and Civilization*, except to deny its importance.[142]

It was not Marcuse's intention in *Eros and Civilization* simply to dissect the relation between political domination and sexual repression—to augment Marx's classical analysis of exploitation with the critical insights of psychoanalysis. Similarly, the message he wished to convey was not merely the desirability of abolishing sexual repression (or surplus sexual repression). The tone of *Eros and Civilization* was much more urgent than this. Hanging over repressive civilization was not only the prospect of continued, even augmented, unpleasure and toil, but also the threat of self-destruction. Moreover, Marcuse felt that the possibility of self-annihilation was intimately connected with the very repressiveness—that is, sexual repressiveness—of the established civilization. It was this perception which led him to Freud's concept of the death instinct.

The death instinct was easily one of the most unpopular

[140] *Ibid.*, pp. 96–100.

[141] *Ibid.*, p. 96.

[142] *Ibid.*, p. 204. "The Oedipus complex, although the primary source and model of neurotic conflicts, is certainly not the central cause of the discontents in civilization, and not the central obstacle for their removal."

of Freud's conceptions, and admittedly the clinical evidence for it was meager. Yet I must confess that I share Marcuse's fascination with the idea; it has about it an undeniable philosophic grandness and mystery. Destructiveness seems to have reached a qualitatively new stage in the twentieth century, with two world wars, mass exterminations, and, of course, Hiroshima. I sense that Marcuse felt the need for some conceptual means with which to come to terms with twentieth-century violence, and Freud's death instinct fulfilled that need ideally. The notion suited Marcuse's propensity for ambitious abstractions—his residual Hegelianism—and his sense of outrage and horror at the historical events he saw unfolding before him.[143]

In the first chapter of *Eros and Civilization,* Marcuse presented the results of his confrontation with Freud's theory of the instincts. The analysis was brilliant, but the outcome curiously inconclusive. Marcuse correctly emphasized Freud's proclivity for dualistic conceptions and described the theoretical process through which Freud's early dualism of Love and Hunger gave way to the final dualism of Eros and Thanatos, sexuality and death. However, the most impressive aspect of Marcuse's analysis was the manner in which he explored the ambivalent character of Freud's final dualism. He noted the regressive tendency common to both the erotic and destructive instincts, the fact that Eros seeks to lower the level of psychic energy (the highest sexual pleasure of the orgasm being in fact the result of a sudden release of pent-up libidinal energy), while Thanatos strives to return to the

[143] *Ibid.,* pp. 4, 87, 101–2.

quiescence of the inorganic world. The dualism of Eros and Thanatos was thus constantly threatening to turn into "a monism of death."[144] This notion of the underlying unity of the instincts naturally appealed to Marcuse the inveterate antidualist. Yet in the last analysis he stressed that despite this monistic tendency, Freud continued to insist on the fundamental antagonism of the two instincts:

> The primacy of the Nirvana principle, the terrifying convergence of pleasure and death, is dissolved as soon as it is established. No matter how universal the regressive inertia of organic life, the instincts strive to attain their objective in fundamentally different modes. The difference is tantamount to that of sustaining and destroying life. Out of the common nature of instinctual life develop two antagonistic instincts.[145]

Marcuse chose to side with Freud's dualistic tendencies for purposes of his own argument, and here he diverged sharply from Norman O. Brown. Moreover, this choice was, I think, quite uncharacteristic and perhaps inconsistent with his long-established philosophical prejudices.

Marcuse adopted Freud's instinctual dualism in order to argue that the future of humanity depended on man's ability to reverse the basically repressive trend of modern civilization. He viewed civilization as a dialectical struggle between the forces of Love and Death, in which the defeat of Thanatos could be assured only through the liberation of Eros. Marcuse adopted Freud's hydraulic or

[144] *Ibid.*, p. 28; cf. pp. 23–29.
[145] *Ibid.*, p. 25. Permission to reprint this passage from *Eros and Civilization* granted by Beacon Press, © 1955, 1966, and Routledge & Kegan Paul Ltd.

economic conception of psychic energy—in a rather un-usual form, to be sure—in order to argue that there was a quantitative interaction between libidinal and destructive energies in the evolution of civilization. Destructive energy could manifest itself only in the "space" made available by the withdrawal of libidinal energy. If de-structiveness was to be eliminated or curtailed, it was necessary that libido not be attenuated, not siphoned off into the various sublimations, such as work. Only when libido remained strong and unsublimated—only when sexuality was given free reign, both in the quantitative sense of a more intense sexual life and in the qualitative sense of a more varied (polymorphous) sexuality—could destructiveness be held to a minimum. Marcuse termed this libidinal economy the "dialectic of civilization," and it was his main concern in *Eros and Civilization* to demon-strate that modern civilization, under the aegis of the performance principle, was in fact stifling Eros. It was thus hell-bent on its own destruction.[146]

It is important to note that Marcuse's analysis of "the dialectic of civilization" differed significantly from that suggested by Freud in *Civilization and Its Discontents*. There are in fact passages in Freud's writings which seem to imply the psychic process outlined by Marcuse, but for the most part Freud's own analysis diverged sharply from Marcuse's. For Freud the antagonism of Eros and Thanatos implied that the arrest of destructiveness de-pended not on the liberation of Eros, but on its repression. The only force which could counteract man's hostility to his fellow man was love. However, it was not unrepressed

[146] *Ibid.*, pp. 54, 80–83, 139.

sexual love which held man's destructive energies in check, but rather its opposite: repressed, "aim-inhibited," or sublimated love—in a word, "affection." The libidinal energy with which these affective ties were created was *withdrawn* from the realm of overt sexuality. For Freud, then, the curtailment of destruction, which made civilization possible in the first place, implied not sexual permissiveness but sexual restrictions.[147] Marcuse's argument that only unrepressed sexuality could counter the force of destructiveness thus contradicted Freud's analysis of the libidinal dynamics of civilization.

Marcuse also seemed to misinterpret Freud's remarks concerning the increased sense of guilt which accompanies the advance of civilization. He equated this sense of guilt with his own conception of increased destructiveness.[148] But for Freud guilt represented the economic antithesis of destructiveness. Modern man felt guilty precisely because he was *not* able to destroy. In economic terms, guilt represented the new form which destructiveness assumed when it was denied expression in the world of interpersonal relations. It was an inward manifestation of Thanatos, in which the destructive energies which would naturally have been directed against other men were in fact directed against one's own ego.[149] I do not mean to imply in this comparison that I feel Freud was right and Marcuse wrong in their respective analyses of the "dialectic of civilization," but only to indicate that

[147] Freud, *Civilization and Its Discontents, The Standard Edition* . . . , XXI, 103–4, 108–16.
[148] *Eros and Civilization*, p. 78.
[149] Freud, *Civilization and Its Discontents*, pp. 123–39.

Marcuse did not explicitly acknowledge the manner in which his own analysis diverged from Freud's.

VI

Eros and Civilization contained a great deal more than an analysis of the sexual and political dilemma in which modern man finds himself. It was also a book of prophecy, outlining in a general fashion the contours of a nonrepressive civilization and the intellectual and practical means by which such a civilization might be realized. Marcuse defended the possibility of a nonrepressive civilization on two fronts, one theoretical, the other historical. In historical terms he attempted to identify certain trends in the development of contemporary civilization which moved in the direction of a nonrepressive order, or created the historical preconditions for such an order. At the level of theory, he tried to demonstrate how the inner logic of Freud's thought, and that of several other major nineteenth- and twentieth-century theorists, suggested a way out of the dilemma of repression.

Characteristically, Marcuse devoted much less attention to the historical trends facilitating a nonrepressive civilization than to the matter of demonstrating its theoretical legitimacy. Indeed, the historical component of his argument was fairly simple and straightforward. In brief, he argued that the development of technology had substantially eliminated the need for alienated labor, and that automation had brought us close to the point where work could be disposed of altogether. If the economic apparatus was all but completely self-sustaining, it followed that there was no longer any *technical* need for the kind of sexual repression which had accompanied the rise of modern capitalism. Men's bodies could once again become organs of pleasure rather than of toil. The resexualization of the body would revitalize the libidinal energies of mankind and assure the ultimate triumph of Eros over Thanatos. The imminent possibility of self-annihilation would thus be effectively eliminated. In short, Marcuse argued that the performance principle had created the historical preconditions for its own abolition.[150]

I do not intend to imply that Marcuse's treatment of the historical trends leading to a nonrepressive society was in any sense perfunctory. In later writings, particularly *One-Dimensional Man*, he devoted increasing attention to this matter. But I want to emphasize that *Eros and Civilization* was for the most part a book of theory, moving along at a high level of abstraction. Even the treatment of historical material was cast in categorical language, and theoretical matters were taken very seriously indeed. Marcuse seemed to imply that the mere conceptualization of a particular historical possibility (such as that of a nonrepressive civilization) represented more than half the battle. The simple fact that the writings of Hegel, Marx, Freud, and others contained such splendid indictments of the existing order, such trenchant arguments for a nonrepressive society, tended to make Marcuse speak as if the new order were already an actuality. Theories were forever "suggesting," "symbolizing," "envisioning," "envisaging," "indicating," and "betokening" the nonrepressive

[150] *Eros and Civilization*, pp. 92–93, 101–2, 105, 129–31.

civilization about to descend upon us. In other words, Marcuse often intimated that the possibility was on the verge of becoming a reality *because of* the various theoretical indictments and promises contained in the writings of Hegel, Freud, Schiller, Nietzsche and other critics.

I have already presented the major theses of Marcuse's critical reinterpretation of Freudian theory. By distinguishing between repression and surplus repression, reality principle and performance principle, Marcuse was able to show that Freud's equation of civilization with repression was premature. He thus liberated the critical tendencies in Freud's thought from their pessimistic and unhistorical fetters, and Freud emerged as the great twentieth-century prophet of a nonrepressive civilization. Not even Freud's death instinct had blunted Marcuse's optimism, since he had shown that aggression could be held in check through the release of erotic energies. It remained only to eliminate one final stumbling block: Freud's theory of sublimation. This theory suggested that civilization (both in the sense of man's collective existence per se, and in the sense of a series of economic, political, and cultural projects) was based on the suppression of sexuality. According to Freud, the affective ties which bound men to one another required a curtailment of the erotic life, and the "work" of civilization was in fact nothing other than sublimated sexual energy.[151] As the apologist of a nonrepressive civilization, Marcuse was thus forced to come to terms with the pessimistic implications of the theory of sublimation.

Marcuse treated the problem of sublimation as at bot-

[151] *Ibid.*, pp. 81–83.

tom the problem of work. Physical and mental labor was the chief manifestation of the cultural enterprise, and therefore if one could resolve the antagonism of sexuality and work, one might be able to escape the unhappy conclusion that culture necessarily involved a vast attenuation of sexuality. Marcuse tried to suggest such a resolution, first by arguing that automation was rapidly diminishing the amount of energy which had to be invested in work, and secondly by setting forth the possibility of what he termed "nonrepressive sublimation." I find the argument concerning automation perfectly consistent with the precepts of psychoanalytic theory. Marcuse envisioned a radical reduction of the working day, which would occur when production and distribution were organized "in such a manner that the least time is spent for making all necessities available to all members of society."[152] He admitted that such a reduction of the working day would involve "a considerable decrease in the standard of living prevalent today in the most advanced industrial countries,"[153] but he regarded this decrease as in and of itself desirable, since the demand for automobiles, television sets, airplanes was a manifestation of repressive affluence. The vast reduction in the time and energy devoted to work would permit both a greater intensity and a greater variety of erotic expression.[154]

Marcuse's complementary notion of nonrepressive sublimation fitted rather badly with the economic conception of psychic energy which he had been prepared to accept

[152] *Ibid.*, pp. 195.
[153] *Ibid.*, pp. 152–53.
[154] *Ibid.*, pp. 152–57.

in his analysis of the dialectic of civilization, and it is quite evident that Marcuse chose to adopt or discard the hydraulic metaphor as it suited the purposes of his argument. He based his case for nonrepressive sublimation on the assumption that the new erotic order would represent such a radical departure from the world of the performance principle that work itself would assume a new character. His hope was that work relations in the new order would take on the character of play relations, and he even suggested that work might become a form of erotic release: "If work were accompanied by a reactivation of pregenital polymorphous eroticism, it would tend to become gratifying in itself without losing its *work* content."[155] I find it difficult to imagine how work could ever be anything but work—that is, sublimation—even in a nonrepressive order, and I think Marcuse was on firmer ground when he demonstrated the possibility of a massive quantitative reduction in the working day, which would leave men free to devote an increasing number of hours to playful and erotic pursuits.

It was Freud's theory which, more explicitly than any other, suggested the possibility of a libidinal organization of society. However, Freud's was only one—albeit the most important—of several critical philosophies which Marcuse felt opened up the prospect of a nonrepressive order. I want to mention briefly his discussion of several other theorists, in particular Nietzsche, Fourier, and Schiller, whom he regarded as prophets of such an order. In terms of the argument of *Eros and Civilization*, Marcuse's treatment of these theorists was of course intended

[155] *Ibid.*, p. 215; cf. pp. 155, 157–58, 212–17, 220.

to lend added authority to the notion of a nonrepressive civilization. But from the more neutral viewpoint of the intellectual historian, his analysis can be regarded as an imaginative exploration of the erotic or Freudian themes in the thought of three major nineteenth-century intellectuals. He argued, in effect, that psychoanalysis was heir to a well-established tradition in European thought, regardless of whether or not Freud had been directly influenced by this tradition.

It was not difficult for Marcuse to discern a note of sexual protest in Nietzsche and Fourier. In Nietzsche's critique of Western rationalism, his insistence on Joy (*Lust*) and enjoyment as the measure of fulfillment, and his analysis of the bad conscience which results from denying the life instincts, Marcuse detected "an *erotic* attitude toward being."[156] Similarly, he argued that Fourier's peculiar brand of utopian socialism was based on a clear perception of the interdependence of political freedom and sexuality. Marcuse also found in Fourier a notion of the transformation of work into pleasure (*travail attrayant*), which he identified with his own concept of nonrepressive sublimation.[157]

More interesting, and certainly more ingenious, was the manner in which Marcuse turned Schiller into a proponent of sexual release. He argued that Schiller's concept of aesthetic education stressed the impulsive, erotic, and playful character of the aesthetic attitude, which would

[156] *Ibid.*, pp. 122, 121–24.
[157] *Ibid.*, pp. 217–18. This theme in Fourier's thought has been emphasized by Marcuse's one-time colleague at Brandeis, Frank Manuel, particularly in his *Prophets of Paris* (Cambridge, Massachusetts, 1962).

serve to transform the repressive *political* order into one
of freedom and instinctual fulfillment. Schiller's sensuous
conception of reason represented a critique of "the reason
of domination," which had long held sway over Western
philosophy.[158] In effect, Marcuse had taken a second
look at the German intellectual revolution of the early
nineteenth century and found that Schiller rather than
Hegel was the true critical spirit of the movement.

Schiller's erotic aestheticism also embodied the critical
conception of art which Marcuse had articulated already
in the 1930's. *Eros and Civilization* further pursued this
theme through an analysis of certain literary archetypes
which served to undermine the repressive sexuality of the
established order. Marcuse stressed in particular the
Orphic and Narcissistic myths of Greek culture, contrasting them with the Prometheus legend ("the archetype-
hero of the performance principle")[159] as images of
erotic fulfillment and political liberation. Orpheus and
Narcissus had failed to become the cultural heroes of the
Western world precisely because they refused to accept
the constraints of the reality principle. Orpheus was "the
voice which does not command but sings,"[160] and Narcissus turned away from the world of productivity to the
voluptuous contemplation of his own body. Both were
classic embodiments of the critical function of art, the
unwillingness to accept the sexual deprivations and the
compulsive toil which have accompanied the progress of
civilization.

[158] *Ibid.,* pp. 111–12, 124, 179–82, 186–93.
[159] *Ibid.,* p. 161.
[160] *Ibid.,* pp. 162, 161–70.

Eros and Civilization rarely descended to the level of tactics. Marcuse considered the problem of how the non-repressive order was to be realized in only a few scattered passages. As tactician the usually bold and emphatic philosopher grew evasive and diffident. He toyed with the Platonic notion that the new order might be initiated by a dictatorship of the enlightened, but his sense of realism and his democratic commitments forced him to abandon this idea almost as he introduced it.[161] In the final pages of the book Marcuse spoke of the liberating function of memory, the *recherche du temps perdu,* which he equated with Freud's notion of the return of the repressed. He apparently hoped that memory might function as a tactical device for realizing the nonrepressive order. As with his suggestion of an enlightened vanguard, however, Marcuse quickly conceded that memory was not enough: "Remembrance is no real weapon unless it is translated into historical action."[162] In the last analysis, Marcuse offered no clear tactical program for the sexual revolution. He was no Lenin; indeed, he did not even share Reich's talents as a political and sexual activist. Ultimately *Eros and Civilization* remained a work of theory, but at its own chosen level of discourse it was, I feel, a powerful piece of critical analysis.

VII

At the beginning of this chapter I noted that *Eros and Civilization* shared much in common with another radical

[161] *Ibid.,* p. 225.
[162] *Ibid.,* p. 233.

Freudian critique of modern civilization, Norman O. Brown's *Life Against Death*. These two works have often been compared with one another, and they are indeed remarkably similar not only in the general point of view they espouse, but even in the particular Freudian concepts which they single out for special analysis. However, I have chosen in what follows to emphasize the very important differences which separate Brown from Marcuse, and I have done so in order to underline the particular strengths of *Eros and Civilization*.

Life Against Death is unquestionably a powerful book. Brown came to psychoanalysis from literature and the classics, rather than philosophy and political theory. *Life Against Death* is consequently more elegantly written than *Eros and Civilization*, and Brown was also able to employ literary authorities more effectively than Marcuse (himself no cultural philistine). There is a strong mystical strain in Brown's intellectual makeup, completely absent in Marcuse, and *Life Against Death* drew effectively on certain revolutionary themes in Western religious thought, most notably the body mysticism of Jakob Böhme and William Blake. Moreover, in some respects Brown explored the radical implications of psychoanalysis in a more rigorous and systematic fashion than Marcuse. He stated in the introduction to *Life Against Death* that he had not hesitated "to pursue new ideas to their ultimate 'mad' consequences, knowing that Freud too seemed mad."[163] And from a psychological point of view, his analysis was consistently more radical than Marcuse's.

[163] Norman O. Brown, *Life Against Death* (New York, 1959), p. xiv.

But if Brown was psychoanalytically more adventurous than Marcuse, he was at the same time more timid politically. Indeed, I have come to the conclusion that *Eros and Civilization* is a more persuasive piece of analysis than *Life Against Death* precisely because Marcuse succeeded, where Brown failed, in transforming psychoanalytic theory into historical and political categories. Marcuse alone managed to synthesize the legacy of Freud with the revolutionary historical criticism of Marx.

The similarities between Brown and Marcuse are at once obvious. Like Marcuse, Brown set out to show that the ultimate implications of psychoanalysis were critical rather than conservative. Similarly, he saw Freud's greatness in his ambitious metahistorical analysis of "the general neurosis of mankind."[164] Like Marcuse, Brown argued that modern man was sick with the burdens of sexual repression and uncontrolled aggression, and he sought to bring out the hidden trend in psychoanalysis which offered a way out of the dilemma of modern unhappiness—to uncover the promise of a nonrepressive civilization beneath Freud's manifest historical pessimism. Most important, Brown pursued the same dialectical tack which Marcuse had adopted, beginning his analysis with a wholehearted acceptance of the most radical and most discouraging of Freud's psychological assumptions: the all-pervasive role of sexuality and the irreducible fact of the death instinct. Here the similarities ended, however, and Brown in fact offered a highly individual analysis of the problems of sexuality and death, and an equally idiosyncratic solution to those problems.

[164] *Ibid.*, p. xiii.

Like Marcuse, Brown expounded in admirable fashion the underlying ambivalence of Freud's late instinctual dualism. Eros and Death were seen as antagonistic psychological principles which constantly threatened to collapse into one another. However, where Marcuse had chosen to emphasize the antithetical nature of the two instincts, Brown quite self-consciously opted to stress their underlying unity.[165] He did so because this tactic suggested a way of averting Freud's unhappy conclusion that aggression or destructiveness was inevitable.

One easily forgets, as Brown noted, that Freud did not in fact consider aggression a basic psychological fact. Aggression was rather a *secondary* manifestation of the more fundamental instinctual force, the death instinct. It was the external expression of an impulse originally directed against the self, i.e., the desire to die or to destroy oneself. Aggression thus became a problem because Eros could carry out its project of creating life only when the death instinct was frustrated in its original enterprise. In order that men might live (and love), they were inevitably forced to destroy, to direct the energies of the death instinct away from themselves onto their fellowmen.

Brown, however, argued that Freud was mistaken in this analysis of the dynamics of Life and Death. Freud's own discovery of the ultimate identity of the two instincts, their primordial union, implied there was no necessary antagonism between Eros and Thanatos. At a deeper level of psychic life, the two instincts existed in harmony with one another. Aggression was thus not the inevitable by-product of life.[166] The death instinct would

[165] *Ibid.*, pp. 77–91.
[166] *Ibid.*, pp. 99–101.

not need to be externalized in the form of destructiveness if men could recapture the original undifferentiated harmony of Life and Death. Brown clearly felt that men *could* learn to contain Death within Life. He called for an end to the "repression of death," or the "flight from death," which perpetuated aggression.[167] In short, men had to learn how to die, which meant, in more concrete psychological terms, learning how to grow old.[168]

This was a daring piece of analysis. As a solution to the problem of aggression it was light years away from that proposed by Marcuse. Marcuse, of course, had chosen to take Freud's dualism seriously, and this led him to formulate the problem of aggression in terms of a psychological and historical struggle between the forces of Life and the forces of Death. Using his particular version of the hydraulic argument, he envisioned a triumph over aggression resulting from the massive accumulation of erotic energy which would be released in a nonrepressive civilization. And this development was in turn a matter of politics and economics, of freeing Eros from the fetters of unnecessary repressive work. By way of contrast, Brown's solution to the problem of aggression implied an entirely different instinctual dynamic, stressing not instinctual antagonism but instinctual reconciliation. Moreover, Brown's solution was exclusively psychological; it was a matter of a new *attitude* toward death. It entailed no political or economic revolution.

An analogous contrast between Marcuse and Brown can be drawn from their treatment of sexuality. One is

[167] *Ibid.*, pp. 100, 109.
[168] *Ibid.*, p. 103.

impressed at first by the remarkable similarity in their respective analyses of sexual repression. Brown, like Marcuse, criticized Reich for misrepresenting the problem of repression as one of genital sexuality.[169] Man did not long for more and better orgasms, but rather for the anarchic and total sexuality of early infancy; a truly nonrepressive civilization was one in which sexuality would be allowed to reassume its polymorphous and "perverse" form.[170] However, Brown interpreted polymorphous perversity in a much more radical (and, I think, more consistent) fashion than did Marcuse. At the same time, he was unable to provide the kind of historical and economic explanation for the establishment of genital tyranny which one finds in *Eros and Civilization*. His argument was once again exclusively psychological.

Brown recognized that if undifferentiated sexuality were the ultimate measure of human happiness, then *any* form of sexual organization was already repressive. In general Marcuse had complained only of the tyranny of genital sexuality, suggesting that the pregenital libidinal organizations had to be reactivated in a nonrepressive civilization. But Brown insisted that the pregenital organizations were just as tyrannical as adult sexuality. The earlier organization of libidinal energy into oral, anal, and phallic syndromes was as foreign to the undifferentiated eroticism of early infancy as was the final tyranny of genitality. Brown was thus unwilling to accept Marcuse's characterization of the sexual deviant as a prophet of polymorphous perversity: "The adult sexual perversions,

[169] *Ibid.*, pp. 140–42.
[170] *Ibid.*, pp. 23–39.

like normal adult sexuality, are well-organized tyrannies: they too represent an exaggerated concentration on one of the many erotic potentialities present in the human body."[171] In a truly nonrepressive civilization sexuality would be completely undifferentiated. Not only would all parts of the body share equally in the release of libidinal energy, but even the distinction between male and female would pale into insignificance.[172] Brown thus took up the androgynous theme in the writings of Geza Roheim (whom Brown admired and quoted frequently throughout *Life Against Death*) and argued for a kind of sexual "perversion" which was much more extreme than anything Marcuse had imagined.

Polymorphous perversity was the original fact of human existence and the ultimate measure of psychic health. Brown then attempted to explain how it came to pass that mankind had abandoned his primeval happiness. He was unwilling to accept Freud's thesis of an innate biological dynamic which led from the undifferentiated sexuality of infancy, through the various pregenital organizations, to the final tyranny of adult genitality.[173] He suggested early in the book that the correct explanation was to be found in man's social history, in the "social organization which marks the transition from ape to man."[174] In fact, however, one looks in vain in *Life Against Death* for any historical analysis of the social and economic factors which might have initiated the organization of sexuality under the various tyrannies. Instead, Brown offered an

[171] *Ibid.*, p. 27.
[172] *Ibid.*, pp. 122–27, 131–34.
[173] *Ibid.*, p. 111.
[174] *Ibid.*, p. 24.

exclusively ontogenetic explanation of this process, and, moreover, one which I find inconsistent with the prophetic intentions of his larger argument.

Brown found the key to repressive differentiation in Freud's famous statement that "it was anxiety which produces repression and not, as I formerly believed, repression which produces anxiety."[175] Like Roheim, Brown considered the basic form of anxiety to be separation anxiety. Because the human infant experienced a prolonged period of dependency, the inevitable fact of separation presented itself in the form of a problem. Brown identified separation with death, the breakdown of that interdependent union of child and mother, child and universe, "which is the essence of life."[176] I find this identification of life with union and death with separation difficult to understand, but I don't think it was essential to Brown's argument. It was sufficient for him to identify anxiety with separation, and to show that separation caused anxiety because union had been so long and lovingly indulged. The child responded to the anxiety caused by separation through various projects to reestablish the original unity, projects which Brown identified as "flights from death," but which could have been described more simply as flights from separation.

These projects involved precisely the various organizations of libido which Brown characterized as repressive; they required abandoning the polymorphous perversity of earliest infancy—that undifferentiated eroticism which remained forever in the individual memory the sole ex-

[175] *Ibid.*, p. 112; Freud, *Inhibitions, Symptoms and Anxiety, The Standard Edition* . . . , XX, 108–9.
[176] *Ibid.*, p. 114.

perience of unqualified happiness. For example, in the oral project the child tried to overcome separation through "the hypercathexis of the act of suckling," reuniting itself with the mother by means of the mouth (and, in fantasy, by ingesting the mother entirely).[177] The anal project involved "symbolic manipulation of feces as a magic instrument for restoring communion with the mother."[178] Following Ferenczi's *Thalassa*, Brown interpreted the phallic project as "the genital re-establishment of the inter-uterine situation," that is, the attempt to be reunited with the mother through the penis, which was identified with the entire body.[179] All of these projects involved a reorganization of the libidinal economy, whereby sexual energy was transferred from the body in its entirety to a particular organ. Furthermore, all of the tyrannical organizations were self-imposed. The repressive differentiation of sexuality was not the result of some external force, least of all some social or economic exigency; in the last analysis repression was "self-repression."[180]

One must admire the rigor and imagination displayed in Brown's argument. However, in his analysis of the genesis of sexual differentiation he unwittingly subverted his larger purpose of demonstrating the real possibility of a nonrepressive organization of sexual life. If the tyrannical sexual organizations result from an inability to accept separation, or in Brown's own terms to accept death, and if this flight from separation is in turn based on the fact of

[177] *Ibid.*, p. 116.
[178] *Ibid.*
[179] *Ibid.*, p. 115.
[180] *Ibid.*, p. 112.

prolonged infantile dependence, then sexual repression appears to be a biological inevitability. The human animal is physically incapable of the early autonomy which animals enjoy, and if Roheim was correct, infantile dependency is growing progressively more extreme. Brown made no effort to dispute this fact in *Life Against Death*. Thus, despite himself, he ultimately offered a counsel of despair. His analysis of sexual repression failed to offer even a theoretical rationale for a nonrepressive civilization. The repressive organization of sexuality was psychological in origin, but the psychological dynamic of repression was itself firmly based upon the facts of human biology.

Marcuse succeeded where Brown failed largely because his analysis of sexual repression was genuinely historical. He was able to correlate the repression of pregenital sexuality with the economic needs of the capitalist order —the requirement that libido be concentrated in the genitals in order that the rest of the body might be transformed into an instrument of labor. Thus repression was based upon social and political domination, and the historical possibility of eliminating domination preserved the promise of instinctual liberation. Brown was unwilling to accept the sexual compromises inherent in Marcuse's nonrepressive order; he was consistently more radical than Marcuse in disallowing any distinction between legitimate and illegitimate repression (basic repression and surplus repression), between repressive and nonrepressive sublimation, or between erotic and nonerotic work.[181] At the same time he was unable to account for

[181] Cf. Part Four of *Life Against Death*: "Sublimation."

the historical rise of repressive civilization (the subtitle of *Life Against Death*, "The Psychoanalytical Meaning of History," was both pompous and misleading), and equally incapable of envisioning any historical escape from the dilemma of modern unhappiness. His analysis moved exclusively at the level of individual psychology, and even at this level it provided no "way out." Repression remained grounded in the unhappy peculiarities of human biology.[182]

VIII

Marcuse has published a good deal since *Eros and Civilization*. I want to treat these writings in a rather selective fashion, first in order to indicate the general direction his thought has taken since the great Freudian exercise of the mid-1950's, and secondly to characterize the manner in which his ideas about Freud have changed in recent years. Both Marcuse and Brown have in a sense passed beyond Freud to other preoccupations, and I find it revealing that they have moved in very different directions. Brown's only major publication since *Life Against Death* has been *Love's Body* (1966), a book which makes quite clear that psychoanalysis was only a stage in Brown's development toward a rather curious (and radical) brand of religious mysticism. The very concrete body

[182] Frederick C. Crews has written a trenchant critique of Brown, emphasizing, as I have, the unhistorical character of Brown's thinking: "Love in the Western World," *Partisan Review*, XXXIV, 2 (Spring, 1967), 272–87.

of Freudian psychology has been absorbed into the Mystical Body of traditional Christian theology. To be sure, Freud remains an important authority, and there is a racy (and confusing) display of sexual rhetoric. But the erotic language is largely metaphorical; as Brown himself says, "Everything is symbolic, . . . including the sexual act."[183] Most significant, Brown has been candid enough to make explicit the pronounced antipolitical assumptions which were only implicit in *Life Against Death.* He now argues that politics can never be the vehicle of liberation, not merely because political action is invariably corrupt, but also because politics don't really exist. Political behavior is theatrical behavior. Political revolutions are "reorganizations of the theater, of the stage for human action. The matter remains the same."[184]

Marcuse, it seems to me, has developed in the opposite direction from Brown. Particularly in *One-Dimensional Man* (1964) he has reverted to the political, and explicitly Marxian, preoccupations of his early writings. Perhaps this return to politics can be explained in terms of the changed political atmosphere of America in the 1960's, where, after a decade of reaction (McCarthyism) and inertia (the Eisenhower Administration), the left has experienced a surprising renaissance. Marcuse's perennial radicalism was forced underground in the 1950's; he found in psychoanalytic theory an outlet for his critical

---

[183] Norman O. Brown, *Love's Body* (New York, 1966), p. 131.
[184] *Ibid.,* p. 115. See Marcuse's review of *Love's Body* in *Commentary,* where he effectively points out the antisexual, collectivist, and apolitical implications of Brown's latest position: "Love Mystified: A Critique of Norman O. Brown," *Commentary,* XLIII, 2 (February, 1967), 71–75.

energies in a period between the collapse of European Marxism in the 1930's and the revival of leftist politics in America in the 1960's.

The muting of Marcuse's political consciousness during the 1950's was reflected in the strangely academic and bloodless character of his only major political writing of that decade, *Soviet Marxism* (1958). Marcuse was at work on the research and writing of *Soviet Marxism* simultaneously with *Eros and Civilization*,[185] and clearly his very substantial critical and imaginative faculties were more justly represented in the latter work. For all its scholarly competence, *Soviet Marxism* is the least interesting of Marcuse's writings. In its marked hostility to Soviet communism, it reflected the Cold War atmosphere of the period, although Marcuse did attempt to explain the unhappy course of Soviet political and social development in terms of the persistent vitality of Western capitalism and the aggressive character of Western, particularly American, foreign policy.[186] In general, the book lacked the critical edge of C. Wright Mills's contemporaneous analysis of the Cold War in *The Power Elite*, where blame was placed squarely on the shoulders of the American economic, political, and military establishments.[187] One would hardly guess from reading *Soviet Marxism* that its author was simultaneously at work on an ambitious excursion into psychoanalytic theory. The book was psychologically quite cautious. Freud was mentioned only once, and even that reference was entirely perfunctory.[188] The repressive char-

[185] *Soviet Marxism*, "Acknowledgments."
[186] *Ibid.*, pp. 6–7, 33–35, 38–39, 195.
[187] C. Wright Mills, *The Power Elite* (New York, 1956).
[188] *Soviet Marxism*, p. 224.

acter of Soviet sexual ethics was criticized, but with neither the energy nor the theoretical insight of Reich's more extensive critique of the 1930's ("The Struggle for the 'New Life' in the Soviet Union").[189]

By way of contrast, *One-Dimensional Man* was a worthy successor to *Eros and Civilization*. The book represented a powerful indictment of American politics and culture. Marcuse pursued his critique in a systematic and detailed fashion, and I want to discuss here only those elements of his analysis which bear upon the thesis of *Eros and Civilization*. Two themes in particular seem to me of great significance for Marcuse's earlier appraisal of the future of repression: his reevaluation of the technological project, the progress toward total automation upon which the possibility of erotic release had been predicated, and his negative assessment of the sexual permissiveness of contemporary American society.

One of the most important of Marcuse's contentions in *Eros and Civilization* was that the performance principle had created the preconditions for its own abolition. He argued that modern economic and technological rationality, although itself the product of tremendous sexual repression, had brought about a situation in which the working day could be drastically reduced, thus freeing men from the repressive necessity of work and opening up the possibility of a massive escalation of eroticism. In other words, Marcuse had assumed that science, technology, and economic efficiency were, in theory, politically and sexually neutral. If they had served the interests of repression in the past, they could just as easily form the

[189] *Ibid.*, pp. 244–253.

basis of liberation in the future. By the mid-1960's, however, Marcuse had come to doubt the neutrality of the technological and scientific projects.[190] The scientific *Weltanschauung* now appeared to him irrevocably repressive. In the 1930's he had critized modern science as implicitly conservative because of its uncritical or passive attitude toward "the facts." But the strictures contained in *One-Dimensional Man* were much more extreme: science was faulted not only for its anticritical bias, but also because it contributed positively to the ideology of domination and manipulation. Marcuse argued that science treated nature as an object of control; its basic categories were operational, thus setting a precedent for the manipulative economic and political enterprises of the modern period:

> The principles of modern science were *a priori* structured in such a way that they could serve as conceptual instruments for a universe of self-propelling, productive control; theoretical operationalism came to correspond to practical operationalism. The scientific method which led to the ever-more-effective domination of nature thus came to provide the pure concepts as well as the instrumentalities for the ever-more-effective domination of man by man *through* the domination of nature.[191]

No revolution, whether political, economic, or sexual, would be successful without a transformation in the conception and function of science. Marcuse demanded not a

[190] Marcuse, *One-Dimensional Man* (Boston, 1964), pp. xvi, 17–18.
[191] *Ibid.*, p. 158; cf. pp. 153–60. Reprinted by permission of Beacon Press, © 1964, and Routledge & Kegan Paul Ltd.

return to the pre-Galilean qualitative conception of science, but rather "the scientific quantification of new goals, derived from a new experience of man and nature—the goals of pacification."[192]

As in the case of science, Marcuse now argued that technology contained an inherently repressive dynamic, which prevented it from serving the purposes of liberation:

> In the medium of technology, culture, politics, and the economy merge into an omnipresent system which swallows up or repulses all alternatives. The productivity and growth potential of this system stabilize the society and contain technical progress within the framework of domination. Technological rationality has become political rationality.[193]

Marcuse was not always consistently pessimistic about technology in *One-Dimensional Man;* there were in fact passages which upheld the older ideal of its liberating potential.[194] But the dominant note was one of skepticism and despair. In particular, Marcuse argued that the technological revolution had created a whole series of false and repressive needs—for refrigerators, television sets, superpowered automobiles, gadgets, and, more ominous, for the elaborate machines of destruction—which "contained" the liberating potential of technology.[195]

[192] Marcuse, "Remarks on a Redefinition of Culture," *Daedalus,* XCIV, 1 (Winter, 1965), 203; *One-Dimensional Man,* pp. 166–167.

[193] *One-Dimensional Man,* p. xvi. Reprinted by permission of Beacon Press, © 1964, and Routledge & Kegan Paul Ltd.

[194] *Ibid.,* pp. 34–37, 230–35.

[195] *Ibid.,* pp. 3–7.

Marcuse was thus no longer able to envision political and sexual liberation on the basis of the existing technology. The pacification of existence would require a complete reversal of the technological project itself, "a change in the *technical* basis" of the established order.[196] To a certain extent such a reversal implied a modified primitivism (a *"reduction of overdevelopment"*),[197] such as appears in the critical anthropological speculations of Roheim. At the same time, however, Marcuse insisted that "liberation from the affluent society does not mean return to healthy and robust poverty, moral cleanliness, and simplicity."[198] The point to be emphasized is that the critique of technological rationality contained in *One-Dimensional Man* substantially undermined Marcuse's argument in *Eros and Civilization*. The technology of automation no longer appeared as the foundation of erotic liberation, but rather as the principal support of an increasingly irrational and repressive organization of men's lives.

Marcuse's pessimistic evaluation of modern technology was complemented by an equally dismal assessment of the sexual permissiveness of advanced industrial society. Apparently Marcuse feared having been misinterpreted as an apologist for the sexual promiscuity which has become so prominent a feature of contemporary American life. I sometimes supect that there is a barely repressed strain of puritanism in Marcuse's makeup, a fastidiousness which allows him to treat sexuality with great abandon at the

---

[196] *Ibid.*, pp. 18, 227–28.
[197] *Ibid.*, p. 242.
[198] *Ibid.* Cf. also pp. 238, 251–52.

level of theory, but results in a squeamish "That's not what I meant at all!" when confronted with the untidy reality of sex. At the same time, I think one is obliged to respect Marcuse's integrity as a critic of modern permissiveness; he presented a strong empirical case for his contention that the overt manifestations of sexuality permitted within our society are in fact conducive to the continued survival of the repressive order in its larger contours.

Marcuse formulated the concept of "repressive desublimation" to characterize this type of permissiveness. The concept was anticipated in isolated passages of *Eros and Civilization*,[199] but it achieved explicit and detailed elaboration only in *One-Dimensional Man*. Repressive desublimation connoted the manner in which sexuality has been put to work in the service of the established order, particularly the established economic system: "It has often been noted that advanced industrial civilization operates with a greater degree of sexual freedom—'operates' in the sense that the latter becomes a market value. . . . The sexy office and sales girls, the handsome, virile junior executive and floor walker are highly marketable commodities."[200] The fact that sex has been incorporated into the workaday world contributes to the voluntary compliance of the repressed individual with the regulations and goals of the repressive order. Work is still work, but it has been made to appear more attractive.

Marcuse contrasted this libidinalization of the economy with the complementary "de-erotization of the environ-

[199] *Eros and Civilization*, pp. 94–95, 202.
[200] *One-Dimensional Man*, pp. 74, 72–79.

ment" through mechanization, a process which he loosely identified with the establishment of genital tyranny:

> Compare love-making in a meadow and in an automobile, on a lovers' walk outside the town walls and on a Manhattan street. In the former cases, the environment partakes of and invites libidinal cathexis and tends to be eroticized. Libido transcends beyond the immediate erotogenic zones—a process of nonrepressive sublimation. In contrast, a mechanized environment seems to block such self-transcendence of libido. Impelled in the striving to extend the field of erotic gratification, libido becomes less "polymorphous," less capable of eroticism beyond localized sexuality, and the *latter* is intensified.[201]

Marcuse now insisted that the older Christian hostility to sexuality was much to be preferred, since it at least prevented the revolutionary oppositional force of sexuality from being compromised. Sublimation had the virtue of preserving "the consciousness of the renunciations which the repressive society inflicts upon the individual."[202] Thus where the sexual deviant had been the hero of *Eros and Civilization,* the highly repressed neurotic assumed the role of chief social critic in *One-Dimensional Man.* The neurotic's sickness represented an uncompromised protest against the repressive world in which he lived.[203] Marcuse also argued that the repressiveness of traditional schooling was preferable to the license of progressive education, since the former kept alive that sense

[201] *Ibid.,* p. 73. Reprinted by permission of Beacon Press, © 1964, and Routledge & Kegan Paul Ltd.
[202] *Ibid.,* p. 75.
[203] *Ibid.,* p. 183.

of alienation which alone could defeat the repressive order.[204] As final proof of the conformist character of the contemporary sexual revolution, Marcuse pointed out that advancing permissiveness has been accompanied not by a decline but rather by an augmentation of destructiveness. He had demonstrated in *Eros and Civilization* that a genuine release of erotic energies would result in a curtailment of aggression. However, aggressiveness was in fact "rampant throughout contemporary industrial society,"[205] leaving little doubt about the spuriousness of the contemporary relaxation of sexual mores.

One senses in Marcuse's recent thought both a more sober assessment of man's future than one finds in *Eros and Civilization* and a mild disenchantment with psychoanalytic theory.[206] Marcuse has not repudiated Freud, but his enthusiasm for psychoanalysis has certainly slackened. Moreover, it is probably symptomatic of the darker atmosphere of his most recent work that the one psychoanalytic insight which he now values above all others is Freud's concept of the death instinct.[207] However, if Marcuse has grown more pessimistic in recent years, he has at the same time become increasingly vocal, some would say strident, as a political critic. The second edition of *Eros and Civilization* contained a new introduc-

---

[204] Marcuse, "Repressive Tolerance," in *A Critique of Pure Tolerance* (Boston, 1965), pp. 113–15.

[205] *One-Dimensional Man*, p. 78.

[206] Marcuse, "Das Veralten der Psychoanalyse" ("Obsolescence of Psychoanalysis"), a paper presented in 1963 in New York at the convention of the American Political Science Association, reprinted (in German) in *Kultur und Gesellschaft II*, pp. 85–106.

[207] Marcuse, in interview of November 15, 1965.

tion entitled, appropriately, "Political Preface 1966." Here Marcuse confessed his earlier overestimation of the revolutionary potential of advanced industrial society and his feeling that the sexual revolution had been betrayed.[208] At the same time, in the "Political Preface" and in other recent writings (most notably in "Repressive Tolerance"), he announced his endorsement of the most radical forms of political protest. The only legitimate political posture, he argued, was one of "absolute refusal," which included refusing to extend the usual toleration to the apologists of reaction.[209] Marcuse has in effect become one of the chief ideologues of the New Left, leading the assault on repressive affluence at home and neocolonial wars abroad.[210] He has assumed this political role quite readily. He now identifies student antiwar demonstrators, civil rights workers, the oppressed victims of colonialism in Africa and Asia (Frantz Fanon's "wretched of the earth"), even hippies as the true descendants of the classical Marxian proletariat.[211] And although he is still willing to employ the rhetoric of psychoanalytic theory, he insists emphatically on the primacy of politics, both political criticism and political action: "Today the fight for life, the fight for Eros, is the *political* fight."[212]

[208] Marcuse, "Political Preface 1966," *Eros and Civilization,* pp. xi, xiii–xv.
[209] *One-Dimensional Man,* p. 255; "Repressive Tolerance," *passim.*
[210] "Political Preface 1966," pp. xvii–xviii. Irwin Unger, "The 'New Left' and American History: Some recent Trends in United States Historiography," *American Historical Review,* LXXII, 4 (July, 1967), 1242 n.
[211] *One-Dimensional Man,* p. 257; "Political Preface 1966," pp. xvi, xxv, xxi.
[212] "Political Preface 1966," p. xxv.

In the most general sense, then, Marcuse's recent development can be characterized as a return from Freud to
Marx, from psychology to politics. At the present time the
future of Freudian radicalism lies in doubt. It may be that
the tradition has worked itself out and that its permanent
legacy will be to have corrected the prevailing interpretation of Freud as conservative. Yet even in the midst of his
exclusively political preoccupations, Marcuse seems unwilling to relinquish entirely his earlier vision of a union
of political and erotic protest. The "Political Preface"
culminates in a curiously ambivalent reassertion of that
synthesis of political and sexual energies which was the
leitmotiv of *Eros and Civilization*:

> Can we speak of a juncture between the erotic and poli-
> tical dimension? In and against the deadly efficient or-
> ganization of the affluent society, not only radical protest,
> but even the attempt to formulate, to articulate, to give
> word to protest assumes a childlike, ridiculous immaturity.
> Thus it is ridiculous and perhaps "logical" that the Free
> Speech Movement at Berkeley terminated in the row
> caused by the appearance of a sign with the four-letter
> word. It is perhaps equally ridiculous and right to see
> deeper significance in the buttons worn by some of the
> demonstrators (among them infants) against the slaughter
> in Vietnam: MAKE LOVE, NOT WAR.[213]

[213] *Ibid.*, p. xxi. Reprinted by permission of Beacon Press, ©
1955, 1966, and Routledge & Kegan Paul Ltd.

INDEX

245